India through Hindu Categories

Contributions to Indian Sociology

OCCASIONAL STUDIES

(Included in this Series are selected numbers of *Contributions*)

1. T.N. MADAN, ed. 1975. *Muslim communities of south Asia: society and culture* [vol. 6, 1972]. New Delhi: Vikas.*

2. SATISH SABERWAL, ed. 1978. *Process and institution in urban India: sociological studies* [vol. 11, no. 1, 1977]. New Delhi: Vikas. Second impression (New Delhi: Vikas), 1978.*

3. T.N. MADAN, ed., 1982. *Way of life: king, householder, renouncer. Essays in honour of Louis Dumont* [vol. 15, nos. 1&2, 1981]. New Delhi: Vikas; Paris: Maison des Sciences de l'Homme. Second impression (New Delhi: Vikas), 1982. Second edition (Delhi: Motilal Banarsidass), 1988.

4. VEENA DAS, ed. 1986. *The word and the world: fantasy, symbol and record* [vol. 19, no. 1, 1985]. New Delhi: Sage.

5. MCKIM MARRIOTT, ed. 1989. *India through Hindu categories* [vol. 23, no. 1, 1989]. New Delhi: Sage.

* Out of print.

India through Hindu Categories

Edited by

McKim Marriott

SAGE Publications
New Delhi/Newbury Park/London

First published in 1990 by

SAGE Publications India Pvt Ltd
M-32, Greater Kailash Market, I
New Delhi 110 048

SAGE Publications Inc
2111 West Hillcrest Drive
Newbury Park, California 91320

SAGE Publications Ltd
28 Banner Street
London EC1Y 8QE

Published by Tejeshwar Singh for Sage Publications India Pvt Ltd, phototypeset by Mudra Typesetters and printed at Chaman Offset Printers.

Fourth printing, 1995

ISBN 0–8039–9636–5 (US)
81–7036–176–1 (India)

In memoriam

RADHAKAMAL MUKERJEE

1889–1968

Contents

Preface
T.N. Madan ix

Introduction
McKim Marriott xi

1. *Constructing an Indian ethnosociology*
McKim Marriott 1

2. *Is there an Indian way of thinking? An informal eassy*
A.K. Ramanujan 41

3. *The original caste: power, history and hierarchy in South Asia*
Nicholas B. Dirks 59

4. *Centrality, mutuality and hierarchy: shifting aspects of inter-caste relationships in north India*
Gloria Goodwin Raheja 79

5. *Hindu periods of death 'impurity'*
Diane Paull Mines 103

6. *Eating sins in Karimpur*
Susan S. Wadley and Bruce W. Derr 131

7. *Humoral transactions in two Tamil cults: Murukan and Mariyamman*
Manuel Moreno and McKim Marriott 149

8. *The Kerala house as a Hindu cosmos*
Melinda A. Moore 169

About the contributors 203

Index 205

Errata

A.K. Ramanujan, 'Is there an Indian way of thinking?'

p. 47, par. 5, line 9: for 'Manu 7.41' read 'Manu 8.41'

p. 50, par. 2, lines 5–6: read '(where a shark does not have to work for the mango, it falls into his open mouth)'

par. 3, line 2: before 'shark' insert 'the'

par. 5, line 6: for 'confuses' read 'con-fuses'

p. 52, par. 4, line 8: for 'Roland (1979)' read 'Roland (1988)'

p. 58, line 40: for 'ROLAND, ALAN. 1979.' read 'ROLAND, ALAN. 1988.'

Gloria Goodwin Raheja, 'Centrality, mutuality and hierarchy'

p. 94, Figure 1, title: for 'Configuration' read 'Configurations'

Diane Paull Mines, 'Hindu periods of death "impurity" '

p. 112, par. 3, line 11: for 'ranks' read 'rank'

p. 125, par. 2, line 2: for 'suffers' read 'suffer'

p. 129, line 31: for '———. 1980. *Karma and rebirth* . . .' read 'O'FLAHERTY, WENDY D., ed. 1980. *Karma and rebirth* . . .'

Manuel Moreno and McKim Marriott, 'Humoral transactions in two south Indian cults'

p. 156, line 11: for 'Beck 1969' read 'Beck 1972'

Melinda A. Moore, 'The Kerala house as a Hindu cosmos'

p. 190, Figure 5: for '975: 23' read '1975: 23'

p. 196, par. 6, line 8: for 'not labelled' read 'not inappropriately labelled'

p. 201, line 9, DAS, VEENA: for '1977' read '1982'

line 16: for '———. 1982. *Banaras:* . . .' read 'ECK, DIANA L. 1982. *Banaras:* . . .'

Preface

The early 1950s saw a surge of interest in India among American anthropologists. Where David Mandelbaum and Murray Emeneau had been ploughing rather lonely though adjacent furrows in the earlier decade or so, we witnessed the arrival of Oscar Lewis, Morris Opler, Robert Redfield and Milton Singer, and of a steadily increasing stream of graduate students. Their contributions in the last forty years have greatly enriched the ethnography of India and provided paradigms for the understanding of society in India.

During the 1970s several new theoretical orientations made their appearance in the work of American anthropologists and were called by names such as 'cognitive anthropology', 'cultural analysis' and 'ethnosociology'. Naturally, these developments were also reflected in the work of those specialising on South Asia. What these new departures imply has not always been clear because even those who would agree that they are ethnosociologically inclined do not speak with one voice. The differences do not reflect only differences of institutional location or temperament but also and more significantly of theory and method.

I was therefore much interested to learn that Michael Moffatt had, with encouragement from the Joint Committee on South Asia (JCSA) of the Social Science Research Council and the American Council of Learned Societies, organised and chaired a panel on ethnosociology at the 1983 meetings of the American Anthropological Association. I knew from my contact with David Szanton that SSRC had resolved in 1976 to encourage the development of South Asian conceptual systems in all fields of the humanities and social sciences, and many scholars, notably McKim Marriott and A.K. Ramanujan, had been involved in this enterprise.

Moffatt again organised a workshop on the same subject at the Annual Conference on South Asia at Madison, Wisconsin, in November 1984. I happened to be at the Conference, though not at the workshop, and heard from Moffatt about the discussions and of his hope eventually to produce a volume of papers on the ethnosociology of India. Being interested, I kept in touch and things were moving, though very slowly. In 1987 I agreed, after some correspondence with Susan Wadley, to propose to the editors of *Contributions* to publish some of the resultant papers in the journal. This was done in a special number of *Contributions* (vol. 23, no. 1, January–June 1989). The present volume is a reprint of the same with some additional materials, namely an introduction by McKim Marriott, an index, revised notes on contributors, and errata.

I would like to point out here that the present collection of papers is of interest inasmuch as it offords us an opportunity to examine between the covers of one volume carefully prepared specimens of the results of work, which has been going on in several areas (anthropology, folklore, history, etc.), exploring the scope of 'ethnosociological' approaches developed by some American scholars. Needless to emphasise, there is no single established conception of 'ethnosociology' and not all American scholars in the twin fields of social sciences and the humanities follow such an approach in their work on India. This does not, however, diminish the importance of the experiment.

This is not the place to go into the genesis of various approaches to the study of Indian society which have characterised the work of Indian and non-Indian scholars in the last half century or so. The subject is much too important for *obiter dicta*, and should be considered comprehensively and in depth. All that is possible here is to note that, in an interesting flow of events, the importance of the dialectic of the people's own categories of thought and of other categories (from other cultures and from scholarly discourses) has rightly gained wide acceptance in Indianist studies in the last five decades. Not that all questions have already been answered satisfactorily, but that at least some significant questions have been posed.

I would like to place on record my gratitude to McKim Marriott, Michael Moffatt, and Susan Wadley for their collaboration. In the final stages of editorial work, Professor Marriott shouldered the burden all by himself, incorporated in his own essay a commentary on the other papers comprising this volume and, finally, wrote an introduction for this edition. His name therefore appears appropriately as the editor of the volume.

Finally, I should thank the officers of the Social Science Research Council in New York for support, Bernard Cohn for sage advice, Omita Goyal (at SAGE) for her inexhaustible patience and good humour, and Aradhya Bhardwaj (at IEG) for editorial assistance.

This volume is dedicated to the memory of Radhakamal Mukerjee (1889–1968) on the centenary of his birth. One of the founding fathers of social science in India, he was also a great humanist. From his early work in what he then called comparative economics to his later ecological, sociological, historical, cultural and religious studies, he affirmed the importance of inter-civilisational comparison and cultural dialogue—of the dialectic of the view from within and the view from without.

T.N. Madan

Introduction

This volume is about some ideas that are useful for understanding the social behaviour of people of South Asian and possibly other civilisations. Ideas are drawn here from Hindu cultural categories, not simply because those categories offer coherent and comprehensive systems of thought, but especially because they illuminate dimensions of variation that escape the notice of conventional social science.

To explore the connections between cultural knowledge and life as it is lived is a commitment shared by all the South Asianists who write herein. They would synthesise humane and social science learning, transcending one-time distinctions such as those between textual indology and contextual, on-the-ground 'area studies'. In this they share a goal for social research that was long advocated by Robert Redfield (1955, 1962), that was pursued by him and Milton Singer (1972) in their thinking about India as a 'social organisation of traditions', and that has been realised through the broad multidisciplinarity of civilisational studies at Chicago (R.H. Davis 1985: 29–64) and elsewhere.

The present authors could have addressed their topics as broadly at any of the other centres where such a commitment is honoured—Delhi, London, New York, Paris, Seattle, or elsewhere. But each of their essays happens to have taken shape partly or wholly at Chicago, and in its critical awareness of its terms of analysis each is also typically (if not uniquely) Chicagoan. A demand that anthropology both use and where necessary revise the concepts of other disciplines was articulated there from the 1920s onward by Redfield (1955, 1962: 23–31), later by others such as Clifford Geertz (1966, 1976) and David M. Schneider (1968, 1976); it is currently urged and extended by Paul Friedrich (1988) and many others.

From linguistic structuralism social-cultural anthropology during the 1960s borrowed an interest in relationships. Field studies in rural South Asia were simultaneously beginning to notice that units such as kin (Inden 1976; Inden and Nicholas 1977; Yalman 1967) and castes (Marriott 1968, 1976; Silverberg 1970) are treated not as fixed, but as transformable through certain transactions of substantive properties among them. Summarising such studies, Marriott and Inden (1974, 1977; Marriott 1977) proposed that South Asian research be rethought overall to take account of the more exact and dynamic perceptions available in the region's implicit 'ethnosociology', which is profoundly relational.

The force of their proposal was strengthened by a number of other analytically indigenising South Asianist dissertations and books which were completed about the same time. Arjun Appadurai (1981), Kenneth A. David (1977), Marvin G. Davis (1983), Murray J. Leaf (1972), Michael

Moffatt (1979), Sherry B. Ortner (1979), Akos Ostor (1980), Susan S. Wadley (1975), and Norman Ziegler (1973) all showed some advantages to be gained from attention to the processes cited in native exegesis. Four long-term visitors to Chicago emphasised some of the same points in their exemplary monographs—Lawrence A. Babb (1975), Brenda E.F. Beck (1972), R.S. Khare (1976a, 1976b), and Veena Das (1977).

With the goal of expanding world conceptual resources by similar means, the Joint Committee on South Asia of the American Council of Learned Societies and the Social Science Research Council resolved in 1976 to encourage the development of South Asian analytic ideas for all fields of the humanities and the social sciences (Szanton 1976). Researchers trained in the region's cultural thought and also in the relevant Western theoretical and empirical disciplines were then (and are still) very few, but under the guidance of David L. Szanton of the SSRC, the Joint Committee reconstituted itself of scholars from many disciplines and universities who at least shared that ethnoscientific goal. These at first included Stanley Heginbotham from political science, Michelle MacAlpin from economics, McKim Marriott from anthropology, Barbara D. Metcalf from history, Karl H. Potter from philosophy, and A.K. Ramanujan from folklore and linguistics.

Thus constituted, the Joint Committee on South Asia until 1981 provided the impetus for many studies like those presented here. It deputed McKim Marriott to explore and develop South Asian concepts of 'person and interpersonal relations' that might expand the behavioural sciences of psychology and sociology. It deputed A.K. Ramanujan to develop studies of South Asian folklore and to articulate its categories for wider use. These two conceived their present essays and separately or in combination conducted numerous Joint Committee-sponsored workshops. In these workshops more than fifty researchers, most of them newly developing scholars, were invited to formulate South Asian social and psychological thought and practice in specialised areas such as astrology, biography, geography, kinship, medicine, oneirics, psychopathology, psychotherapy, and ritual. Folklore was also extensively explored through a series of workshops, and other scholars were deputed to investigate the workings of *karma* (Keyes and Daniel 1983; O'Flaherty 1980), the uses of Muslim moral ideologies (Ewing 1988; Metcalf 1984), South Asian notions in dealing with political economy (Desai et al. 1984), and other topics.

The efforts begun then have accelerated since. The present descriptive papers were selected with the help of Susan S. Wadley from a genre that has grown to comprise several dozens of dissertations and uncounted articles in journals and symposia. Analytic uses of South Asian ideas in the present papers resonate with similar usages in recent monographs by other researchers, such as L.A. Babb (1986), E.V. Daniel (1984), Ann Grodzins Gold (1988), Daniel Gold (1988), Ronald Inden (n.d.), Sudhir Kakar

(1982), T.N. Madan (1987), Frédérique Apffel Marglin (1985), Bryan Pfaffenberger (1982), Alan Roland (1988), Margaret Trawick (n.d.), and Francis Zimmermann (1987, 1989).

With the Joint Committee's further encouragement, Michael Moffatt empanelled ten ethnosociological researchers (of whom four write in the present volume) at the 1983 Chicago meetings of the American Anthropological Association. There and in a further workshop and panel at the 1984 Wisconsin Conference on South Asia, he asked them whether their analyses went 'beyond purity and pollution', referring to the narrower model of Indian society constructed with some Western categories by Louis Dumont (1957, 1970). After reformulating Moffatt's question in the more variable terms of their wider Hindu universes, all those researchers who reply below do so in the affirmative.

One peculiarity of the present papers is that they do not posit any single South Asian value or social configuration (such as Dumont's 'purity' or 'hierarchy') toward which all relations must tend. In not positing such uniformity, they diverge from one-dimensional normative analysis, and also from several reified versions of structuralism. Another peculiarity of the papers is that they do not assume (as social anthropologists often do) the invariance of units like caste, house, and person. They privilege neither the 'forces of production' from which a simpler class analysis usually proceeds, nor the free-floating conceptual categories which are often the only givens of an older philological indology or cognitive anthropology.

Rather than bind themselves by any of these familiar humanistic or social science conventions, the present researchers locate themselves in the many-layered, many-dimensioned contexts of Hindu life. There they analyse behavioural variation by reasoning in terms derived from the civilisation's own recognised systems of categories. They work with and from the elements, humours, strands, or divergent aims of action that are taken as axiomatic in South Asian exegesis.

The often surprising variations explored in these papers—differentiated dependencies among castes and kin, varied periods of healing after death, diverse imputations of cause, distinct kinds of political power, contrasting transactions with the gods, specialisations of domestic space—can be interpreted by Hindus as paradigms repeatedly generated through combinations and permutations of known components. Like the diverse fabrics that can be woven of the same threads, or the diverse utterances that can be spoken in one language, the varied people of the Hindu world can themselves also be seen as composite and contingent outcomes of that world's multivariate processes.

That such variabilities are assumed to be potential in and around all beings may be sufficient reason for Hindus variously to embrace flux, to make some counterassumptions of constancy (as in postulating the categories themselves), and to attempt counterpolicies, such as constraint, opposition, and disengagement (which are misunderstood in characterisations of Hindu culture as generally static or otherworldly). The history, politics, and developmental psychology of the Hindu categories are not deeply discussed here, but some of the active human logics and dialectics commonly operating within that categorically multidimensional and dynamic South Asian social world are made uncommonly evident in the present book.

The authors are collectively indebted to David L. Szanton for his early initiatives and to the Social Science Research Council for its financial support; to the Lichtstern Fund of the University of Chicago for further support; to Susan S. Wadley for arranging the original appearance of these papers in *Contributions to Indian sociology*; and to T.N. Madan, both for taking extraordinary pains over the papers' production and for facilitating their republication in this volume. The editor is singularly indebted to the authors and to Bernard S. Cohn for their cooperation and good counsel.

McKim Marriott

REFERENCES

Appadurai, Arjun. 1981. *Worship and conflict under colonial rule*. Cambridge: Cambridge University Press.

Babb, Lawrence A. 1975. *The divine hierarchy: popular Hinduism in central India*. New York: Columbia University Press.

———. 1986. *Redemptive encounters: three modern styles in the Hindu tradition*. Berkeley: University of Chicago Press.

Beck, Brenda E.F. 1972. *Peasant society in Konku: a study of right and left subcastes in south India*. Vancouver: University of British Columbia Press.

Daniel, E. Valentine. 1984. *Fluid signs: being a person the Tamil way*. Berkeley: University of California Press.

Das, Veena. 1977. *Structure and cognition: aspects of Hindu caste and ritual*. Ist ed. Delhi: Oxford University Press.

David, Kenneth A. 1977. Hierarchy and equivalence in Jaffna, north Sri Lanka: normative codes as mediator. *In* K. A. David, ed., *The new wind: changing identities in South Asia*, pp. 179–226. The Hague: Mouton.

Davis, Marvin G. 1983. *Rank and rivalry: the politics of inequality in rural West Bengal*. Cambridge: Cambridge University Press.

Davis, Richard H. 1985. *South Asia at Chicago: a history*. Chicago: Committee on Southern Asian Studies, University of Chicago.

Desai, Meghnad, Susanne Hoeber Rudolph, and Ashok Rudra, eds. 1984. *Agrarian power and agricultural productivity in South Asia*. Berkeley: University of California Press.

Dumont, Louis. 1957. For a sociology of India. *Contributions to Indian sociology* 1: 7–22.

———. 1970. *Homo hierarchicus: the caste system and its implications* (trans. Mark Sainsbury). Chicago: University of Chicago Press.

Ewing, Katherine P., ed. 1988. Shari'at *and ambiguity in South Asian Islam*. Berkeley: University of California Press.

FRIEDRICH, PAUL. 1988. Multiplicity and pluralism in anthropological construction/synthesis. *Anthropological quarterly* 61: 103–12.

GEERTZ, CLIFFORD. 1966. *Person, time and conduct in Bali: an essay in cultural analysis.* Cultural report series n.14. New Haven: Yale Southeast Asia Program.

———. 1976. 'From the native's point of view': on the nature of anthropological understanding. *In* Henry A. Selby and Keith M. Basso, eds., *Meaning in anthropology*, pp. 221–37. Albuquerque: School of American Research.

GOLD, ANN GRODZINS. 1988. *Fruitful journeys: the ways of Rajasthani pilgrims.* Berkeley: University of California Press.

GOLD, DANIEL. 1988. *The lord as guru: Hindi sants in north Indian tradition.* New York: Oxford University Press.

INDEN, RONALD B. 1976. *Marriage and rank in Bengali culture: a history of caste and clan in middle period Bengal.* Berkeley: University of California Press.

———. n.d. *Imagining India.* Oxford: Basil Blackwell (in press).

INDEN, RONALD B., and RALPH W. NICHOLAS. 1977. *Kinship in Bengali culture.* Chicago: University of Chicago Press.

KAKAR, SUDHIR. 1982. *Shamans, mystics and doctors: a psychological inquiry into India's healing traditions.* New York: A.A. Knopf.

KEYES, CHARLES F., and E. VALENTINE DANIEL, eds. 1983. *Karma: an anthropological inquiry.* Berkeley: University of California Press.

KHARE, RAVINDRA SAHAI. 1976a. *The Hindu hearth and home.* New Delhi: Vikas Publishing House.

———. 1976b. *Culture and reality: essays on the Hindu system of managing foods.* Simla: Indian Institute of Advanced Study.

LEAF, MURRAY J. 1972. *Information and behavior in a Sikh village.* Berkeley: University of California Press.

MADAN, TRILOKI NATH. 1987. *Non-renunciation: themes and interpretations of Hindu culture.* Delhi: Oxford University Press.

MARGLIN, FRÉDÉRIQUE APFFEL. 1985. *Wives of the god-king: the rituals of the devadasis of Puri.* Delhi: Oxford University Press.

MARRIOTT, MCKIM. 1968. Caste ranking and food transactions: a matrix analysis. *In* Milton Singer and Bernard S. Cohn, eds., *Structure and change in Indian society*, pp. 133–71. Chicago: Aldine.

———. 1976. Hindu transactions; diversity without dualism. *In* Bruce Kapferer, ed., *Transaction and meaning: directions in the anthropology of exchange and symbolic behavior*, pp. 109–42. Philadelphia: Institute for the Study of Human Issues.

———. 1977. [Remarks in] Symposium: changing identities in South Asia. *In* Kenneth A. David, ed., *The new wind: changing identities in South Asia*, pp. 423–28. Chicago: Aldine.

MARRIOTT, MCKIM, and RONALD B. INDEN. 1974. Caste systems. *Encyclopaedia Britannica, macropaedia* 3: 982–91. Chicago: Helen Hemenway Benton.

———. 1977. Toward an ethnosociology of South Asian caste systems. *In* Kenneth A. David, ed., *The new wind: changing identities in South Asia*, pp. 227–38. The Hague: Mouton.

METCALF, BARBARA DALY, ed. 1984. *Moral conduct and authority: the place of* adab *in South Asian Islam.* Berkeley: University of California Press.

MOFFATT, MICHAEL. 1979. *An Untouchable community in South India: structure and consensus.* Princeton: Princeton University Press.

O'FLAHERTY, WENDY D., ed. 1980. *Karma and rebirth in classical Indian traditions.* Berkeley: Univeristy of California Press.

ORTNER, SHERRY B. 1979. *Sherpas through their rituals.* Cambridge: Cambridge University Press.

OSTOR, AKOS. 1980. *The play of the gods: locality, ideology, structure, and time in the festivals of a Bengali town.* Chicago: University of Chicago Press.

PFAFFENBERGER, BRYAN. 1982. *Caste in Tamil culture: the religious foundations of Sudra domination in Tamil Sri Lanka*. Foreign and Comparative Studies, South Asian series, n. 7. Syracuse: Maxwell School of Citizenship and Public Affairs, Syracuse University.

REDFIELD, ROBERT. 1955. *The little community: viewpoints for the study of a human whole*. Chicago: University of Chicago Press.

———. 1962. *Human nature and the study of society: the papers of Robert Redfield, Volume I* (ed. Margaret Park Redfield). Chicago: University of Chicago Press.

ROLAND, ALAN. 1988. *In search of self in India and Japan: toward a cross-cultural psychology*. Princeton: Princeton University Press.

SCHNEIDER, DAVID M. 1968. *American kinship: a cultural account*. Englewood Cliffs NJ: Prentice-Hall.

———. 1976. Notes toward a theory of culture. *In* Keith H. Basso and Henry A. Selby, eds., *Meaning in anthropology*, pp. 197–220. Albuquerque: School of American Research.

SILVERBERG, JAMES, ed. 1970. *Social mobility in the caste system in India: an interdisciplinary symposium*. Comparative studies in society and history, supplement iii. The Hague: Mouton.

SINGER, MILTON B. 1972. *When a great tradition modernizes: an anthropological approach to Indian civilization*. New York: Praeger.

SZANTON, DAVID L. 1976. South and Southeast Asia: new concerns of the council. *Social science research council items* 30: 2: 1–2.

TRAWICK, MARGARET. n.d. *Notes on love in a Tamil family*. Berkeley: University of California Press (in press).

WADLEY, SUSAN SNOW. 1975. *Shakti: power in the conceptual structure of Karimpur religion*. The University of Chicago studies in anthropology, series in social, cultural, and linguistic anthropology, n. 2. Chicago: Department of Anthropology, University of Chicago.

YALMAN, NUR. 1967. *Under the bo tree: studies in caste, kinship, and marriage in the interior of Ceylon*. Berkeley: University of California Press.

ZIEGLER, NORMAN P. 1973. *Action, power and service in Rajasthani culture*. Chicago: University of Chicago Library.

ZIMMERMANN, FRANCIS B. 1987. *The jungle and the aroma of meats: an ecological theme in Hindu medicine*. Berkeley: University of California Press.

———. 1989. *Le discours des remèdes au pays des épices: enquête sur la médecine Hindoue*. Paris: Éditions Payot.

1

Constructing an Indian ethnosociology[1]

McKim Marriott

It is an anomalous fact that the social sciences used in India today have developed from thought about Western rather than Indian cultural realities. As a result, although they pretend to universal applicability, the Western sciences often do not recognise and therefore cannot deal with the questions to which many Indian institutions are answers. In the interest of dealing with Indian questions and answers, this volume explores social science ideas that can be developed from the realities known to Indian people.

Attending to what is perceived by Indians in Indian categories should at least promote a more perceptive Indian ethnography, and the papers of this volume are offered as specimens. Recognition of Indian realities should also promote more incisive analysis, inference, hypothesis formation, and positive theoretical growth—in other words, the development of Indian ethnosocial sciences.

This volume aims by the same attention to Indian realities to increase the range and power of the social sciences generally. All social sciences develop from thought about what is known to particular cultures and are thus 'cultural' or 'ethno-' social sciences in their origins.[2] All are initially parochial in scope. Since thought originating outside of Europe and America has not yet been recognised or developed as 'social science', the world has thus far had to manage with ethnosocial sciences of only one limited, Western type. By working with a culturally related, but non-European people's thought about their own realities, the authors of this volume aim to expand the world repertory of social sciences.

[1] This paper has grown out of an initial three-month fellowship from the Social Science Research Council. Its ideas are a cumulation of the experiences reported to me by the many investigators named herein. I must especially thank Margaret Trawick for numerous valuable suggestions as well as Michael Moffatt and Melinda Moore for comments which I have attempted to take into account.

[2] The assertion that all social sciences are cultural (and therefore '-emic') amounts to denying the privileged position claimed for an imaginary '-etic' social science, which is really derived from the investigator's emics.

If their efforts help in developing at least one non-Western social science (many more are desirable), the authors may well contribute to a third purpose: assisting social scientists working in a Western, Indian, or any other tradition to become conscious of their presuppositions—their cultural biasses and blindspots. What a culture presupposes may, like a language's grammar, remain unconscious just because it seems to be universally accepted, to have no alternative. An Indian ethnosociology could offer a conscious alternative. It could offer a second lens through which all could look, a second language in which all could speak.[3]

Preoccupied with answering questions about the kinds of entities, relationships, media, and states of being that others of his common sense or limited professional culture take to be real, the social scientist of any tradition may be unaware that the traditional categories of sociological questioning themselves impose a culture upon respondents. Whether aware or not, however, the investigator who seeks ways of asking in rural India about equivalents of Western 'individuals', 'social structures', 'kinship', 'classes', 'statuses', 'rules', 'oppositions', 'solidarities', 'hierarchies', 'authority', 'values', 'ideology', 'religion', 'purity', etc., risks imposing an alien ontology and an alien epistemology on those who attempt to answer.

Such terms of questioning are precipitates of Western social, intellectual, and particularly academic history.[4] Many of them also remain as commonplaces of Western popular thought. But they rarely fit Indian definitions of reality. For example, Marx's distinction between a 'material' base and an 'ideological' superstructure, like Lévi-Strauss' distinction between 'nature' and 'culture', is commonsensical in the West, but is overridden by Hindu notions that natural matter, actions, words and thoughts are all substances and all imbued with relational properties: by Hindu definitions there are no insignificant material facts, no nonmaterial ideas (e.g., Ramanujan 1967: 105–08). Similarly, Durkheim's (1915) definition of 'religion' as a separation of 'profane' from 'sacred' things, like the

[3] In the interest of heightening awareness of the analytical terms used, English words which closely gloss Indian concepts are given in double quote marks, while quoted Western analytic terms are given with the usual single quote marks.

[4] The Western ethnodisciplines themselves reflect the historic circumstances of their origins. The Reformation split 'spirit' from 'matter', 'value' from 'fact', and the 'humanities' (*Geisteswissenschaften*) from the 'natural sciences' (*Naturwissenschaften*); the Enlightenment further split 'mind' from 'body', 'philosophy' from 'biology', 'subjective' from 'objective', and 'idealism' from 'materialism' (Uberoi 1978); liberal capitalism split 'markets' from 'government', and 'economics' from 'political science'; the industrial and political revolutions split 'urban' from 'rural', 'individual' from 'society', and 'psychology' from 'sociology'; European expansion split 'anthropology' from 'sociology'. The separateness of the domains of the present Western ethnodisciplines from each other is itself one of their most striking and troubling cultural characteristics; there is no reason to suppose that a society which has not shared the Western historic experiences would wish so to divide them.

common Western definition of 'purity' as 'spirit' from which 'flesh' has been separated, has little useful applicability to the *dharma* of Hindus, which is principally concerned with the ways in which all such categories are connected (Mines 1989; Waghorne and Cutler 1985). Weber's (1968: 926–40) social differentiations by 'class' or economic position and by 'status' or style of life are obviously helpful concepts in the West, but cannot separately or together define the transactional ways in which Hindu institutions order castes or persons (Marriott 1968, 1976). The 'solidarity' that Durkheim (1933) presumes as a normal, healthy social state in the Western world may be extraordinary or pathological for the inhabitants of a Hindu world which "moves" (*jagat*) or "flows together" (*saṃsāra*); for them, 'fluidarity' may be preferable. Justifying behaviour by citing precedents and rules—the issue of 'legitimation' on which Weber focuses his famous typology of traditional and bureaucratic 'authority'—is irrelevant to Indian concerns with continual flux and with the *dhārmik* consequences of material and power relations, such as feeding and violence (e.g., Chakravarti 1975: 10–20; Heginbotham 1975). The 'means-end' and 'actor-action' dichotomies with which Parsons and Shils (1952) accurately summarise many of the above Western theoretical distinctions and concerns may seem like universal and unexceptionable notions, yet they are overridden by Hindu notions of *karma*, according to which ends inhere in means and actors are products of actions (Potter 1980).

Are Indian perceptions of a variable and interactive world then of interest largely as negations of all Western distinctions, and of value only as refutations of the Western ethnosocial sciences' claim to analytic universality? Do Indian institutions presume a single, undifferentiated cosmos—one which is impregnable to analysis, and therefore unlikely to produce an analyti ystem? The authors of this volume think otherwise; they find that Indian joinings of what the West would split often point to alternative, especially transactional concepts of integrative value. Their papers also tell of Indian perceptions and kinds of analytic relations (other than dichotomous distinctions) that are ignored by Western social science conventions (including those of structuralism) to the detriment of all.

Thus, a positive impetus for this volume comes from the hope that more fully developed Indian ethnosocial sciences may take their place beside the Western ethnosocial sciences. Together with the ethnosciences of other lands they may provide better bases for the future claim of an expanded, multicultural set of sciences to have that '*universal* significance and value' which Weber in 1904 (1952: 13) prematurely reserved for rational social thought in the West.

Developing indigenous sciences

How can Indian ethnosocial sciences develop today? Potentialities have long existed, both in learned thought and in the perceptual and cognitive categories of everyday Indian life and discourse. These potentialities have been neglected for some centuries as other intellectual technologies were imported from the West. Increasingly since Independence, however, some researchers in every Western discipline have noted that their imported concepts do not fit Indian perceptions and meanings (Mukerji 1986). Many are now seeking to incorporate indigenous definitions of the underlying realities in their discovery procedures (Szanton 1976).

The imperial style of Western ethnosocial science excludes competing definitions of reality from its published reports. A more cosmopolitan, self-critical Western style of 'comparative sociology' allows the reporting of non-Western phenomena (such as *varṇa* and *āśrama*) which can be described by permutations of authoritative Western notions (e.g., Dumont 1970); but its results tend to include a patchwork of negations and unresolved paradoxes. The more humanistic style of ethnography called 'cultural' takes care to report local social concepts that have no ready translations into Western natural languages or existing social science jargons; but its results tend to be richly idiographic, rather than adding to any systematic general model of the culture studied. A 'cultural interpretation' or 'a cultural account' goes further toward systematising: it takes indigenous words and concepts around Dilthey's 'hermeneutic circle' of meaning, building evocatively from smaller local details to more general concepts, and then using the general to inform and enlighten the particulars (Geertz 1983).

Constructing a theoretical social science for a culture requires somewhat more than providing a meaningful cultural account: it requires building from the culture's natural categories a general system of concepts that can be formally defined in relation to each other; it requires developing words and measures that can be used rigorously for description, analysis and explanation within that culture; and it especially requires developing deductive strategies that can generate hypotheses for empirical tests in order that the science may criticise itself and grow. It requires doing all this in terms that will be analytically powerful enough to define all the major parameters of living in that culture without violating the culture's ontology, its presuppositions, or its epistemology.

Talcott Parsons and his many collaborators exemplify some success toward meeting these requirements for the West in their syntheses of the Western social sciences as a 'system of action' (Parsons and Shils 1952). They build on the shared categories of major European and American theorists of the late 19th and early 20th centuries (psychologists, sociologists, economists, anthropologists) who use categories like 'personality', 'society', 'biology', 'culture', etc. Behind these categories, they infer metacategories, such as the 'actor-action' and 'means-end' dichotomies. They take these dichotomies as the axioms—the smallest possible set of basic ideas—from whose combinations and replications the major institutional forms and dilemmas of modern Western life can be deduced. Among common dilemmas they deduce and define are five 'pattern variables'—'affectivity' versus 'affective neutrality', 'self-orientation' versus 'collectivity orientation', 'particularism' versus 'universalism', 'qualities' versus 'performance', and 'functional diffuseness' versus 'functional specificity'. These variables are postulated as potentially recurring in all institutions, in all interactions among persons.

The Parsonian synthesis has been influential and productive in research on Western society, where its general theoretical system has been used to generate hypotheses for studies of kinship systems, social stratification, occupational role structures, politics, etc. As with other Western theories, its resulting hypotheses, rather than its method for *developing* a general theoretical system, have been applied also to non-Western societies. Investigators working in this applied manner assume the universality of the Western axioms; they would research the Western cultural categories among people of different cultures (e.g., Damle [1965] for India). A common result of such applications has been to fault the non-West for failing to recognise the Western categories or for failing to resolve the Western dilemmas in the 'modern' manner (Kapp 1963; Parsons 1966, 1971; Shils 1961). Rarer but theoretically more constructive results have included the discovery that non-Western societies may presuppose other categories and have other questions to deal with—questions demanding answers in terms of alternative percepts and concepts which may not now exist in the Western social sciences (e.g., for Japan, Lebra [1976]; for India, McClelland [1975: 123–68]).

None appears yet to have attempted what is proposed here—following the Parsons and Shils method all the way to constructing an alternative general theoretical system for the social sciences of a non-Western civilisation, using that civilisation's own categories. Some anthropologists have developed theoretical accounts from folk notions of Western institutions (e.g., Schneider [1968] on American kinship). Many have formulated parts of general theoretical systems from the categories presented by the institutions of smaller, more homogeneous non-Western communities, where the materials for synthesis have been relatively few and largely ethnographic (e.g., Fernandez 1982; Geertz 1966; Leaf 1972; Meggitt 1972; Rosaldo 1980). Sociologists who have set out to systematise the categories of Indian social theory have limited themselves to summarising existing *dharmaśāstra* (e.g., Motwani 1934), or to selecting just those features of it that seem to have Western analogues or contraries (e.g., Saksena 1965: 4). The task envisaged here for social scientists is a broader one—to synthesise a theoretical general system accommodating the realities known to Hindus, using both India's multiple textual sources and the evidence of its highly varied social life.

This task should not be begun without taking cognisance of Piatigorsky's (1985) admonition (addressed to researchers on Indian religion) that an investigation needs to work out metaconceptual categories and descriptive terms which are (*i*) congruent with the indigenously cognised features of the phenomena under study, and which also (*ii*) facilitate comparison with other phenomena (here the Western social sciences) having different features. Since vedic Hindus see their society as based directly upon understandings of nature (Dumont 1961: 36–37), the metaconcepts and terms employed here are largely drawn from the natural sciences. The perfect natural science for Hindu India has long been linguistics, this paper and the papers by Ramanujan and Raheja in this volume all illustrate the usefulness of some concepts drawn from that science. But the ideal natural science for the West has long been geometry, and the mathematical concepts also employed in this essay as translations, while partly shared between India and the West, no doubt involve some shifting of Indian meanings in a Western direction. The present results are thus inevitably compromises—equitable ones, it is hoped.

Materials for Hindu ethnosocial sciences

Comprehensive abstract categorisations suggestive of a general theoretical system are plentiful in Hindu thought; they are in fact so many and so variously labelled as to raise doubts about the possibility of their successful synthesis into one scheme. There are widely known classical lists of three "strands" (*guṇa*s), three "humours" (*doṣa*s), three + one "human aims" (*puruṣārtha*s), four "classes" (*varṇa*s), four "stages" (*āśrama*s), five "elements" (*bhūta*s), five "senses" (*indriya*s), five "sheaths" (*kośa*s), six "savours" (*rasa*s), eight + one "sentiments" (*rasa*s), eight + one "feelings" (*bhāva*s), and so on. Lists bearing such titles respectively suggest specialised metaphysical, biological, moral, economic, developmental, physical, psychological, and aesthetic subject matters whose historical and analytic differences in the modern West would locate them in widely separated academic departments and exclude any expectations of a common conceptual framework. Yet all these lists and more have been maintained simultaneously over some centuries by large numbers of learned but unspecialised Indians. If Pugh (1984: 88–95), Raheja (1976: 45–47) and Trawick (1974) are right, these lists describe what are felt to be concentric domains: they are understood as differently labelled, but approximately congruent overlays on a common underlying set of processes whose complexity is less than its many surface appearances would suggest.

The multiple layering of conceptualisations is not less in daily life. Foods are regionally varied, yet the modes of classification in different regions seem mutually consistent: they imply similar variables and the same sort of layered complexity that appears in the above-mentioned, more abstract lists (Ferro-Luzzi 1977, 1978; Khare 1976; Nichter 1986; Rizvi 1986). The dozens of modes of healing (dietary, medicinal, religious, magical, astrological) applied to one ailment, through which suppositions much like those of the food classification can again be read, are sometimes called 'pluralistic' by observers applying the Western distinctions (Beals 1976); yet an Indian patient may try all modes, feeling them to involve mutually implicated levels of reality—such are the field and clinical reports of many anthropologists (Amarasingham 1980; Egnor 1983; Pugh 1984; Weiss et al. 1986).

The implicit congruences and lived-in mutualities among the many layers—"sheaths" (*kośa*s), "bodies" (*śārīra*s), or on the larger scale, "spheres" (*loka*s)—of Hindu reality are such that no learned text nor ethnographer's informant seems to have felt the need to either deny any of them or provide a definitive ordering or articulation of them all. Different lists or layers are often compared, usually only two at a time, and then variously, according to the purpose at hand (S.B. Daniel 1983; Ramanujan 1989; Trawick 1988a). An explicit analysis of the common properties, if any, of these layers is thus an urgent task, preliminary to constructing a general theoretical system for the Indian social sciences.

The general nature of the compatibilities and partial congruences among the layers, whether of learned or popular formulation, should be evident from any group of lists like the above, but may be easier to see among the shorter ones. Four of these—classical and still widely repeated lists of "elements" (*bhūta*s), "humours" (*doṣa*s), "strands" (*guṇa*s), and "human aims" (*puruṣārtha*s)—are taken together below as possible bases for a general theoretical system. Each list is given in the order in which it is conventionally recited.

Table 1
Some Classical Lists of Categories

Elements (*a*)	*Humours* (*b*)	*Strands* (*c*)	*Human Aims* (*d*)
1. ether	1. wind	1. goodness	1 coherence-incoherence
2. air	2. bile	2. passion	2. advantage-disadvantage
3. fire	3. phlegm	3. darkness	3. attachment-nonattachment
4. water			+1. release
5. earth			

The contents of these lists at first appear heterogeneous, yet certain resemblances among them are also striking. That physical phenomena like "fire" and "darkness" appear in them as well as do human moral qualities like "attachment" and "goodness" is itself one striking fact: it suggests that such categories may be seen as somehow of one genre. The implication that moral and physical are mutually translatable replicates the *sāṃkhya* postulate that the world and everything in it comes into being through a merger of "pure consciousness" (*puruṣa*) and "materiality" (*prakṛti*) (Larson 1987: 23, 43). It recalls the observation by Potter (n.d.) that in Sanskrit *karma* is not just a 'doing', but also a 'making' of something substantial, and the observation by Inden (1976: 21) that "substance" (*dhātu*) and "code" (*dharma*) are of one etymology (*dhṛ*) and need not be dichotomised in the world of constituted things. Inden's observation is documented in his account of medieval Bengali social theories and social histories. It is illustrated in other analyses and ethnographic reports connecting substantive qualities with actions, such as those by Babb (1970, 1981, 1983); E.V. Daniel (1984); Davis (1983); Inden and Nicholas (1977); Marriott (1976); and Marriott and Inden (1974).[5] If physical, biological and social things do have common conceptual denominators, those denominators must be of rather abstract, metaconceptual kinds, like 'relationships' or 'processes'.

That none of these lists contains less than three items is a second striking commonality, contrasting especially with the insistent dualising of the Western typologies: three appears to be the irreducible number of properties or components with which Hindus will comfortably think about human affairs. Thinking about constituted things in dualities is often condemned. At least three terms are always present, always combined.[6]

Leaving aside the aim of "release", which is an all-or-nothing event, the incidence of each other item is said to be variable. This is a third striking common fact. Each element and humour is said to be more or less strongly present in every food or bodily tissue, each strand more or less predominant in every action, each human aim more or less prominent in any person's motivation. Learned texts display few type-entities illustrating just one item taken in isolation. Thus binary, all-or-nothing measures of an item's total presence or absence will rarely apply; analog or proportional measures

[5] Against this mutual translatability of substance and action or code, McGilvray (1982a: 90–94) objects that the Mukkuvar-dominated order of castes in Batticaloa, Sri Lanka, is explained by informants as resulting from a historical imposition of rules, and not from transactions in any medium that he would recognise as a 'substance'. If commands or statements of rules along with other words, gestures and signs are admitted (as previously proposed) to the analytic category 'substance', then McGilvray's objection would seem to dissolve.

His data, like the reports in this volume by Dirks and Raheja, do however raise important questions about the political circumstances in which different media are foregrounded and regarded as definitive of social relations: actional media may be most prominent among maximal transactors, such as Gujars, Kallars, Mukkuvars and Buddhists, while substantial media are more prominent in defining relations among minimal transactors, such as many Jains and Vaiṣṇavas; translatability may be most typical of transactors of middle type, such as Brahmans and most others. Until this possible range of variation can be more systematically investigated, formulations of the middle range continue to seem worth stating.

[6] It appears to be Western dualistic structuralism, rather than indigenous thinking, that leads to reconceiving Hindu triads as dichotomies mediated by a third term.

will generally be needed to express their relative strengths, for all these items are variables. Furthermore, the relative strengths of the variables in each list are not indicated by their places in the recitational or in any other fixed orders: examinations of their uses in their respective contexts show that each may vary independently of the other items on its list.[7]

Three-dimensional graphing

Mathematical conventions of graphing would not leave any triad of independent variables in a one-dimensional column, as each appears in Table 1; they would instead depict each variable as a numbered line turned at right angles where it intersects the other two, thus creating a three-dimensional property-space. Hindu conventions might prefer to draw three such variables as the petals of a flowering lotus, emerging from a centre at various angles in open space, and such a representation might in fact serve quite well. But a rectangular cube with the familiar properties of breadth, height and depth can make three-dimensional relations easier to specify and compare (e.g., Mitchell 1980), at least for scholars used to living in and with such structures. Cubes are therefore offered here provisionally as geometric metaphors and mnemonics for Indian spaces within which everything must be rated along at least three different dimensions. Of course, a cubic graph's right angles should be altered by evidence that the variables are not wholly independent (as exemplified in Hiebert's [1971: 66–67] graphing of relations between personal and caste rank); and the cube's sides, arbitrarily made of equal length, should be altered by evidence that the variables' scales are not commensurate.

Each column of Table 1 (corresponding to columns [*a*] through [*d*] of Table 2) has a corresponding cube in Figure 1 on which the numbered variables (and their contraries, if any) are written. Thus, from Table 2, column (*d*), "advantage" (*artha*) is shown as opposite to "disadvantage" (*anartha*) and so on, in the "human aims" cube of Figure 1. In the other cubes, variables for whose contrary no one Sanskrit word is commonly used are shown opposite to unlabelled sides; the named variable is meant to be present there too, although less so.

Since the cubes are not intended to imply static substance or impenetrability, they are drawn as transparent. Indeed, the variables being graphed by the cubes are said to be anything but static; elements and humours are all

[7] At times, the three strands are treated more simply as high, middle and low degrees along a single scale (e.g., in Manu 12.30–33, 39–51). But elsewhere and more generally (e.g., Manu 12.24–29; Bhagavad Gītā 14.5–17, 17.4–22, 18.18–40) the strands' independent variability is made evident. In some Tamil thinking (reported by Moreno and Marriott 1989), a single "hot-cold" scale seems to do the work of the three classical humours. But popular usages like those reported by S.B. Daniel (1983: 53–54) and by Davis (1983: 49, 51) continue to employ at least three variables.

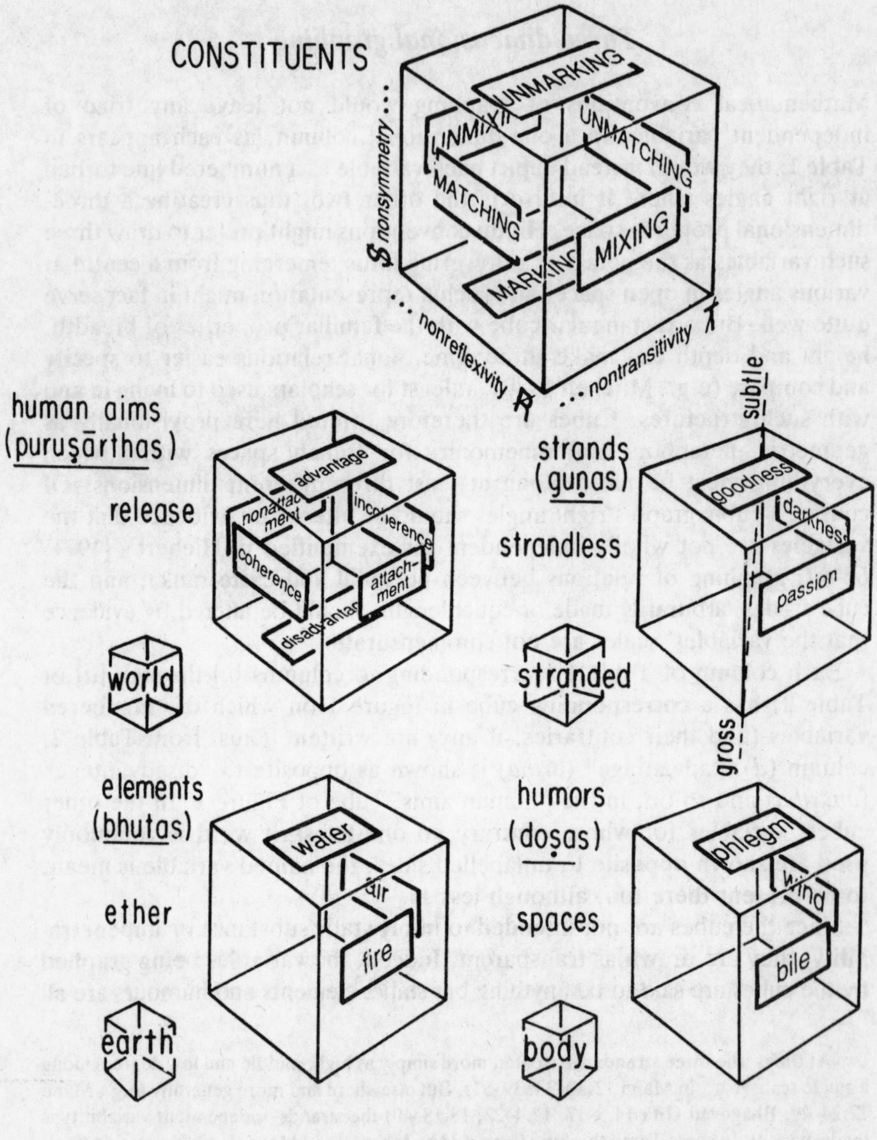

Fig. 1 Derivation of the Hindu Constituent Cube

described as motile substances, while strands and aims are transient relations or processes. All cubes are more or less open to movements between their internal and external spaces, and none is intended to provide an exhaustive accounting of the sphere that it depicts.

Three-dimensional graphing opens the possibility that differing points of view may explain the differing conventional orders for listing the faces of what may still be a single underlying shape. Thus, when "ether" or "sky" (*ākāśa*) as the most inclusive element is named first while "earth" (*pṛthvī*) as the most included is named last, the viewing and starting point seems to be well beyond the earth (outside the cube), looking earthward (inward); this ordering also asserts a process of devolution (explicit in *sāṃkhya* doctrine) from relatively imperceptible or "subtle" (*sūkṣma*) to relatively perceptible or "gross" (*sthūla*) substance (Larson 1987: 50–52). The humours of Hindu biology are conventionally listed starting from the lower backside of Figure 1 "elements" cube with "wind" (*vāyu*) first and with "phlegm" (*kapha*) last, possibly because some physicians think wind is the most troublesome humour and phlegm the least (Caraka 1983 *Sū*. 20.10). Strands are listed in the Bhagavad Gītā, perhaps as they are seen by Lord Kṛṣṇa from the heavens directly above, with "goodness" (*sattva*) first and "darkness" (*tamas*) last. The list of three worldly "human aims" in *dharmaśāstra* usually begins with "coherence" (*dharma*) and ends with "attachment" (*kāma*); this series is read from the upper front of the cube, where the Brahman authors of such books reside, to the lower rear, where their social opposites do. A cube's six sides have no inherent taxonomy, nor do they decree any one, fixed 'value hierarchy', and this fact permits a variety of equally valid but different ordinal readings.

The six sides of a cube can help to visualise the 'revolving hierarchy' that Malamoud (1982) sees as typical in learned debates on "human aims". As the cube is turned by different debaters, different faces come into the foreground, where the items written on them are given broader definitions, while items written on other faces are backgrounded and given narrower definitions. The foregrounding capacity of the cube also facilitates understanding of any relationship among persons which has 'shifting' aspects, like the analytically distinct 'central', 'mutual', and 'hierarchical' aspects of inter-caste relations which Raheja (1989) finds in Pahansu village. Even the 'central conundrum of Indian social ideology', which Trautmann (1981: 285–88) finds in differently ordered transactions between priest and king, may cease to confound when a three-dimensional semantic space is presupposed, for such a space allows different, equally true orderings of the same two persons. Three-dimensional representation further helps to clarify the elaborately 'faceted' or aspectual reasoning of Hindu biology and astrology; these sciences both deal with relationships whose angles shift through several planes, rather than with fixed, linear oppositions (Kemper 1977; Zimmermann 1987: 116–24, 143–48). Three dimensions offer resolutions to many other problems of diversity-within-unity, such as the problem of henotheism, by which, without a sense of contradiction, different deities are exalted at different times. Three-dimensional graphing is obviously congenial also to sculptural representations and to the plural faces and other attributes of one god that appear in Hindu iconography. It accommodates the simultaneous existence of six orthodox "views" (*darśana*s) within Hindu philosophy, and can be expanded, if necessary, to a manifold of many more dimensions (Thurston and Weeks 1984).

Merging the triads

If the four differently labelled cubes drawn in Figure 1 are understood as overlays of a single underlying structure (a simplifying assumption that may be essential for communication and social functioning),[8] then the general meanings of that structure, if any, might be discovered by merging the meanings of the four overlays. Merging requires first orienting the four cubes so that the faces which are most alike are aligned. It also requires construing each item in its broadest significance.[9]

The mutual orientations of the cubes shown in Figure 1 and the alignments of items in the rows of Table 2 are not supplied by the usual orders of the items' recitation. For example, arranging the four cubes so that all of the items numbered '1' face the same way or occupy the same row would group together "ether", "wind", and "goodness"—a set of items that no Indian usage seems to endow with a common meaning.

The more generally felt resemblances can, however, be determined through many other textual and ethnographic evidences. The homology or metonymy shown in columns (*a*) and (*b*) between elemental "fire" and humoral "bile", elemental "water" and humoral "phlegm", and elemental "air" and humoral "wind", is explicit in *āyurveda* (e.g., Caraka 1983 *Sū.* 12.11–12). The correspondence between these humours and the respective strands "darkness", "passion", and "goodness" (column [*c*]) is also explicit in those sections of *āyurveda* which deal with psychological health (Caraka 1983 *Sū*. 1.57, 1985 *Śā*. 4.34–36). Similar world qualities are assumed by the Hindu set of four "human aims" or concerns (*puruṣārtha*s), which work sometimes with those qualities, sometimes against them. The aims are shown in column (*d*) with their opposites in additional rows of the same column. These are sought in varying combinations by all living beings, but by different persons at different times. Thus, seeking and maintaining "attachment" (*kāma*) may be desirable for many, especially in earlier phases of life, yet developing nonattachment may be desirable for some,

[8] Ambiguous exegesis may be equally essential to communication and social functioning in a system that is assumed to have a single structure (Trawick 1988a).

[9] Merging the four cubes in order to find possible shared meanings among them is not intended to eliminate consideration of their other, more distinctive meanings.

and especially in later phases of life; seeking "advantage" (*artha*) may be preferable when one has the means to obtain it, but submitting to disadvantage may be preferable when one does not; seeking "coherence" (*dharma*) may be suitable among good and stable circumstances, but cultivating incoherence may be more suitable among bad or changing times. Divergences of orientations, motivations and behaviours among the above three pairs of aims may be judged minor in comparison with the divergence of the '+ 1' aim—obtaining "freedom" or "release" (*mokṣa*) from the world of seeking. Release is not for everyone, nor is it for anyone at all times. Thus, again there can and need be no one 'hierarchy' of these 'values': time in its many Indian senses is intrinsic to choices among them.

Human aims are extensively linked with the triad of strands in popular texts of *dharmaśāstra*, as shown in the third and fourth columns of Table 2.[10] Thus, the Bhagavad Gītā speaks of the "attachment" aim (*kāma*) as a direct expression of the "passion" strand (*rajas*) (Bhagavad Gītā 17.5, 18.34). It speaks of the strand called "darkness" (*tamas*) as promoting ignorance (18.22) and as reversing judgments of right and wrong (18.32), etc., all of which are tantamount to "incoherence" (*adharma*) and opposite to the goal of "coherence" (*dharma*). These pairings implicitly leave the third strand, "goodness" (*sattva*), to be linked with the remaining aim, "advantage" (*artha*). Both goodness and advantage help one to be "strong" (17.8), to move "upward" (14.18) and to achieve the "highest" (14.14). That achievement of advantage of any kind, especially material or political, is a sign of virtue is also strongly attested in Hindu ethnography, for example, by Chakravarti (1975: 49, 53–54) and Wadley (1975: 183). (Also see Madan 1987: 121.)

Elements and humours are also linked directly with human aims by many usages, without recourse to the scheme of strands. Attachment is expressed and described as accompanied by a "hot" bodily surface, nonattachment by a cool one (the "heat" having gone inward as *tapas*), thus implicating fire. Persons of "bilious type" (*pitta prakṛti*) are aggressive, lecherous, greedy—all ways of being externally attached (Caraka 1985 *Sa*. 4.38). Air is the

[10] Manu (at 12.38) differs from these alignments and seems to be unique among the classical authors of *dharmaśāstra* in linking (*i*) "coherence" (*dharma*) with "goodness" (*sattva*), (*ii*) "advantage" (*artha*) with "passion" (*rajas*), and (*iii*) "attachment" (*kāma*) with "darkness" (*tamas*). Manu's linkages would result from simply placing the lists of aims and strands side by side, each in its conventional order, and reciting them together. These pedantic linkages may also express (*i*) a professional *dharmaśāstri*'s exaltation of *dharma* as the most inclusive aim, (*ii*) an ascetic's devaluation of other upward striving by construing it narrowly as the pursuit of wealth, and (*iii*) a vedic teacher's sense that the warm attachments which flourish in darkness most threaten the chastity demanded of students, and deserve last listing. Manu's alignments in this verse are no doubt congenial to some others who are situated as he is, but they conflict with more widespread understandings. They have been influential (for example on Motwani 1934), but would confound development of a more generalisable and realistic sociology.

Table 2

Derivation of Postulates for a Processual Hindu Social Science

Hindu Analytic Sets				Mathematical Analogues		FIVE PROCESSES POSTULATED (and further defined)
Elements (*mahābhutas*) *(a)*	Humours (*doṣas*) *(b)*	Strands (*guṇas*) *(c)*	Human Aims (*puruṣārthas*) *(d)*	Fundamental Properties *(e)*	Set Theory Operations *(f)*	*(g)*
3. Fire (*agni*) ...	2. Bile (*pitta*) ...	2. Passion (*rajas*) ...	3. Attachment (*kāma*)... ...nonattachment (*niṣkāma*)	Nonreflexivity / reflexivity	Intersection	**MIXING** (opening, expanding)... ...unmixing (closing, condensing)
4. Water (*ap*) ...	3. Phlegm (*kapha*) ...	1. Goodness (*sattva*) ...	2. Advantage (*artha*) ... ...disadvantage (*anartha*)	Nonsymmetry	Inclusion	**UNMARKING** self (outranking, pervading other neutralising self).. ...marking self (being outranked being pervaded)

2. Air (*vāyu*) …	1. Wind (*vāta*) …	3. Darkness (*tamas*) …	…incoherence (*adharma*)	Nontransitivity	Disjunction, Complementation	UNMATCHING (reversing, negating, separating)…
			1. Coherence (*dharma*)…	/ transitivity	/ Union	…matching (continuing, affirming, uniting)
5. Earth (*pṛthvī*)	[gross body (*sthūla śārīra*)]	[depends on: more *rajas* less *sattva* less *tamas*]	[birth, life, (*janma*)]	[example]	Set	GROSSENING (materialising, localising, synthesising)
1. Ether, sky (*ākāśa*) …	[subtle body (*sukṣma śārīra*)]	[depends on: less *rajas* more *sattva* more *tamas*]	[death, (*mṛtyu*)]	[definition]	Universal set	…subtilising (abstracting, universalising, analysing)
0. none (*brahman*)	[soul (*ātman*)]	No strand (*nirguṇa*)	4. Release (*mokṣa*)	[none]	Empty set	CONSCIOUSNESS (nonrelationality).

medium of spirit possession, a kind of "play"-filled communication that deals with incoherent states (e.g., Gold 1988: 165, 182). Humoral "wind" is characterised by unrestrainable motion (Caraka 1983: *Sū.* 12.8; Manu 12.120), as are the strand of darkness (Das 1985: 187) and the negative aim of *adharma* (Selwyn 1982). Water falls from above—from places of advantage and influence—while phlegm as "unctuousness" (*sneha*) is another way of referring to the love that descends from caring superiors, such as gods and parents (Inden and Nicholas 1977: 87).

Figure 1 (in its top cube) and Table 2 (in its final column) summarise the above linkages and give each metonymic set a new, generalised name intended to indicate some shared meanings and uses of the Sanskrit-named categories that it summarises. 'Unmarking' appears on the top side of the cube and in the same row with "advantage" and with other superior items like "goodness", "phlegm" and "water"; it contrasts with 'marking', which falls in the place of "disadvantage" below it. 'Mixing' appears with "attachment" on the "fire", "bile" and "passion" (cube right) side and row; it contrasts with 'unmixing' on the left. 'Unmatching' appears with "incoherence" on the "dark", "airy", and "windy" backside and row, contrasting with 'matching', which joins (bright, anaerobic, calm) "coherence" on the front.

Each row of items, each set of similarly oriented cubic sides is incorporated in one of the general processual constituents that is postulated—mixing, unmarking and unmatching. These incorporations are possible because of mutual homologies or metonymies among the items. 'Metonymy' and 'homology' do not refer to a complete identity of meaning between "fire" and "bile", for example, but do indicate partial identities—sharings of some properties—which justify substituting one of these words for the other in many contexts.[11] Thus, 'mixing' is intended to stand for what any two of these items—"fire", "bile", "passion", "attachment"—have in common. "Fire", "bile", and "attachment" are of one metonymic set, yet also belong to separable, partly differing layers or spheres; they may at times be felt as conflicting—as partly unmatching with each other—perhaps especially because they *are* otherwise presumed to be metonymous. Das (1976) gives many examples of the anguish experienced in Hindu families when personal feelings conflict with other definitions of members' relatedness.

What the layered cube postulates is that anything in the Hindu world which partakes of "substance" (*dravya, dhātu, prakṛti*)—an atom, an organism, a group, a time, a place, a relationship, a feeling, etc.—requires characterisation along at least the three processual dimensions of variation that such a cube represents; and then that this construct may be viewed from many angles.

[11] The relations among items in these rows are of the kind that Wittgenstein (1958: 17) has called 'family resemblances'.

Antiequivalence relations

If the above alignments of variables are accepted as common and meaningful, then a highly systematic set of further analogues comes into view: the metonymic sets of variables summarised as 'mixing', 'unmarking' and 'unmatching' point respectively to notions that concern three of the fundamental relational properties of mathematics and symbolic logic—reflexivity, symmetry and transitivity (column *e*). They also point to partly corresponding operations of set theory—intersection, inclusion and union (column *f*).

Their names are less abstract, yet the Hindu variables (especially the strands) are used in ways that approximate the wide range (the analytic 'power') of the three fundamental relational properties. These three relational properties are defined by logicians (such as Langer 1967: 246–49) as potentialities, respectively, of the numbers one, two, and three. They function as axioms for all formal structural analyses. As such, they have been applied to studies of marriage (beginning with Weil in Lévi-Strauss 1949: 278–85), group dynamics (Lindzey and Borgatta 1954), and social relations generally (Doreian 1971: 15–20; Harary et al. 1965: 7–9; Kemeny et al. 1966: 385–406). They have been successfully used to design models of many cultural systems (Hage and Harary 1983).

The Hindu variables revise the standard Western version of the fundamental relational properties called 'equivalence relations'. Equivalence relations have tended to be assumed in recent Western popular thought and social science as essential to the organisation of human personality and society. Thus, persons and many other entities are postulated as being normally self-reflexive ('individuals', having identity with and being sufficient to themselves), and as symmetrical (equal) and transitive (consistent) in their relations with each other. 'Individuals' are indivisible, integrated, self-developing units, not normally subject to disjunction or reconstitution. Given such units, interpersonal influences, inequalities, and changes have to be brought in as external factors or pathologies. Other Western examples of equivalence thinking are a Euclidean plane and solid geometry, an Aristotelian syllogistic logic, and notions of legislation as fixed and uniformly applicable to all.

The Hindu postulations of mixing, unmarking and unmatching instead assert that persons are in various degrees nonreflexive (not necessarily identical with or otherwise related only to themselves), nonsymmetrical (not necessarily equal), and nontransitive (not necessarily consistent) in their relations. They emphasise that persons are composite and divisible (what one might better call 'dividuals') and that interpersonal relations in the world are generally irregular and fluid, if not entirely chaotic. Such Hindu postulations in effect constitute the universe as a set of 'antiequivalence relations'.

Antiequivalence relations are necessarily variable, since while they deny perfect reflexivity, symmetry and transitivity, they do not postulate the dichotomous opposites of these—absolute irreflexivity, asymmetry and intransitivity. Instead, they assert that various imperfect and inconstant intermediate states are to be expected, and thus that processes and intermediate states, rather than any fixed or polarised structures, are basic. Yet, since antiequivalence relations are understood by Hindus to inhere also in matter, they may appropriately be called 'substances' as well as 'processes'.

Matter that is subject to such variations may well be called 'fluid', and indeed Hindus generally refer to the world they must live in as "[that which is] moving" (*jagat*) and as a "flowing together" (*saṃsāra*). Such a world has its channels, basins and pools—even its temporary dams and dikes—but knows no absolute or enduring partitions (Zimmermann 1979). It and its inhabitants are generated by, and constituted of, more or less malleable substance that is continually moving in and out of them and also moving, like other features of the hydrosphere, under the variable influences of heat, gravity, currents and wind.[12] As a people who are etymologically "riverine", it is serendipitous that Hindus should have a set of sciences that respond so well to hydraulic metaphors.

The approximations of any abstract, analytic axioms—even antiequivalence axioms—to Hindu constituents would seem to be limited by Hindu presuppositions of a wholly substantial and fluid world. Unlike any ideal and universalising logic, Hindu social formulations inhere always in substantial agencies which necessarily differ in particulars (Ramanujan 1989). Unlike points in a Euclidean geometric space, imperfectly bounded fluid entities can never be presumed to be fixed, discrete, or absolutely measurable. Modellings of Hindu phenomena thus seem to require algorithms more like those used in the sciences of oceanography or meteorology. Meanwhile, for starting to think about Hindu social realities, several simple and relatively precise techniques of relational modelling and measuring based on irreflexive and asymmetrical axioms are already available, as mentioned below.

Mixing, unmarking and unmatching

'Mixing' is the nonreflexive (intersective, externalising, expanding) process

[12] In proposing that the strands may be understood as three kinds of motion—stasis (*sattva*); controlled movement (*rajas*); and both inertia and uncontrolled, riotous movement (*tamas*)—Veena Das (1985: 187) comes close to what is noted here. In a wholly moving world, however, a concept like 'stasis' is not strictly allowable. An entity such as an earth satellite may, however, gain apparent stability by applying equal force against its own potential drift, thus moving along with the earth's rotation. What is called *sāttvik* action is often such a counteractive movement that gives relative stasis.

implied in common Hindu assertions that the substantial universe with all its human and other contents is more or less "hot", being made up of "fire" (*agni*) or "bile" (*pitta*), moved by "passion" (*rajas*) and "attachment" (*kāma*), and affected by temporal "conjunctions" (*parvans*), spatial "crossings" (*tīrthas*), a logic of "combinations" (*yukti*), etc.

To say that 'mixing' (rather than unmixing) is a general property of the Hindu world is to assert the rarity of reflexivity, the improbability that any entity in that world can relate only to itself, even by a relationship of equality or identity. Mixing thus suggests the probability that any entity will be found nonself-sufficient, incompletely related to itself, not even equivalent to itself—being to a greater or lesser degree open and dependent for its qualities and processes upon exchanges with others.[13] Mixing's nonReflexivity and its *rājasik* nature are both suggested in the figures by use of the slashed 'R' symbol for the incidence of this variable.

The mixing variable is illustrated by David's (1974, 1977) ethnographies from Jaffna. Its formulation as 'maximal' and 'minimal transacting' is available in Marriott's (1976) unconventional matrix analysis of inter-caste and other relations in seven villages, a formulation which is replicated and critically examined in a single Tamil village by Levinson (1982). Mixing is particularly well analysed through the graph-theoretical procedures of Harary et al. (1965), which are further developed and applied in Hage and Harary (1983).

'Unmarking' (out-ranking, pervading others, neutralising self) is the nonsymmetrical process implied by Hindu postulations of "water" (*āpaḥ*), "phlegm" (*kapha*), and "goodness" (*sattva*) as universal constituents. All of these have a property of initial altitude and a directional tendency to descend, like rain and rivers, from "origin" to "end", "wet" to "dry", "pure" to "impure", "subtle" to "gross", "essence" to "residue", etc. Gravitational orientations and movements of substance are expected everywhere—in ancestry, birth, alimentation, top-down bathing, ranked feeding, deference, tutelage, obedience to commands, speaking and listening, and worship. A *sāttvik* person is one who faces into the prevailing gravitational direction of flow and successfully swims upstream.

Transfers of any entity's constituent properties are also understood to occur by transactions, such as those from gods to humans through natal "headwriting" (*talai eṛuttu*) (S.B. Daniel 1983: 28–40), and by the carefully matched personal "polishings" or "markings" called *saṃskāras*. The subtle karmic "traces" (*vāsanās*) left by personal action are markings that continue to affect future life (Potter 1980).

As the only reliable, directional force, unmarking-marking is what seems to Hindus to give continuity and relative stability to social relations. Its

[13] An example in this volume is Wadley and Derr's finding that no survivor of the Karimpur fire fails to share his sins.

reality is affirmed by Hindu attention to relative "advantage" (*artha*), to priority in time sequence, and to evaluative preferences. In the figures, the nonSymmetrical (and anti-*sāttvik*) direction of marking is suggested by use of a slashed 'S' as its abbreviation. Measures of relative marking as evaluations and as transactions among castes and persons are readily available (Freed 1970; Garbett 1980; Hiebert 1971: 54–67; Mahar 1959; Marriott 1968, 1976).

Calling this process 'marking' is here meant to evoke the image of a substance (such as a sediment or pigment) moving from a marker to a marked object, one-way, as some property (tangible or intangible) is so often felt to do in Hindu interpersonal relations. Animal behaviourists use the term 'marking' in this way for the scents that animals use to claim territories. 'Marking' is also meant to evoke uses of this word for partly similar phenomena by linguists.[14] Hindu marking shares with linguistic marking the notion that unmarked (neutral) or less marked entities are more inclusive (in substantial terms, more 'pervasive') and thus taxonomically 'higher' than are the more marked and specialised entities included under (that is, pervaded by) them. The term 'marking' was first used for Hindu phenomena by Wadley (1975: 56) in analysing a local 'hierarchy' of deities, arranged by the scope of their powers. Substantial marking in the Hindu world particularly resembles morphological marking in linguistics (as in the comparison of 'man' and 'woman'), but does not so closely resemble nonmorphological, semantic marking, which may occur without the addition of sound features (as in different meanings of the word 'man'). The substantialistic Hindu notion that entities become 'unmarked' or neutralised by transferring markings to others distinguishes Hindu marking from both linguistic and animal marking.

'Unmatching' (which could alternatively be called 'messing' or 'nixing') is the nontransitive (reversing, negating, separating) constituent process. A slashed 'T', referring to nonTransitivity, is used as its abbreviated sign in the two figures. It summarises the fluctuating movement, sometimes the disorder which is anticipated in Hindu postulations that "air" or "wind" (*vāyu, vāta*) is an element and a "fault" or "humour" (*doṣa*) of all life (as are also "bile" and "phlegm"), and that "darkness" (*tamas*) and "incoherence" (*adharma*) are expectable constituents of the universe generally. Inaction when action is needed, chaotic action when controlled action is needed (Das 1985: 204, fn. 5); separating when unity is needed, joining when separation is needed—are all examples of unmatching. Hindu notions of "inappropriateness" (*pratiloma, asātmya*, etc.), "unwisdom" (*avidyā*) and "uncertainty" (*adṛṣta*) are other examples of the richly developed Hindu notions of unmatching—these approximating statistical concepts of

[14] Others (such as Allen 1985: 22–25) note that Dumont's uses of the term 'hierarchy' are often synonymous with linguistic 'marking'

'negative correlation' and 'error', respectively. That orderings of entities not much more inconsistent than those of Hindu society may be realised by chickens (who lack any axiom of transitivity) has been shown by Chase (1984), giving credence to the less extreme characterisation of Hindu society as nontransitive in its axioms.

Unmatchings occur continually through the permutations of astral "time" (*kāla*), through spatial dislocations, and through "impure" (*aśuddha, āśauca*) and "inauspicious" (*aśubha*) events (Madan 1987: 50–58). Unmatching is a secular trend of the universe as it devolves through increasingly corrupt "ages" (*yuga*s) and falls into states of "emergency" (*āpad*). 'Ritual'—"coherent action" (*dharmakārya*)—the principal means of rematching (which may itself involve negations, reversals and separations), is the ubiquitous but not wholly effective Hindu antidote to all sorts of disorder.

Earth, ether and consciousness

Hindu thought generally, following the ancient ideas of *sāṃkhya*, assumes at least two other elements, "ether" (*ākāśa*) and "earth" (*pṛthvi*) as variable constituents of the material universe. Ether and earth are respectively understood in *sāṃkhya* and elsewhere as upper and lower points of a devolving, increasingly marked, self-depleting series of elements running from a relatively "subtle" (*sūkṣma*) or ethereal and inclusive source to a sink of "gross" (*sthūla*) materiality, the included remainder of the other elements (Larson 1987: 51–52). Accordingly, they are here tentatively treated as one variable, titled in Table 2 as 'Grossening and subtilising'.

Following no *sāṃkhya* text, but using the *sāṃkhya*-influenced semantic space defined above, one could plot the idea of a subtle-gross continuum as the diameter shown in the cube of "strands" (*guṇa*s) in Figure 1. This diameter runs from the far, upper corner where things are particulate—small (unmixed) and loose (unmatched) but pervasive (unmarked)—to the opposite near, lower corner, where things are large (mixed), unified (matched), and pervaded (marked). Table 2, column *c*, defines the same, grossening diameter in *guṇa* terms.

In the texts of Hindu biology, the constituents "sky" or "ether" (*ākāśa*) and "earth" (*pṛthvī, kṣiti*) are in the background and are discussed much less fully than are "air", "fire", and "water". They seem to function mostly as temporary containers for other elements, actions and processes. Ether supplies cavities or empty spaces—for movements outside, through, and within substances—while earth constitutes the limits of loci—defined places, tangible shapes, partial boundaries, routes with termini (Manu 12.120; Caraka 1985 *Śā*. 7.16). Given the bulk and motility of the other Hindu elements, such localising containers seem indispensible, and Hindu discourse accordingly postulates many sorts of "channels" (*srotase*s), "vessels" (*pātra*s), places of "rest" (*āśrama*s), "wombs" (*yoni*s), "bodies" (*śārīra*s), "genera" (*jāti*s), "fields" (*kṣetra*s), and "spheres" (*loka*s). "Earth" and "ether" thus together provide temporary loci for birth, aggregation, death, rebirth, and all else that passes among people. In the figures in this essay, such loci are represented by cubes, cubes within cubes, and arrows.

Affected by what flows through them, much as any karmic agent is understood to be affected by its actions, these containers of earth and ether appear to be partly dependent on variations in the three more motile constituents. Earth can evidently be reshaped by sun, wind and irrigation, while ether is expandable and contractable. The temporary 'incapacities' of human bodies during death and birth are the subject of Mines' (1989) study, which confirms that repairs to these containers are affected by the other variables. Table 2 therefore excludes earth and ether from the list of independent variables.

Generally also, earth and ether appear to be in mutually complementary distribution—where one is strong the other is weak (Caraka 1983 *Sū.* 26.40)—supporting the interpretation that these two elements are opposed poles of a single variable. They are so listed in Table 2. As containers of terminal but contrary kinds, their functions seem to be to transform—to recombine, reproduce and reissue what they receive, earth in relatively gross, ether in relatively subtle forms.

The Hindu sciences also generally postulate one nonelement and antiaim—the omnipresent, reflexive, nonmaterial, constant process(es) commonly glossed as "self" or "soul" (*brāhman, ātman*), or "consciousness" (*puruṣa*). Its function of total, passive consciousness is normally available to humans only on release from the stranded, substantial and fluctuating world. Only through a released consciousness, conceivable as the empty and static complement of the universal set (of the foregoing particulars), does a sense of wholeness ordinarily arise. By conceptually aggregating all points of view (those of all differently situated, embodied souls) on a fluid world, however, this Hindu notion of a ubiquitous consciousness seems to point to the multiperspectival and multidimensional kind of thought about relationships and processes which a Hindu ethnosociology, too, may well attempt. Such consciousness is, of course, the subject of a vast speculative literature, but has only begun to be a focus of ethnography.[15]

The five common processes described above, listed in Table 1 and shown as constituents in Figure 1, are summarised as postulates in column (*g*) of Table 2.

Other spheres, other cubes: homologies and deductions

Up to this point, this essay has been concerned with defining the general semantic property-space in which Hindus conceptually and perceptually

[15] Gold's (1988) ethnography of pilgrimages to and from a Rajasthan village shows the large, yet intermittent and peripheral relevance of such consciousness in social life.

dwell. If that space has been correctly defined in the postulates and diagrams above, other realities of the civilisation—processes, actions, entities, institutions, issues, etc.—should readily find places to function meaningfully within that same space. This seems to be the case, as illustrated by the other papers in this volume.[16]

In each sphere, such as those of religion, architecture, kinship, village organisation, disaster, and state politics investigated in the other studies of this volume, one finds definitions of particular property-spaces and contents that are metonymous and partly homologous with the general properties of the constituent cube postulated above. Thus, the festivals and castes of a Tamil town observed by Moreno are characterised and operate in terms of the system of humours which itself helps to define the general cube. Similarly, the household activities, deities, and structures described by Moore are aligned with the physical elements which also define the cube. Likewise, the rates of survivors' healing after death are calculated by Mines for *varṇas* and *āśramas* from the defining system of qualitative "strands" and from the transactions that the triad of strands imply. Political powers (Dirks 1989), karmic speculations (Wadley and Derr 1989), and inter-caste relational patterns (Raheja 1989) are all found to proceed in various terms which correspond well with the three classical aims—another scheme contributing to the general cube. Each of the primary analyses thus implies or explicitly refers to other schemes labelling the same general, multi-dimensional space. Some homologies among the schemes of the several social spheres are listed in Table 3 and diagrammed in Figure 2. More of them are shown in the several figures in Moore's paper.

Anything that is described by a combination of three or more of the processual variables can be located in any sphere or cube. The four *āśramas*, if one follows Mines' characterisation of them by their strands and interactions (as in Table 3), would occupy four sides of the cube, two at the more matched front, two further back. The four *varṇas*, if characterised by the three strands as Davis (1983: 51) found them to be in a Bengal village, occupy the two upper front and two lower rear corners of that cubic "sphere". The year can be shown to rotate counter-clockwise through the same plane of the cube which is described by the *varṇas*, since it follows the six seasons, whose "savours" (*rasas*) are similarly located by the humours and elements (as in Caraka 1983 *Sū*. 6 and elsewhere).[17] If characterised by their predominant constituents and effects (tabulated by

[16] As an alternative to descriptive, field testing, such as the present papers provide, assessment of the processual variables' adequacy may be made through the experimental game 'SAṂSĀRA' (Marriott 1987). Reborn into a game world in which the above five variables are postulated, uninstructed players regularly generate institutions that resemble *jātis*, *varṇas*, *āśramas*, karmic philosophies, etc.

[17] Zimmermann (1980, 1987: 146–48) offers two-dimensional, triangular and hexagonal analyses of this plane that might more easily be accommodated in a cube of three humoral dimensions.

Table 3

Some Social Examples of Three Processual Variables

Processual Variables	**Classic Categories (Mines)**		**Transactional Strategies**	**Prestational Values**	**Political Issues (Dirks)**
	vārṇas (Davis)	*āśramas*	(Marriott, Raheja)	(Raheja)	
MIXING	Kṣatriya, Vaiśya/	householder/	maximal	mutuality	territory wider
. . . unmixing	Brahman, Śudra	renouncer	. . . minimal		. . . territory narrow
UNMARKING	Brahman, Kṣatriya/	forest-dweller/	optimal	hierarchy	command, honour
. . . marking	Vaiśya, Śudra	student	. . . pessimal		. . . [obey, defer]
UNMATCHING	Vaiśya, Śudra/	renouncer/	peripheral		[violence]
. . . matching	Brahman, Kṣatriya	householder	. . . central	centrality	. . . constraint

Processual Variables	**Impurity** (Mines, Moore)	***karma* Operation** (Wadley and Derr)	**Effects of Action, Social and Personal** (various authors)	**Worship Offerings** (Moreno)	**Cosmic Orientations** (Moore)
MIXING	mixed	large network	external power	hot (sugar)	east/
. . . unmixing	moderate	. . . small unit	. . . internal power	. . . cold (water)	west
UNMARKING	less	high agent	superiority	wet (milk)	up, source/
. . . marking	. . . more	. . . low patient	. . . inferiority	. . . dry (shoes)	down, sink
UNMATCHING	more	unmerited	sin, inauspiciousness	kill (burn, impale)/	north/
. . . matching	. . . less	. . . merited	. . . merit, auspiciousness	marry	south

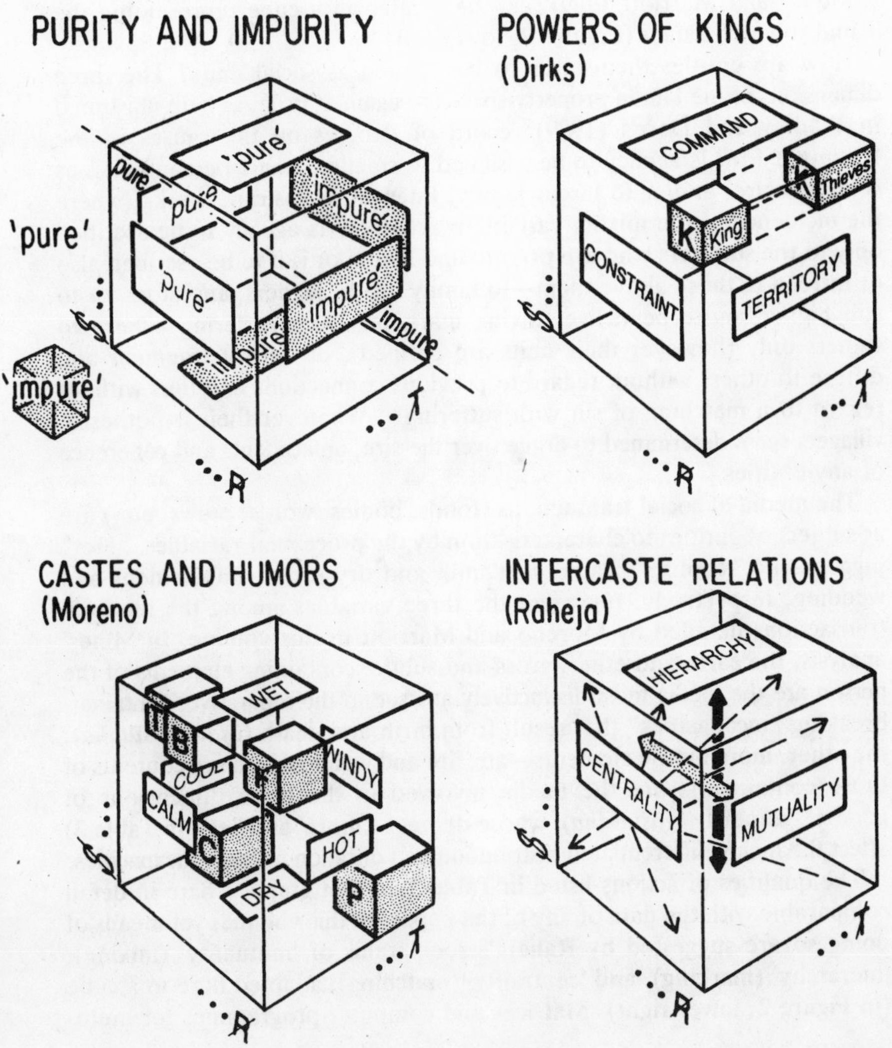

Fig.2 Uses of the Constituent Cube

Pugh 1983b, 1984: 90), most of the nine celestial bodies can also be located in a cube of the heavenly sphere. Returning to the human sphere of local social organisation, the Right- and Left-hand divisions as well as five occupational castes, all characterised by their humoral reputations (Moreno and Marriott 1989), can be located in a cube representing the Tamil town of Palani (Figure 2, lower left).[18]

How are entities themselves to be defined as social units? The three dimensions of the Hindu property-space are again at issue, as here illustrated in Wadley and Derr's (1989) record of debates on the causes of the Karimpur fire. Is agency to be assigned to smaller, single-person units, as some declare, and/or to larger family, lineage, or caste networks (where the incidence of the mixing variable is greater)? Is agency to be ascribed only to the sufferers who are present and living, or is it to be ascribed also or instead to those above them—to family heads, leaders, ancestors, or to still higher, more pervasive, divine markers? Does suffering adhere to sinners only (however their units are defined), or does it fragment and diffuse to others without regard to previous connections and thus without regard to a matching of sin with suffering?[19] Whatever their hypotheses, villagers seem determined to argue over the size, antecedents and coherence of any entities.

The media of social transactions (foods, bodies, words, blows, etc.) are as subject as entities to characterisation by the processual variables. "Hot" jaggery and "cooling" water, wet milk and dry shoes, impalement and wedding, respectively, represent the three variables among the humoral transactions detailed by Moreno and Marriott in this volume. In Mines' analysis, the earth-and-ether, gross-and-subtle, containing elements of the person are the media most distinctively at issue in the separative, container-breaking "incapacities" that result from birth and death (*āśauca, sūtaka*); the other, more motile elements—air, fire and water (which are contents of those containers)—are the media involved in the three dimensions of general "impurity" (*āśuddha*), whose degrees ('more' and 'less' in Table 3) affect the highly differentiated distribution and duration of these incapacities.

The qualities of actions listed in Table 3 are not graphed here in detail comparable with the data of any of the papers in this volume, yet means of doing so are suggested by Raheja's sociograms of 'mutuality' (mixing), 'hierarchy' (marking), and 'centrality' (matching), adapted here to a cube (in Figure 2, lower right). Matrices and computer programmes for multi-

[18] The castes located in Figure 2, lower left cube are:

LEFT		RIGHT
	B = Brahman	
T = Traders (Naṭṭukkottai Ceṭṭiyar)		F = Farmers (Kavuṇṭar)
C = Cobblers (Cakkiliyan)		P = Pallan Labourers

[19] Ramanujan (1980) correlates the difference between matched (karmic) and unmatched agency with the difference between classical and folk codes, both of which may be available within the repertoire of any sophisticated speaker.

dimensional scaling and graphing may be used to manage the much fuller depictions that will be required for rigorous and detailed studies of such actions; for these, previous efforts (Hage and Harary 1983; Levinson 1982; Marriott 1968, 1976; Mitchell 1980) are only beginnings.

The differentiated Hindu property-space presents problems and opportunities for action to be not merely typed, but also either mixed or unmixed with (intensifying or reducing), marked or unmarked by (influenced or influencing), and matched or unmatched to (conforming with or opposing) the properties of its locus. When Palani Farmers heat themselves by cooling an overheated goddess (Moreno and Marriott 1989), when Kallar kings constrain their thieving cousins (Dirks 1989), when Gujar *jajmāns* distribute potential disaster (Raheja 1989), when survivors subtly re-embody the spirit of a deceased relative (Mines 1989), they all counteract features that the varying world presents. Kerala householders (in Moore 1989) locate some of their activities (cooking, entertaining, conserving, menstruating) at similarly propertied places within the cube they inhabit, but they also exploit the house's contrasting properties by moving hot sexual activities to cool places, and disorderly death to orderly places; they even counteract the house's properties by putting light into the darkest region and by recycling life-sustenance through what would otherwise be the most polluted and inauspicious corner.

The processual variables are found in other spheres of action, such as time, that may at first seem remote from the human world of variable substance. In astrology, for example, (*i*) combinatory relations (mixing), (*ii*) ascendant relations (marking), and (*iii*) permutative (unmatching) spatio-temporal relations are among the most prominent variables of its interpretive logic (Kemper 1977, 1980; Pugh 1983a, 1983b). The shifting relations of seasonal time are as much "substance" (*dravya*) to Hindu biological thought (Caraka 1983 *Sū*. 6 and 11.42; Zimmermann 1980) as are the other physical elements of which human and celestial bodies are constituted (Pugh 1984).

So it is also with human events. If one rephrases past Pudukkottai politics (Dirks 1987, 1989) in Hindu spatio-temporal terms (rather than splitting 'history' as dynamics apart from 'cultural' statics, Western-style), one deals with three analogous variable processes of time-space: (*i*) coincidence (intensities of mixing in the territorial concentration, distribution, and confrontation of clans); (*ii*) precedence (marking, emphasised in the sequential narratives of genealogy, settlement, and temple-founding); and (*iii*) cycling (unmatching or reversal—here the transformation of violent Kallar bandits into *dhārmik* kings) (Dirks 1982; Shulman 1980). These three temporal vectors are diagrammed spatially in Figure 2 (upper right) as the powers of larger "territory", higher "honour" or "command", and greater "constraint", respectively; their higher scores on all three of these scales thrust some Kallars into the royal corner of the cube.

Temporal processes are similarly categorised in the sphere of karmic calculation, where in Wadley and Derr's account of a recent disaster, villagers debate the relative causal weights of (*i*) simultaneous and immediate intersections of circumstances (mixtures), (*ii*) prior and predetermined qualities (karmic markings), and (*iii*) unpredictable, unconnected (unmatched) factors. All three sorts of time are involved, and villagers' several particular explanatory resolutions of the debate are products of their various combinations. Rhodes (1984) has reported just such a triad of kinds of time in Sinhalese medical treatment.

Once the data (on entities, actions, or processes) within any sphere are mapped in a three-dimensional property-space, both Hindus and social scientists thinking with Hindu concepts may exploit the adjacent layers' meanings. By metonymic deduction, one may hypothesise, for example, that a group acknowledged to be of the Kṣatriya *varṇa* (whose strands are imagined in Bengal as much passion and goodness, but little darkness [Davis 1983: 51]) will have a humoral profile of much bile and phlegm, but little wind; will be much concerned with their attachments, advantages and coherence; and will generally evidence processes of mixing, unmarking and matching in their lives. Following the layer-to-layer analogical reasoning so richly developed in all the Hindu sciences, one may go much further in hypothesising their social organisation, diet and temperament, as well as compatible and incompatible times, spaces, directions, flavours, colours, textures, powers, styles of action, etc. The extent to which they disconfirm such hypotheses will indicate problems for further, meaningful investigation. The authors of most of the following papers have used such reasoning many times in constructing their interpretations. The empirical proofs or disproofs of their hypotheses lead them, and should lead others, to more accurate articulations of the dynamics and dialectics of Hindu life.

Layering seems intrinsic to the overlapping, homologous systems explored in these papers, as three-dimensional conceptions are replicated in sphere after sphere, providing similar orientations in each. Layers are explicit in widespread Hindu theories of homology between the inner and outer minds (Raheja 1976); they are supported by yogic doctrine, which posits five outer and inner bodily "sheaths"—a mixing-to-unmixing sort of variation—and by the devolutionary orders of *sāṃkhya*, which generally devolve "gross", outer substance from "subtle", inner substance (Larson 1987: 49–65). In astrological interpretation a different, possibly contrary ordering of layers prevails in which the divine, celestial sphere marks all the layers contained within it (community, family, body, psyche). But the four inner layers interpenetrate and have no fixed order among them (Pugh 1984). Layers of expansion (mixing) and of danger (unmatching) both appear intermingled as physical features in planning house-to-land ratios in Kerala (Moore 1989). Castes living away from the centre are generally more marked and more unmatched both in themselves and in their relations with other castes (Hiebert 1971: 59–62; Pfaffenberger 1982; Raheja 1988a, 1988b, 1989). Such "others" residing in peripheral layers are appropriate recipients of inauspiciousness (a kind of unmatching) in the Tamil ritual complexes detailed elsewhere by Shulman (1985) and by Raheja (1988a, 1988b, 1989) and also by Moreno and Marriott (1989). Thus it appears that the orderings and meanings of layers differ, following all of the three regnant variables, much as any ordering of aspects or entities depends on the locus of the viewer. Layering is nevertheless a recurrent consequence of dealing with a world whose every sphere replicates a similar underlying relational structure.

Moore (1989) discovers the special importance of the innermost layer—the middle of a cube—where the atrium of Kerala houses is conceived to be. This is the point where conventional Western graphing would put its zeros, but where Hindu calculation finds all of its substantial variables present and in a perfect state of matching, or balance. (They would be numbered 5, 5, 5 on the scales of 1 to 9 that are favoured by the Kerala building manuals.) Being a place of matching, and being protected from the dangerously unmatched outer layers, it is a good place for carefully matched rituals. An equipoise of physical elements, humours and strands is similarly Tamil villagers' idea of the divine original state (E.V. Daniel 1984: 3–5). The person whose humours are so balanced is free of disease, according to *āyurveda* (Caraka *Sū*. 7. 39–40). The ideally all-competent Sikh yeoman would command his world from such a balanced middle locus, needing none of the Hindu *varṇa*s' division of labour (Uberoi 1967: 100). The many Western theorists who, following Durkheim (1915: 47), suppose that sacred things must be set apart may be surprised to come upon this most perfect spot in the middle of life. The "sacred" (*tiru*) "middle" of the Kerala house is, like the "heart-mind" (*manas*), a divinely illuminated special locus where humans can cultivate the fifth and constant process—pure consciousness.

Diametric concepts: 'purity', 'dominance' and 'hierarchy'

Three-dimensional analysis can provide perspectives on two pairs of Hindu concepts that have been much debated among researchers on caste in India—'pure-impure' and 'great-small' (the last more often called 'dominance' by social scientists of Western type). These are rarely defined concepts, essentially contested among Hindus, with which social scientists have nevertheless often attempted to analyse Indian materials, usually with ambiguous results. 'Hierarchy' is a disagreed dimension that partakes of the difficulties of both 'purity' and 'dominance'.

Like the "subtle-gross" continuum plotted above and also like the "violent-nonviolent" distinction which is not much discussed in this volume, "purity" (*śuddha* with its synonyms) and "dominance" (*adhikāra*, etc.) are potentially three-dimensional ideas that can generally be interpreted as lines running diametrically from corner to corner of the constituent cube. While the cube can be correctly labelled with these words, and while it could even be redefined by these four main diameters—by its corner-to-corner axes, rather than its face-to-face axes—to do so would be to open theory to the claims of rival ideologies and contentions. The three rectangular dimensions actually used are preferable because of their parsimony and their neutrality. They are less contested as presuppositions.

The ambiguities of the diametric concepts are illustrated by some of the many meanings of "purity" diagrammed in the first cube of Figure 2. "Purity" as used by Hindus may refer to being relatively unmixed (e.g., "cool", non-*rājasik*), unmarked (e.g., "virtuous", *sāttvik*), and matched (e.g., "coherent", *dhārmik*); or to any two of these properties, but not the third; or to any one of these properties, but not the other two; or to none of these properties (Carman 1985). Only the last, socially peripheral Hindu usage approximates the usual Western meanings of 'spirit without flesh', or 'rule without deviation'. Analytic clarity requires specifying which of these eight meanings is intended. In this volume, the papers of Mines and Moore especially achieve and illustrate such clarity.

The alien term 'hierarchy' seems to have suffered because of its naively one-dimensional participation in the three-dimensional Hindu semantic space. The word is given at least three meanings in the descriptive papers of this volume: (*i*) the 'purity' diameter of the first cube in Figure 2 (cited by Dirks, criticising this Brahman-oriented usage by Dumont); in the next cube, (*ii*) the 'dominance' or 'power' diameter (from 'King' to the hidden back, bottom corner—the meaning that best suits Pudukkottai kingship as described by Dirks; (*iii*) any chord moving through the vertical dimension of the constituent cube. The last is Raheja's usage, depicted by the dark arrow in the cube of inter-caste relations in Figure 2, and is formally equivalent to what is here called 'marking'.

'Hierarchy' is strongly identified with 'purity' in Dumont's usage. He translates Hindu 'purity' into a Western ideal—the separation of spirit from 'biological' or 'organic life'—even though, paradoxically, he notes that Hindu thought generally ignores or denies such a typically Western 'rift between man and nature' (Dumont 1970: 59, 61). His analytical application of this alien ideal locates the apogee of 'purity' at what he sees as the most 'encompassing' (*englobant*) end of a partly asymmetrical series of operations that he calls 'hierarchy'.

'Encompassing' is not a canonical operation of set theory, but is Dumont's condensation of a complex model of two mutually excluding 'hierarchies' called 'inclusion-exclusion' by its inventor, Raymond Apthorpe (1984). Apthorpe devised 'inclusion-exclusion' in 1956 to describe the unresolved contention between the Tutsi and Hutu tribes for inclusive dominance over the state of Ruanda in Africa, a territory from which each tribe would exclude the other. As used by Dumont, 'to encompass' shows the same irresolution, for it means 'to include', as when an orientation to purity-impurity is said to encompass the 'whole' of society; and also means 'to surround, but not include', as when the purity orientation is said to be ignored by Kṣatriyas and other 'power'-oriented groups, who are alleged to occupy a disordered 'middle' region—separated but surrounded. 'Encompassment' is thus an oxymoron: it asserts that Hindu society is both split and not split, both ranked and not ranked. Dumont (1979: 809) defends such a characterisation of Hindu society as necessary, but admits that such self-contradictory usages of 'encompassment', or 'hierarchy', create a 'logical scandal'.

The present model avoids such scandal. It postulates 'unmarking' as a dimension of its entire property-space, and thus returns to noncontradictory relations more like those that set theory calls 'inclusion' and linguistics calls 'taxonomic hierarchy'. It adds two other variable dimensions (which approximate the set-theory terms 'intersection' and 'union') to its presupposed property-space. It conceives the top of this space not as narrowing to a point on a single line, but as a broad and deep rectangular region capacious enough to accommodate Kṣatriyas, gods, bandits, and others as well as Brahmans. Brahman and Kṣatriya *varṇa*s are both controlling elites, each of them relatively unmarked (pervasive or inclusive in their scope) and strongly matching (nondisjunctive, capable of union); they differ mostly along the one dimension of mixing (intersection), popularly known as "cold" and "hot". The "purity" and "dominance" diameters which they respectively head intersect with each other: they are alternative lines across the same diagonal (top front to bottom rear) plane of the cube. As a cube or a plane may be viewed in more than one way, the orderings of the marked or backgrounded entities will be seen to vary, depending on whether the angle of vision is that of king, thief, priest, village *jajmān*, or some other. Diversity of ranking is an intrinsic potentiality of such a model.

After reading Raheja's evidence (1989; also 1988a and 1988b) for the actuality of such diverse and shifting three-dimensional views, and Beck's (1972: 154–81) and Marriott's (1976) similar reports of diverse rankings from elsewhere, one might hope that the supposition of a single-dimensional space will henceforth be abandoned. After seeing Moore's evidence (1989, Figures 4 and 6) for a Hindu consciousness of many diagonal "slopes", one might hope that the utility of a multidimensional model will be clear. One might hope also that the oxymoronic term 'encompassment' will be dropped and the now heavily overburdened word 'hierarchy' will be either restored to its unambiguous meaning of an order of inclusions, or else given a rest.

Other possible Indian social sciences

The foregoing constructs by no means form a complete ethnosociology, nor do they exhaust the materials from which Indian social sciences may be developed. They leave untouched the Hindu systems of "senses", "savours", "sentiments" and "feelings"—materials for concentric indigenous psychologies. The model outlined above is undoubtedly biassed in the direction of its sources, which are mostly Hindu, more north Indian than southern, more learned than popular, more of *sāṃkhya-yoga* than of any other *darśana*, more *āyurvedic* than astrological, more orthodox than devotional, more high caste than low, and more male than female.

The different general theoretical systems that could develop from other, one- or two-dimensional humoral schemes have yet to be fully imagined. Suggestive examples are the Tamil humoral notions described by McGilvray (1982b) and E.V. Daniel (1984) (noted by Moreno and Marriott in this volume), and the highly developed fire- and water-based, but windless Greco-Muslim humoral scheme reflected in the notions of Muslim farmers of Panjab and Sindh (Kurin 1981).

Ether and earth have been interpreted above as secondary if necessary elements, providing containers and recycling for the world's otherwise highly motile substances. But earth as regenerative mother and ether as spirit or feeling might become central understandings of these categories if a general theoretical system were built from Tamil women's views of the world (Egnor 1978, 1984). Sky and earth would also play far larger and very different roles in a science developed from the theories of Muslim farmers in Bangladesh (Thorp 1982), for whom the analogous god and man are the principal duality of the universe, and for whom other elements (fire, water) are mere media or qualifiers.

Differences of aspect or point of view on the cubic structure have been noted repeatedly above. But the cube has been pictured so far from just one angle. The differences of aspect stressed in the papers by Moreno and Marriott, Raheja, and Dirks result from shifts only among the elites who occupy the edge joining its top and forward (unmarking and matching) faces. Views from along this edge may well be the most influential and prevalent ones: the replication of a "purity" diameter by Tamil Untouchable castes who are excluded from direct participation in elite celebrations has been richly demonstrated by Moffatt (1979). But suppose one takes a sampling of other views: Jaini's (1979: 138–87) account of Digambar Jains' single-minded avoidance of mixing and of marking (which they consider a particularly violent kind of mixing); or Trawick's (1988b) reports on systematic verbal inversions of marking relationships, sung out loud by Untouchable Tamil women; or Parry's (1985) account of the ritual joinings of all opposites by *tāntrik* Aghori Sadhus; or Khare's (1984) reports of how Lucknow Untouchables perceive humans as bodiless souls. These views, from what cubists would regard as the lower left side, the backside, all sides, and the inside-outside of the cube, can alternatively be regarded as implying radically different topologies which should yield radically different general theoretical systems.

Conclusions

The constructs developed here and in the other essays of this collection may be regarded as belated carryings forward of what has long been potential, but has remained implicit or neglected in the Indian sciences. On the other hand, the novel verbal and mathematical translations and geometric mappings used here can be taken as proof of alienation from truly Indian ways of constructing sciences. Both views seem correct.

There is no doubt that the present interpretations *are* constructs, and that they will look strange to scientists of both Western and Hindu traditions. Still, they were developed through profound and active intellectual participation in both Western and Indian life and ideas by all the authors of the following papers and many others whose works are cited. Western and Indian sciences cannot easily be made one, yet they are enough alike that those who practise both can heighten their awareness of common underlying issues, such as equivalence and antiequivalence relations, or context-free and context-sensitive variations (Ramanujan 1989), on which very different perspectives exist. Deep comparisons are possible.

The plethora of Sanskrit words here and in the following papers may give rise to a suspicion that the constructs offered here are anachronisms irrelevant to the present Indian or any other region of the modern world. The possibility of irrelevance or anachronism appears remote, however, since liquid, antiequivalent Hindu presuppositions, while old, are nonetheless resonant with a great body of living Indian literature and with the findings of much recent ethnography. These presuppositions are in many ways also compatible with the findings of current linguistics, of molecular and atomic physics, of ecological biology, and of social systems theory (Buckley 1967; Capra 1975; Marriott 1977; Prigogine and Stengers 1984). They are more compatible than are the presuppositions of Western theology, law, or common sense which generally underlie the concepts of conventional Western social science. In other words, the constructs explored here may be as much for the present and future as for past Hindu and wider worlds.

Breaking with some aspects of the established Western ethnosocial sciences and cultivating other-regional rivals may also raise fears of parochialism and relativism. But the processual relativism that the Hindu ethnosocial sciences would indulge is potentially the least parochial, the most ecumenical of urges. Hindu ontology and epistemology, whether labelled as fire, water, and air, or as more learned notions of strands and humours, can be said to deal more directly with some ideas of greater universality—the fundamental relational axioms of mathematics, or the fact of universal flux, for example—than conventional Western social science does with its parochial, equivalence-based ideas of discrete, static and uniform entities. One cannot in fact avoid parochialism in the present state of the social sciences. If Indian sciences are developed, however, one may at least be able to choose whether to practise with alien and often inappropriate concepts or with indigenous, appropriate ones.

REFERENCES

Allen, N.J. 1985. Hierarchical opposition and some other types of relation. *In* R.H. Barnes, Daniel de Coppet, and R.J. Parkin, eds., *Contexts and levels: anthropological essays on hierarchy*, pp. 21–31. JASO occasional papers, n. 4. Oxford: JASO.

Amarasingham, Lorna Rhodes. 1980. Movement among healers in Sri Lanka: a case study of a Sinhalese patient. *Culture, medicine, and psychiatry* 4: 71–92.

Apthorpe, Raymond. 1984. Hierarchy and other social relations: some categorial logic. *In* Jean-Claude Galey, ed., *Différences, valeurs, hiérarchie: textes offerts à Louis Dumont*, pp. 283–98. Paris: Éditions de l'École des Hautes Études en Sciences Sociales.

Babb, Lawrence A. 1970. The food of the gods in Chhattisgarh: some structural features of Hindu ritual. *Southwestern journal of anthropology* 26: 287–304.

———. 1981. Glancing: visual interaction in Hinduism. *Journal of anthropological research* 37: 387–401.

———. 1983. The physiology of redemption. *History of religions* 22: 298–312.

Beals, Alan R. 1976. Strategies of resort to curers in south India. *In* Charles M. Leslie, ed., *Asian medical systems: a comparative study*, pp. 184–200. Berkeley: University of California Press.

Beck, Brenda E.F. 1972. *Peasant society in Konku: a study of right and left subcastes in south India*. Vancouver: University of British Columbia Press.

Bhagavad Gītā. 1969. *The Bhagavad-gītā* (trans. R.C. Zaehner). London: Oxford University Press.

Buckley, Walter. 1967. *Sociology and modern systems theory*. Englewood Cliffs: Prentice-Hall.

Capra, Fritjof. 1975. *The Tao of physics: an exploration of the parallels between modern physics and Eastern mysticism.* Boulder: Shambhala Publications.

Caraka. 1983. *Agniveśa's Caraka saṃhita* (trans. Ram Karan Sharma and *Vaidya* Bhagwan Dash). Vol. 1, *Sūtra sthāna*. Varanasi: Chowkhamba Sanskrit Series Office.

———. 1985. *Agniveśa's Caraka saṃhita* (trans. Ram Karan Sharma and *Vaidya* Bhagwan Dash). Vol. 2. Varanasi: Chowkhamba Sanskrit Series Office.

Carman, John B. 1985. Conclusion: axes of value in Hindu society. *In* John B. Carman and Frédrique Apffel Marglin, eds., *Purity and auspiciousness in Indian society*, pp. 109–20. Leiden: E.J. Brill.

Chakravarti, Anand. 1975. *Contradiction and change: emerging patterns of authority in a Rajasthan village*. Delhi: Oxford University Press.

Chase, Ivan D. 1984. Social process and hierarchy formation in small groups: a comparative perspective. *In* Patricia R. Barchas, ed., *Social hierarchies: essays toward a sociophysiological perspective*, pp. 45–80. Westport: Greenwood Press.

Damle, Y.B. 1965. For a theory of Indian sociology. *In, Sociology in India: Seminar*, pp. 32–52. Agra: Institute of Social Sciences

DANIEL, E. VALENTINE. 1984. *Fluid signs: being a person the Tamil way*. Berkeley: University of California Press.

DANIEL, SHERYL B. 1983. The tool-box approach of the Tamil to the issues of moral responsibility and human destiny. *In* Charles F. Keyes and E. Valentine Daniel, eds., *Karma: an anthropological inquiry*, pp. 27–62. Berkeley: University of California Press.

DAS, VEENA. 1976. Masks and faces in Punjabi kinship. *Contributions to Indian sociology* (n.s.) 10: 1–30.

———. 1985. Paradigms of body symbolism: analysis of selected themes in Hindu culture. *In* Richard Burghart and Audrey Cantlie, eds., *Indian religion*, pp. 180–207. London: Curzon Press.

DAVID, KENNETH A. 1974. And never the twain shall meet? Mediating the structural approaches to caste ranking. *In* Harry M. Buck and Glenn E. Yocum, eds., *Structural approaches to south India studies*, pp. 43–80. Chambersburg: Conocoheague Associates for Wilson Books.

———. 1977. Hierarchy and equivalence in Jaffna, north Sri Lanka: normative codes as mediator. *In* K.A. David, ed., *The new wind: changing identities in South Asia*, pp. 179–226. The Hague: Mouton.

DAVIS, MARVIN GENE. 1983. *Rank and rivalry: the politics of inequality in rural West Bengal*. Cambridge: Cambridge University Press.

DIRKS, NICHOLAS B. 1982. The pasts of a Palaiyakarar: the ethnohistory of a south Indian little king. *Journal of Asian studies* 41: 655–83.

———. 1987. *The hollow crown: ethnohistory of an Indian kingdom*. Cambridge: Cambridge University Press.

———. 1989. The original caste: power, history and hierarchy in South Asia. *In* this volume.

DOREIAN, PATRICK. 1971. *Mathematics and the study of social relations*. New York: Shocken Books.

DUMONT, LOUIS. 1961. Caste, racism and 'stratification': reflections of a social anthropologist. *Contributions to Indian sociology* 5: 20–43.

———. 1970. *Homo hierarchicus: the caste system and its implications* (trans. Mark Sainsbury). Chicago: University of Chicago Press.

———. 1979. The anthropological community and ideology. *Social science information* 18: 785–817.

DURKHEIM, ÉMILE. 1915. *The elementary forms of the religious life* (trans. Joseph Ward Swain). London: George Allen and Unwin.

———. 1933. *The division of labor in society* (trans. George Simpson). London: Macmillan.

EGNOR, MARGARET TRAWICK. 1978. The sacred spell and other conceptions of life in Tamil culture. Ph. D. dissertation in Anthropology. Chicago: University of Chicago Library.

———. 1983. Death and nurturance in Indian systems of healing. *Social science and medicine* 17: 935–45.

———. 1984. The changed mother or what the smallpox goddess did when there was no more smallpox. *Contributions to Asian studies* 18: 24–45.

FERNANDEZ, JAMES W. 1982. *Bwiti: an ethnography of the religious imagination in Africa*. Princeton: Princeton University Press.

FERRO-LUZZI, GABRIELLA EICHINGER. 1977. The logic of south Indian food offerings. *Anthropos* 72: 529–55.

———. 1978. Food for the gods in south India. *Zeitschrift für Ethnologie* 103: 86–108.

FREED, STANLEY A. 1963. An objective method for determining the collective caste hierarchy in an Indian village. *American anthropologist* 65: 879-91.

———. 1970. Caste ranking and the exchange of food and water in a north Indian village. *Anthropological quarterly* 43: 1–13.

GARBETT, G.K. 1980. Graph theory and the analysis of multiplex and manifold relationships. *In* J.C. Mitchell, ed., *Numerical techniques in social anthropology*, pp. 191–232. Philadelphia: Institute for the Study of Social Issues.

Geertz, Clifford. 1966. *Person, time and conduct in Bali: an essay in cultural analysis.* Cultural report series n. 14. New Haven: Yale Southeast Asia Program.

———. 1983. 'From the native's point of view': on the nature of anthropological understanding. *In* Clifford Geertz, ed., *Local knowledge: further essays in interpretive anthropology*, pp. 55–70. New York: Basic Books.

Gold, Ann Grodzins. 1988. *Fruitful journeys: the ways of Rajasthani pilgrims*. Berkeley: University of California Press.

Hage, Per, and Frank Harary. 1983. *Structural models in anthropology*. Cambridge: Cambridge University Press.

Harary, Frank, Robert Z. Norman, and Dorwin Cartwright. 1965. *Structural models: an introduction to the theory of directed graphs*. New York: John Wiley and Sons.

Heginbotham, Stanley J. 1975. *Cultures in conflict: the four faces of Indian bureaucracy*. New York: Columbia University Press.

Hiebert, Paul G. 1971. *Konduru: structure and integration in a south Indian village*. Minneapolis: University of Minnesota Press.

Inden, Ronald B. 1976. *Marriage and rank in Bengali culture: a history of caste and clan in middle period Bengal*. Berkeley: University of California Press.

Inden, Ronald B., and Ralph W. Nicholas. 1977. *Kinship in Bengali culture*. Chicago: University of Chicago Press.

Jaini, Padmanabh S. 1979. *The Jaina path of purification*. Berkeley: University of California Press.

Kapp, K. William. 1963. *Hindu culture, economic development and economic planning in India: a collection of essays*. Bombay: Asia Publishing House.

Kemeny, John G., J. Laurie Snell, and Gerald L. Thompson. 1966. *Introduction to finite mathematics*. Second edition. Englewood Cliffs: Prentice-Hall.

Kemper, Stephen E.G. 1977. Sinhalese astrology, South Asian caste systems, and the notion of individuality. *Journal of Asian studies* 38: 477–97.

———. 1980. Time, person, and gender in Sinhalese astrology. *American ethnologist* 7: 744–58.

Khare, Ravindra Sahai. 1976. *The Hindu hearth and home*. New Delhi: Vikas Publishing House.

———. 1984. *The Untouchable as himself: ideology, identity, and pragmatism among Lucknow Chamars*. Cambridge: Cambridge University Press.

Kurin, Richard. 1981. Person, family and kin in two Pakistani communities. Ph.D. dissertation in Anthropology. Chicago: University of Chicago Library.

Langer, Susanne K. 1967. *An introduction to symbolic logic*. Third revised edition. New York: Dover Publications.

Larson, Gerald James. 1987. Introduction to the philosophy of *Sāṃkhya*. *In* Gerald James Larson and Ram Shankar Bhattacharya, eds., *Sāṃkhya, a dualist tradition in Indian philosophy*, pp. 3–103. Encyclopedia of Indian philosophies, vol. 4. Princeton: Princeton University Press.

Leaf, Murray John. 1972. *Information and behavior in a Sikh village*. Berkeley: University of California Press.

Lebra, Takie Sugiyama. 1976. *Japanese patterns of behavior*. Honolulu: University of Hawaii Press.

Lévi-Strauss, Claude. 1949. *Les structures élémentaires de la parenté*. Paris: Presses Universitaires de France.

Levinson, Stephen C. 1982. Caste rank and verbal interaction in western Tamilnadu. *In* Dennis B. McGilvray, ed., *Caste ideology and interaction*, pp. 98–203. Cambridge: Cambridge University Press.

Lindzey, Gardner, and Edward F. Borgatta. 1954. Sociometric measurement. *In* Gardner Lindzey, ed., *Handbook of social psychology*, pp. 405–48. Cambridge MA: Addison-Wesley Publishing Company.

MADAN, TRILOKI NATH. 1987. *Non-renunciation: themes and interpretations of Hindu culture.* Delhi: Oxford University Press.

MAHAR, PAULINE M. 1959. A multiple scaling technique for caste ranking. *Man in India* 39: 127–47.

MALAMOUD, CHARLES. 1982. On the rhetoric and semantics of puruṣārtha. *Contributions to Indian sociology* (n.s.) 15: 33–54.

MANU. 1886. *The laws of Manu* (trans. Georg Bühler). Sacred Books of the East, Vol. 25. Oxford: Clarendon Press.

MARRIOTT, MCKIM. 1968. Caste ranking and food transactions: a matrix analysis. *In* Milton Singer and Bernard S. Cohn, eds., *Structure and change in Indian society*, pp. 133–71. Chicago: Aldine.

———. 1976. Hindu transactions; diversity without dualism. *In* Bruce Kapferer, ed., *Transaction and meaning: directions in the anthropology of exchange and symbolic behavior*, pp. 109–42. Philadelphia: Institute for the Study of Human Issues.

———. 1977. [Remarks in] Symposium: changing identities in South Asia. *In* Kenneth A. David, ed., *The new wind: changing identities in South Asia*, pp. 423–28. Chicago: Aldine.

———. 1987. A description of SAṂSĀRA: a realization of rural Hindu life. Chicago: Civilization Course Materials Project, The College, University of Chicago.

MARRIOTT, MCKIM, and RONALD B INDEN. 1974. Caste systems. *Encyclopaedia Britannica, macropaedia* 3: 982–91.

MCCLELLAND, DAVID C. 1975. *Power: the inner experience*. New York: Irvington Publishers.

MCGILVRAY, DENNIS B. 1982a. Mukkuvar vannimai: Tamil caste and matriclan ideology in Batticaloa, Sri Lanka. *In* Dennis B. McGilvray, ed., *Caste ideology and interaction*, pp. 34–97. Cambridge: Cambridge University Press.

———. 1982b. Sexual power and fertility in Sri Lanka: Batticaloa Tamils and Moors. *In* Carol P. Macormack, ed., *Ethnography of fertility and birth*, pp. 25–73. London: Academic Press.

MEGGITT, MERVYN J. 1972. Understanding Australian Aboriginal society: kinship systems or cultural categories? *In* Priscilla Reining, ed., *Kinship studies in the Morgan centennial year*, pp. 64–67. Washington, DC: Anthropological Society of Washington.

MINES, DIANE PAULL. 1989. Hindu periods of death 'impurity.' *In* this volume.

MITCHELL, J. CLYDE. 1980. *Numerical techniques in social anthropology*. Philadelphia: Institute for the Study of Social Issues.

MOFFATT, MICHAEL. 1979. *An Untouchable community in south India: structure and consensus*. Princeton: Princeton University Press.

MOORE, MELINDA A. 1989. The Kerala house as a Hindu cosmos. *In* this volume.

MORENO, MANUEL and MCKIM MARRIOTT. 1989. Humoral transactions in two Tamil cults: Murukan and Mariyamman. *In* this volume.

MOTWANI, KEWAL. 1934. *Manu: a study in Hindu social theory*. Madras: Ganesh and Co.

MUKERJI, DHURJATI PRASAD. 1986. Presidential address to the Indian Sociological Society. *In* T.K. Oommen and Partha N. Mukherji, eds., *Indian sociology: reflections and introspections*. Bombay: Popular Prakashan.

NICHTER, MARK. 1986. Modes of food classification and the diet-health contingency: a south Indian case study. *In* R.S. Khare and M.S.A. Rao, eds., *Food, society, and culture: aspects in South Asian food systems*, pp. 185–221. Durham NC: Carolina Academic Press.

PARRY, JONATHAN P. 1985. The Aghori ascetics of Benares. *In* Richard Burghart and Audrey Cantlie, eds., *Indian religion*, pp. 51–78. London: Curzon Press.

PARSONS, TALCOTT. 1966. *Societies: evolutionary and comparative perspectives*. Englewood Cliffs: Prentice-Hall.

———. 1971. *The system of modern societies*. Englewood Cliffs: Prentice-Hall.

PARSONS, TALCOTT, and EDWARD A. SHILS, eds., 1952. *Toward a general theory of action*. Cambridge MA: Harvard University Press.

Pfaffenberger, Bryan. 1982. *Caste in Tamil culture: the religious foundations of Sudra domination in Tamil Sri Lanka*. Foreign and Comparative Studies, South Asian series, n. 7. Syracuse: Maxwell School of Citizenship and Public Affairs, Syracuse University.

Piatigorsky, Alexei. 1985. Some phenomenological observations on the study of Indian religion. *In* Richard Burghart and Audrey Cantlie, eds., *Indian religion*, pp. 208–58. London: Curzon Press.

Potter, Karl H. 1980. The karma theory and its interpretation in some Indian philosophic systems. *In* Wendy D. O'Flaherty, ed., *Karma and rebirth in classical Indian traditions*, pp. 241–67. Berkeley: University of California Press.

———. n.d. Karma: the metaphor of making. Typescript, 15 pp.

Prigogine, Ilya, and Isabelle Stengers. 1984. *Order out of chaos: man's new dialogue with nature*. New York: Bantam Books.

Pugh, Judy F. 1983a. Astrology and fate: the Hindu and Muslim experiences. *In* Charles F. Keyes and E. Valentine Daniel, eds., *Karma: an anthropological inquiry*, pp. 131–46. Berkeley: University of California Press.

———. 1983b. Into the almanac: time, meaning, and action in north Indian society. *Contributions to Indian sociology* (n.s.) 17: 27–49.

———. 1984. Concepts of person and situation in north Indian counseling: the case of astrology. *In* E. Valentine Daniel and Judy F. Pugh, eds., *South Asian systems of healing*, pp. 85–105. Contributions to Asian studies, vol. 18. Leiden: E.J. Brill.

Raheja, Gloria Goodwin. 1976. Transformational processes in Hindu ritual: concepts of 'person' and 'action' in the performance of a *vrat*. Unpublished Master's paper. Chicago: Department of Anthropology, University of Chicago.

———. 1988a. *The poison in the gift: ritual, prestation, and the dominant caste in a north Indian village*. Chicago: University of Chicago Press.

———. 1988b. India: caste, kingship, and dominance reconsidered. *Annual review of anthropology* 17: 497–522.

———. 1989. Centrality, mutuality and hierarchy: shifting aspects of inter-caste relationships in north India. *In* this volume.

Ramanujan, A.K. 1967. *The interior landscape: love poems from a classical Tamil anthology*. Bloomington: Indiana University Press.

———. 1980. The relevance of South Asian folklore. Paper presented at the Conference on Models and Metaphors in south Asian Folklore, Berkeley and Mysore.

———. 1989. Is there an Indian way of thinking? An informal essay. *In* this volume.

Rhodes, Lorna Amarasingham. 1984. Time and the process of diagnosis in Sinhalese ritual treatment. *In* E. Valentine Daniel and Judy F. Pugh, eds., *South Asian systems of healing*, pp. 46–59. Contributions to Asian studies, vol. 18. Leiden: E.J. Brill.

Rizvi, Najma. 1986. Food categories in Bangladesh, and its relationship to food beliefs and practices of vulnerable groups. *In* R.S. Khare and M.S.A. Rao, eds., *Food, society, and culture: aspects in South Asian food systems*, pp. 223–51. Durham NC: Carolina Academic Press.

Rosaldo, Michelle Zimbalist. 1980. *Knowledge and passion: Ilongot notions of self and social life*. Cambridge: Cambridge University Press.

Saksena, R.N. 1965. Sociology in India. *In, Sociology in India: Seminar*, pp. 1–13. Agra: Institute of Social Sciences, Agra University.

Schneider, David M. 1968. *American kinship: a cultural account*. Englewood Cliffs NJ: Prentice-Hall.

Selwyn, Tom. 1982. Adharma. *Contributions to Indian sociology*. (n.s.) 15: 381–401.

Shils, Edward. 1961. *The intellectual between tradition and modernity: the Indian situation*. Comparative studies in society and history, supplement 1. The Hague: Mouton.

Shulman, David Dean. 1980. On south Indian bandits and kings. *Indian economic and social history review* 17: 283–306.

———. 1985. Kingship and prestation in south Indian myth and epic. *Asian and African studies* 19: 93–117.

SZANTON, DAVID L. 1976. South and Southeast Asia: new concerns of the Council. *Social science research council items* 30 (2): 1–2.
THORP, JOHN PUTNAM. 1982. The Muslim farmers of Bangladesh and Allah's creation of the world. *Asian folklore studies* 41: 201–15.
THURSTON, WILLIAM P., and JEFFREY R. WEEKS. 1984. The mathematics of three-dimensional manifolds. *Scientific American* 251: 108–20.
TRAUTMANN, THOMAS R. 1981 *Dravidian kinship*. Cambridge: Cambridge University Press.
TRAWICK, MARGARET. 1974. Principles of continuity in three Indian sciences: psychology of sāṃkhya and yoga, biology of āyurveda, sociology of dharmaśāstra and their concentric domains. Unpublished Master's paper. Chicago: Department of Anthropology, University of Chicago.
———. 1988a. Ambiguity in the oral exegesis of a sacred text: *Tirukkovaiyar*. *Cultural anthropology* 3: 316–51.
———. 1988b. Spirits and voices in Tamil songs. *American ethnologist* 15: 193–215.
UBEROI, JIT PAL SINGH. 1967. On being unshorn. *Transactions of the Indian Institute of Advanced Study*, 4: 87–100. Simla: Indian Institute of Advanced Study.
———. 1978. *Science and culture*. Delhi: Oxford University Press.
WADLEY, SUSAN SNOW. 1975. *Shakti: power in the conceptual structure of Karimpur religion*. The University of Chicago studies in anthropology, series in social, cultural, and linguistic anthropology, n. 2. Chicago: Department of Anthropology, University of Chicago.
WADLEY, SUSAN SNOW, and BRUCE W. DERR. 1989. Eating sins in Karimpur. *In* this volume.
WAGHORNE, JOANNE PUNZO, and NORMAN CUTLER, eds., in association with VASUDHA NARAYANAN. 1985. *Gods of flesh, gods of stone: the embodiment of divinity in India*. Chambersburg PA: Anima Books
WEBER, MAX. 1952. *The Protestant ethic and the spirit of capitalism* (trans. Talcott Parsons) New York: Charles Scribner's Sons.
———. 1968. *Economy and society: an outline of interpretive sociology*, 3 vols (eds. Gunther Roth and Claus Wittich). New York: Bedminster Press.
WEISS, MITCHELL G., SUSHRUT S. JADHAV, and S.M. CHANNABASAVANNA. 1986. Relation of humoral imbalance and possession as explanations of mental illness in India. Paper presented to American Anthropological Association. Philadelphia. 23 pp.
WITTGENSTEIN, LUDWIG. 1958. *The blue and brown books*. New York: Harper and Row.
ZIMMERMANN, FRANCIS B. 1979. Remarks on the body in ayurvedic medicine. *South Asian digest of regional writing* 18: 10–26.
———. 1980. *Ṛtūsātmya*: the seasonal cycle and the principle of appropriateness. *Social science and medicine* 14B: 99–106.
——— 1987. *The jungle and the aroma of meats: an ecological theme in Hindu medicine*. Berkeley: University of California Press.

[illegible] (1977) Smith and [illegible] [illegible] [illegible] 30: [illegible]

[illegible]

[illegible] and [illegible] (1984) [illegible]

[illegible]

[illegible]

[illegible]

[illegible] (1975) [illegible]

[illegible] and [illegible] (1983) [illegible] Journal of [illegible]

[illegible] New York: [illegible]

[illegible] (1987) [illegible]

[illegible]

2

Is there an Indian way of thinking? An informal essay

A.K. Ramanujan

Walter Benjamin once dreamed of hiding behind a phalanx of quotations which, like highwaymen, would ambush the passing reader and rob him of his convictions.

I

Stanislavsky had an exercise for his actors. He would give them an everyday sentence like, 'Bring me a cup of tea', and ask them to say it forty different ways, using it to beg, question, mock, wheedle, be imperious, etc. My question, 'Is there an Indian way of thinking?', is a good one for such an exercise. Depending on where the stress is placed, it contains many questions—all of which are real questions—asked again and again when people talk about India. Here are a few possible versions:

Is there an Indian way of thinking?
Is there *an* Indian way of thinking?
Is there an *Indian* way of thinking?
Is there an Indian way of *thinking*?

The answers are just as various. Here are a few: There *was* an Indian way of thinking; there isn't any more. If you want to learn about the Indian way of thinking, do not ask your modern-day citified Indians, go to the pundits, the *vaidyas*, the old texts. On the contrary: India never changes; under the veneer of the modern, Indians still think like the vedas.

The second question might elicit answers like these: There is no single Indian way of thinking; there are Great and Little Traditions, ancient and modern, rural and urban, classical and folk. Each language, caste and region has its special world view. So, under the apparent diversity, there is really a unity of viewpoint, a single supersystem. Vedists see a vedic model in all Indian thought. Nehru made the phrase 'unity in diversity' an Indian slogan. The Sahitya Akademi's line has been, 'Indian literature is One, though written in many languages'

The third question might be answered: What we see in India is nothing special to India; it is nothing but pre-industrial, pre-printing press, face-to-face, agricultural, feudal. Marxists, Freudians, McLuhanites, all have their labels for the stage India is in, according to their schemes of social evolution; India is only an example. Others, of course, would argue the uniqueness of the Indian Way and how it turns all things, especially rivals and enemies, into itself; look at what has happened to Indo-Europeans in India, they would say: their language gets shot with retroflexes, their syntax with nominal compounds, they lose their nerve—the British are only the most recent example (according to Nirad Chaudhuri). Look what happens to Buddhism, Islam, the Parsis. There is an *Indian* way, and it imprints and patterns all things that enter the continent; it is inescapable, and it is Bigger Than All of Us.

The fourth question may question whether Indians think at all: It is the West that is materialistic, rational; Indians have no philosophy, only religion, no positive sciences, not even a psychology; in India, matter is subordinated to spirit, rational thought to feeling, intuition. And even when people agree that this is the case, we can have arguments for and against it. Some lament, others celebrate India's un-thinking ways. One can go on forever.

We—I, certainly—have stood in one or another of these stances at different times. We have not heard the end of these questions—or these answers.

II

The problem was posed for me personally at the age of 20 in the image of my father. I had never taken a good look at him till then. Didn't Mark Twain say, 'At 17, I thought my father was ignorant; at 20, I wondered how he learned so much in three years'? Indeed, this essay was inspired by contemplation of him over the years, and is dedicated to him.

My father's clothes represented his inner life very well. He was a south Indian Brahmin gentleman. He wore neat white turbans, a Śri Vaiṣṇava caste mark (in his earlier pictures, a diamond earring), yet wore Tootal ties, Kromentz buttons and collar studs, and donned English serge jackets over his muslin *dhoti*s which he wore draped in traditional Brahmin style. He often wore tartan-patterned socks and silent well-polished leather shoes when he went to the university, but he carefully took them off before he entered the inner quarters of the house.

He was a mathematician, an astronomer. But he was also a Sanskrit scholar, an expert astrologer. He had two kinds of exotic visitors:

American and English mathematicians who called on him when they were on a visit to India, and local astrologers, orthodox pundits who wore splendid gold-embroidered shawls dowered by the Maharajah. I had just been converted by Russell to the 'scientific attitude'. I (and my generation) was troubled by his holding together in one brain both astronomy and astrology; I looked for consistency in him, a consistency he didn't seem to care about, or even think about. When I asked him what the discovery of Pluto and Neptune did to his archaic nine-planet astrology, he said, 'You make the necessary corrections, that's all.' Or, in answer to how he could read the Gītā religiously having bathed and painted on his forehead the red and white feet of Viṣṇu, and later talk appreciatively about Bertrand Russell and even Ingersoll, he said, 'The Gītā is part of one's hygiene. Besides, don't you know, the brain has two lobes?'

The following poem says something about the way he and his friends appeared to me:

Sky-man in a man-hole
with astronomy for dream,
astrology for nightmare;

fat man full of proverbs,
the language of lean years,
living in square after

almanac square
prefiguring the day
of windfall and landslide

through a calculus
of good hours,
clutching at the tear

in his birthday shirt
as at a hole
in his mildewed horoscope,

squinting at the parallax
of black planets,
his Tiger, his Hare

moving in Sanskrit zodiacs,
forever troubled
by the fractions, the kidneys

in his Tamil flesh,
his body the Great Bear
dipping for the honey,

the woman-smell
in the small curly hair
down there. (Ramanujan 1986: 24)

III

Both Englishmen and 'modern' Indians have been dismayed and angered by this kind of inconsistency. About twenty years ago, *The illustrated weekly of India* asked a number of modern Indian intellectuals to describe the Indian character—they did not seem to be daunted by the assignment and wrote terse, some quite sharp, columns. *They* all seemed to agree on one thing: the Indian trait of hypocrisy. Indians do not mean what they say, and say different things at different times. By 'Indians' they did not mean only servants. In Max Müller's lectures (1883) on India, the second chapter was called 'Truthful character of the Hindus', in answer to many complaints.

Recently I attended a conference on *karma*, a notion that is almost synonymous in some circles with whatever is Indian or Hindu. Brahminical texts had it, the Buddhists had it, the Jainas had it. But when I looked at hundreds of Kannada tales, I couldn't find a single tale that used *karma* as a motif or motive. Yet when their children made a mess, their repertoire of abuse included, 'You are my *karma*!' When Harper (1959) and others after him reported that many Indian villagers didn't know much about reincarnation, such a discrepancy was attributed to caste, education, etc. But the 2,000 Kannada tales, collected by me and others over the past twenty years, were told by Brahmins, Jainas (both of whom use *karma* in their explanations elsewhere quite readily), and by other communities as well. What is worse, Sheryl Daniel (1983) independently found that her Tamil village alternately used *karma* and *talaividi* ('headwriting') as explanations for the events around them. The two notions are inconsistent with each other. *Karma* implies the self's past determining the present, an iron chain of cause and consequence, an ethic of responsibility. *Talaividi* is one's fate inscribed arbitrarily at one's birth on one's forehead; the inscription has no relation to one's prior actions; usually in such explanations (and folktales about them) past lives are not even part of the scheme (see also Wadley, in this volume).

Another related characteristic seems to preoccupy observers. We have already said that 'inconsistency' (like my father's, or the Brahmin/Jaina use of *karma*) is not a matter of inadequate education or lack of logical rigor. They may be using a different 'logic' altogether. Some thinkers believe that such logic is an earlier-stage of 'cultural evolution' and that Indians have not developed a notion of 'data', of 'objective facts'. Edward Said's *Orientalism* cites many such European stereotypes about the 'Third World'. Here is Henry Kissinger's explanation:

> Cultures which escaped the early impact of Newtonian thinking have retained the essentially pre-Newtonian view that the world is almost completely *internal* to the observer . . . [Consequently] empirical reality has a much different significance for many of the new [old?] countries

> than for the West because in a certain sense they never went through the process of discovering it (Said 1978: 47).

Such a view cannot be dismissed as peculiar to Kissinger's version of Newtonian optics. One meets with it again and again in travelogues, psychological writings, novels. Naipaul quotes Sudhir Kakar, a sophisticated psychoanalyst, deeply knowledgeable in matters Indian as well as Western, an insider/outsider:

> Generally among Indians there seems to be a different relationship to outside reality, compared to the one met with in the West. In India it is closer to a certain stage in childhood when outer objects did not have a separate, independent existence but were intimately related to the self and its affective states . . . . The Indian 'ego' is underdeveloped; 'the world of magic and animistic thinking lie close to the surface; so the grasp of reality is 'relatively tenuous' (1977: 107).

In a memorable and oft-quoted section of Foster's *A passage to India*, Mrs. Moore muses vividly on the relations between inside and outside in India; the confounding of the two is not special to humans in India:

> Going to hang up her cloak, she found the tip of the peg was occupied by a small wasp. She had known this wasp or his relatives by song; they were not as English wasps, but had long yellow legs which hung down behind when they flew. Perhaps he mistook the peg for a branch—no Indian animal has any sense of an interior. Bats, rats, birds, insects will as soon nest inside the house as out, it is to them a normal growth of the eternal jungle, which alternately produces houses, trees, houses, trees. There he clung, asleep, while jackals bayed their desires and mingled with the percussion of drums (1952: 35).

And sympaticos, like Zimmer, praise the Indians for not being hung up on an objectivity that distinguishes self from non-self, interior from exterior; what for Naipaul is a 'defect of vision', is for Zimmer vision itself:

> India thinks of time and herself . . . in biological terms, terms of the species, not of the ephemeral ego . . . .We of the west regard world history as a biography of mankind, and in particular of Occidental Man . . . . Our will is not to culminate in our human institutions the universal play of nature, but to evaluate, to set ourselves against the play, with an ego-centric tenacity (1946: 21).

A third trait should be added to 'inconsistency', and to the apparent inability to distinguish self and non-self. One has only to read Manu after a bit of Kant to be struck by the former's extraordinary lack of universality. He seems to have no clear notion of a universal *human* nature from which one can deduce ethical decrees like 'Man shall not kill', or 'Man shall not tell an untruth'. One is aware of no notion of a 'state', no unitary law of all men.

> Manu VIII.267 (quoted by Müller 1883) has the following: A Kshatriya, having defamed a Brahmana, shall be fined one hundred (*panas*); a Vaisya one hundred and fifty or two hundred; a Sudra shall suffer corporal punishment.

Even truth-telling is not an unconditional imperative, as Müller's correspondents discovered.

> An untruth spoken by people under the influence of anger, excessive joy, fear, pain, or grief, by infants, by very old men, by persons labouring under a delusion, being under the influence of drink, or by mad men, does not cause the speaker to fall, or as we should say, is a venial not a mortal sin (Gautama. paraphrased by Müller [1883: 70]).

Alexander Wilder adds, in a footnote, further extensions:

> At the time of marriage, during dalliance, when life is in danger, when the loss of property is threatened, and for the sake of a Brahmana . . . Manu declared . . . . whenever the death of a man of any of the four castes would be occasioned by true evidence, falsehood was even better than truth (Müller 1883: 89).

Contrast this with Kant's well-known formulation of his imperative: 'Act as if the maxim of your action were to become through your will a Universal Law of Nature' (Copleston 1946: 116).

'Moral judgements are universalizable', says Mackie (1977: 83). Universalisation means putting oneself in another's place—it is the golden rule of the New Testament, Hobbes' 'law of all men': do not do unto others what you do not want done unto you. The main tradition of Judeo/Christian ethics is based on such a premise of universalisation—Manu will not understand such a premise. To be moral, for Manu, is to particularise—to ask who did what, to whom and when. Shaw's comment, 'Do not do unto others as you would have they should do unto you. Their tastes may not be the same' (Mackie 1977: 89) will be closer to Manu's view, except he would substitute 'natures or classes' for 'tastes'. Each class (*jāti*) of man has his own laws, his own proper ethic, not to be universalised. Hegel shrewdly noted this Indian slant: 'While we say, "Bravery is a virtue," the Hindoos say, on the contrary, "Bravery is a virtue of the Cshatriyas" ' (Hegel *ca.* 1827: First part, Sect. 2, 'India').

Is there any system to this particularism? Indian philosophers do not seem to make synoptic 'systems' like Hegel's or Kant's. Sheryl Daniel (1983) speaks of a 'tool-box' of ideas that Indians carry about, and from which they use one or another without much show of logic; anything goes into their 'bricolage' (Lévi-Strauss 1962: 16–36). Max Weber, in various writings, distinguished 'traditional' and 'rational' religions. Geertz summarises the distinction better than other writers:

> Traditional religions attack problems opportunistically as they arise in each particular instance . . . employing one or another weapon chosen, on grounds of symbolic appropriateness, from their cluttered arsenal of myth and magic . . . the approach . . . is discrete and irregular . . . . Rationalized religions . . . are more abstract, more logically coherent, and more generally phrased . . . . The question is no longer . . . to use a classical example from Evans-Pritchard, 'Why has the granary fallen on my brother . . .?' but rather, 'Why do the good die young and the evil flourish as the green bay tree?' (Geertz 1973: 172).

IV

It is time to step back and try a formulation. The grammarian sees grammar in all things; I shall be true to my bias and borrow a notion from linguistics and try it for size.

There are (or used to be) two kinds of grammatical rules: the context-free and the context-sensitive (Lyons 1971: 235–41). 'Sentences must have subjects and predicates in a certain relation' would be an example of the first kind of rule. 'Plurals in English are realised as *-s* after stops (e.g., dog-s, cat-s), *-es* before fricatives (e.g., latch-es), *-ren* after the word *child*, etc.'—would be a context-sensitive rule. Almost all language rules are of the latter kind.

I think cultures (may be said to) have overall tendencies (for whatever complex reasons)—tendencies to *idealise*, and think in terms of, either the context-free or the context-sensitive kind of rules. Actual behaviour may be more complex, though the rules they think with are a crucial factor in guiding the behaviour. In cultures like India's, the context-sensitive kind of rule is the preferred formulation. Manu (I have already quoted a law of his) explicitly says: '[A king] who knows the sacred law, must imagine into the laws of caste (*jāti*), of districts, of guilds, and of families, and [thus] settle the peculiar law of each' (Manu 7.41).

In an illuminating discussion of the context-sensitive nature of *dharma* in its detail, Baudhāyana enumerates aberrant practices peculiar to the Brahmins of the north and those of the south.

> There is a difference between the South and the North on five points. We shall describe the practices of the South: to eat with a person not having received Brahmanical initiation; to eat with one's wife; to eat food prepared the previous day; to marry the daughter of the maternal

uncle or paternal aunt. And for the North: to sell wool; to drink spirits; to traffic in animals with two rows of teeth; to take up the profession of arms; to make sea voyages.

After this admirable ethnographic description, he notes that all these practices are contrary to the precepts of *śruti* or *smṛti*, but these *śiṣṭa*s (learned men) know the traditions and cannot be blamed for following the customs of their district. In the north, the southern ways would be wrong and vice versa (Lingat 1973: 196).

Add to this view of right and wrong behaviour, the ethical views of the *āśramadharma* (the conduct that is right for one's stage of life), *svadharma* (the conduct that is right for one's station, *jāti* or class, or *svabhāva* or given nature), and *āpaddharma* (conduct that is necessary in times of distress or emergency, e.g., one may even eat the flesh of dogs to save oneself from death by starvation, as sage Viśvāmitra did). Each addition is really a subtraction from any universal law. There is not much left of an absolute or common (*sādhārana*) *dharma* which the texts speak of, if at all, as a last and not as a first resort. They seem to say, if you fit no contexts or conditions, which is unlikely, fall back on the universal.

I know of no Hindu discussion of values which reads like Plato on Beauty in his *Symposium*—which asks the initiate not to rest content with beauty in one embodiment but to be drawn onward from physical to moral beauty, to the beauty of laws and mores, and to all science and learning, and thus to escape 'the mean slavery of the particular case'. (I am reserving counter-instances for later.)

Or take Indian literary texts. No Indian text comes without a context, a frame, till the 19th century. Works are framed by *phalaśruti* verses—these verses tell the reader, reciter or listener all the good that will result from his act of reading, reciting or listening. They relate the text, of whatever antiquity, to the present reader—that is, they contextualise it. An extreme case is that of the Nāḍiśāstra, which offers you your personal history. A friend of mine consulted the Experts about himself and his past and future. After enough rupees had been exchanged, the Experts brought out an old palm-leaf manuscript which, in archaic verses, mentioned his full name, age, birthplace, etc., and said suddenly, 'At this point, the listener is crossing his legs—he should uncross them.'

Texts may be historically dateless, anonymous; but their contexts, uses, efficacies, are explicit. The Rāmāyana and Mahābhārata open with episodes that tell you why and under what circumstances they were composed. Every such story is encased in a metastory. And within the text, one tale is the context for another within it; not only does the outer frame-story motivate the inner sub-story; the inner story illuminates the outer as well. It often acts as a microcosmic replica for the whole text. In the forest when the Pandava brothers are in exile, the eldest, Yudhiṣthira, is in the very slough of despondency: he has gambled away a kingdom, and is in exile. In the depth of his despair, a sage visits him and tells him the story of Nala. As the story unfolds, we see Nala too gamble away a kingdom, lose his wife, wander in the forest, and finally, win his wager, defeat his brother, reunite with his wife and return to his kingdom. Yudhiṣṭhira, following the full curve of Nala's adventures, sees that he is only halfway through his own, and sees his present in perspective, himself as a story yet to be finished. Very often the Nala story is excerpted and read by itself, but its poignancy is partly in its frame, its meaning for the hearer within the fiction and for the listener of the whole epic. The tale within is context-sensitive—getting its meaning from the tale without, and giving it further meanings.

Scholars have often discussed Indian texts (like the Mahābhārata) as if they were loose-leaf files, rag-bag encyclopaedias. Taking the Indian word for text, *grantha* (derived from the knot that holds the palm leaves together), literally, scholars often posit only an accidental and physical unity. We need to attend to the context-sensitive designs that embed a seeming variety of modes (tale, discourse, poem, etc.) and materials. This manner of constructing the text is in consonance with other designs in the culture. Not unity (in the Aristotelian sense) but coherence, seems to be the end.

Tamil (and Sanskrit) lyrics are all dramatic monologues; they imply the whole 'communication diagram': who said what to whom, when, why, and often with who else overhearing it. Here is an example:

What his concubine said about him (within earshot of the wife's friends, when she heard that the wife had said disparaging things about her):

You know he comes from
where the fresh-water shark in the pools
catch with their mouths
the mangoes as they fall, ripe
from the trees on the edge of the field.

At our place
he talked big.

Now back in his own
when others raise their hands
and feet,
he will raise his too:

like a doll
in a mirror

he will shadow
every last wish
of his son's dear mother.

Kuruntokai 8
(Ramanujan 1967: 22)

The colophons give us the following frames for this poem:
Genre: *Akam*, love poetry, the 'interior'.
Landscape: agricultural, with pool, fresh-water fish, mango trees.
Mood: infidelity, sullenness, lover's quarrels.

The poetry of such a poem (see Ramanujan 1967 for details) depends on a taxonomy of landscapes, flora and fauna, and of emotions—an ecosystem of which a man's activities and feelings are a part. To describe the exterior landscape is also to inscribe the interior landscape. What the man has, he is: the landscape which he owns, in which he lives (where sharks do not have to work for the mango, it falls into its open mouth) re-presents him: it is his *property*, in more senses than one. In Burke's (1946) terms, *Scene and Agent* are one; they are metonyms for one another.

The poem does not use a metaphor. The human agents are simply *placed* in the scene. Both parts of the comparison (the man and shark) are part of one scene, one syntagm; they exist separately, yet simulate each other. The Tamils call such a figure *ullurai* 'inward speaking'; it is an 'inset', an 'inscape'. In such a metonymic view of man in nature—man in context—he is continuous with the context he is in. In Peircean semiotic terms, these are not symbolic devices, but indexical signs—the signifier and the signified belong in the same context (Peirce 1931–58).

One might say, from this point of view, that Hindu ritual (e.g., vedic sacrifice, or a coronation; see Inden [1978]) converts *symbols*, arbitrary signs (e.g., sacrificial horse), into *icons* where the signifier (the horse) is *like* what it signifies (the universe) and finally into *indexes*, where the signifier is *part* of what it signifies: the horse is the Universe is Prajāpati, so that in sacrificing and partaking of it one is sacrificing and partaking of the Universe itself (see the passage on the Horse in *Bṛhadāraṇyaka*, First Adhyāya, First Brāhmana).

Neither in the Tamil poem nor in the upaniṣadic passages (e.g., the Horse), does the Lévi-Straussian opposition of nature-culture make sense; we see that the opposition itself is culture-bound. There is another alternative to a culture vs. nature view: in the Tamil poems, culture is enclosed in nature, nature is reworked in culture, so that we cannot tell the difference. We have a nature-culture continuum that cancels the terms, confuses them even if we begin with them.

Such container-contained relations are seen in many kinds of concepts and images: not only in culture-nature, but god-world, king-kingdom, devotee-god, mother-child. Here is a *bhakti* poem which plays with many such concentric containments:

My dark one
 Stands there as if nothing's changed,

after taking entire
into his maw

all three worlds
the gods
and the good kings
  who hold their lands
  as a mother would
  a child in her womb –

and I, by his leave,
have taken him entirely
and I have him in my belly
for keeps.

Nammāḻvār 8.7.1
(Ramanujan 1980)

Like the Nala story in the Mahābhārata, what is contained mirrors the container; the microcosm is both *within* and like the macrocosm, and paradoxically also contains it. Indian conceptions tend to be such concentric nests: the view of the 'sheaths' or *kośas*, the different 'bodies' or *kāyas* (Egnor 1975) are examples. Such impressions are so strong and even kinesthetic that analysts tend to think in similar terms: one example is Dumont's (1970: Sects. 31, 34, 106, 118; App. E, F) notions of hierarchic encompassment, where each higher category or *jāti* encompasses all the earlier ones: the Kṣatriya is distinct from but includes the Vaiśya, as the Brahmin encompasses the Kṣatriya. Many Indian lists, like *dharma-artha-kāma* tend to be successive encompassments. (For the separation of *mokṣa*, see below.)

Even space and time, the universal contexts, the Kantian imperatives, are in India not uniform and neutral, but have properties, varying specific densities, that affect those who dwell in them. The soil in a village, which produces crops for the people, affects their character (as liars, for instance, in E.V. Daniel's village (1984); houses (containers par excellence) have mood and character, change the fortune and moods of the dwellers. Time too does not come in uniform units: certain hours of the day, certain days of the week, etc., are auspicious or inauspicious (*rāhukāla*); certain units of time (*yugas*) breed certain kinds of maladies, politics, religions, e.g., *kaliyuga*. A story is told about two men coming to Yudhiṣṭhira with a case. One had bought the other's land, and soon after found a crock of gold in it. He wanted to return it to the original owner of the land, who was arguing that it really belonged to the man who had now bought it. They had come to Yudhiṣṭhira to settle their virtuous dispute. Just then Yudhiṣṭhira was called away (to put it politely) for a while. When he came back the two gentlemen were quarrelling furiously, but each was claiming the treasure for himself this time! Yudhiṣṭhira realised at once that the age had changed, and *kaliyuga* had begun.

As hour, month, season, year, and aeon have their own properties as contexts, the arts that depend on time have to obey time's changing moods and properties. For instance, the *rāga*s of both north and south Indian classical music have their prescribed appropriate times. Like the Tamil poems, the genres and moods are associated with, placed in, hours of the day and times of the season. Even musical instruments have their caste properties; a *vīṇā*, no less than the icon of a god, has to be made by a particular caste, or family, after observing certain austerities (*vratā*), made on an auspicious day; the gourd from which it is made has to be taken from certain kinds of places. Their *guṇa*s (qualities of substance) affect the quality of the instrument, the music.

The same kind of contextual sensitiveness is shown in medical matters: in preparing a herbal medicine, in diagnosis and in prescription. As Zimmermann's work (1980) is eloquent on the subject, I shall say little. The notion of *ṛtusātmya* or appropriateness applies to poetry, music, sacrificial ritual, as well as medicine. As Renou (1950a, 1950b) points out, *ṛtu*, usually translated as 'season', means articulation of time; it is also the crucial moment in vedic sacrifice. *Ṛtā* ('order', the original notion behind *dharma*) is that which is articulated. *Kratu*, sacrifice, is a convergence of events, acts, times and spaces. The vocabulary of *ṛtusātmya* 'appropriateness', *rasa* 'essences, flavours, tastes', *doṣa* 'defects, deficiency', and of landscapes is common to both medicine and poetry: the arts of man reading and re-forming himself in his contexts.

Thus, all things, even so-called non-material ones like space and time or caste, affect other things because all things are 'substantial' (*dhātu*). The only difference is that some are subtle (*sūkṣma*), some gross (*sthūla*). Contrary to the notion that Indians are 'spiritual', they are really 'material minded'. They are materialists, believers in substance (Marriott 1976, 1980): there is a continuity, a constant flow (the etymology of *saṁsāra*!) of substance from context to object, from non-self to self (if you prefer)—in eating, breathing, sex, sensation, perception, thought, art, or religious experience. This is the grain of truth glimpsed by many of the stereotypes cited in the earlier parts of this essay. Zimmermann (1979) points out that in Indian medical texts, the body is a meeting-place, a conjunction of elements; they have a physiology, but no anatomy.

Where Kissinger and others are wrong is in not seeing that this view has nothing to do with Newtonian revolution, education, or (in)capacity for abstract thought. Cognitive anthropologists like Richard Shweder (1972) have studied descriptive phrases used by highly intelligent Oriya and American adults and shown that they describe persons very differently: Americans characterised them with generic words like 'good', 'nice', Oriyas with concrete contextual descriptions like 'he brings sweets'. The psychoanalyst Alan Roland (1979) suggests that Indians carry their family-context wherever they go, feel continuous with their family. He posits a familial self, a 'self-we regard', sees no phase of separation/individuation from the parental family as in modern America; hence there seems to be no clear-cut adolescent phase through which one rebels, and thereby separates and individuates oneself in opposition to one's family (the exceptions are in 'modern' urban-centred families). Roland remarks that Indians develop a 'radar' *conscience* that orients them to others, makes them say things that are appropriate to person and context. (No wonder Max Müller had to insist that Indians were truthful!) Roland also found that when directions to places are given, Indians always make reference to other places, landmarks.

Such a pervasive emphasis on context is, I think, related to the Hindu concern with *jāti*—the logic of classes, of genera and species, of which human *jāti*s are only an instance. Various taxonomies of season, landscape, times, *guṇa*s or qualities (and their material bases), tastes, characters, emotions, essences (*rasa*), etc., are basic to the thought-work of Hindu medicine and poetry, cooking and religion, erotics and magic. Each *jāti* or class defines a context, a structure of relevance, a rule of permissible combinations, a frame of reference, a meta-communication of what is and can be done.

It is not surprising that systems of Indian philosophy, Hindu, Buddhist, or Jaina,

> confine themselves to the consideration of class-essences (*jāti*) called genera and species in Western philosophy. They never raise the question of whether there are universals of other types, namely identical qualities and relations. The assumption seems to be that qualities and relations are particulars, though they may be instances of universals (Dravid 1972: 347).

The most important and accessible model of a context-sensitive system with intersecting taxonomies is, of course, the grammar of a language. And grammar is the central model for thinking in many Hindu texts. As Frits Staal has said, what Euclid is to European thought, the grammarian Pāṇini is to the Indian. Even the Kāmasūtra is literally a grammar of love—which declines and conjugates men and women as one would nouns and verbs in different genders, voices, moods and aspects. Genders are genres. Different body-types and character-types obey different rules, respond to different scents and beckonings.

In such a world, systems of meaning are elicited by contexts, by the nature (and substance) of the listener. In *Bṛhadāraṇyaka* 5.1., Lord Prajāpati speaks in thunder three times: 'DA DA DA'. When the gods, given to pleasure hear it, they hear it as the first syllable of *damyatā*, 'control'. The antigods, given as they are to cruelty, hear it as *dayādhvam*, 'be compassionate'. When the humans, given to greed, hear it they hear it as *dattā*, 'give to others'.

V

All societies have context-sensitive behaviour and rules—but the dominant ideal may not be the 'context-sensitive' but the 'context-free'. Egalitarian democratic ideals, Protestant Christianity, espouse both the universal and the unique, insist that any member is *equal* to and *like* any other in the group. Whatever his context—birth, class, gender, age, place, rank, etc.—a man is a man for all that. Technology with its modules and interchangeable parts, and the post-Renaissance sciences with their quest for universal laws (and 'facts') across contexts intensify the bias towards the context-free. Yet societies have underbellies. In predominantly 'context-free' societies, the counter-movements tend to be towards the context-sensitive: situation ethics, Wittgensteinian notions of meaning and colour (against class-logic), the various relativisms including our own search for 'native categories' in anthropology, holistic movements in medicine (naturopaths who prescribe individually tailored regimens) are good examples. In 'traditional' cultures like India, where context-sensitivity rules and binds, the dream is to be free of context. So *rasa* in aesthetics, *mokṣa* in the 'aims of life', *sannyāsa* in the life-stages, *sphoṭa* in semantics, and *bhakti* in religion define themselves against a background of inexorable contextuality.

Where *kāma, artha* and *dharma* are all relational in their values, tied to place, time, personal character and social role, *mokṣa* is the release from all relations. If *brahmacārya* (celibate studentship) is preparation for a fully relational life, *gṛhasthāśrama* (householder stage) is a full realisation of it. Manu prefers the latter over all other states. *Vānaprastha* (the retiring forest-dweller stage) loosens the bonds, and *sannyāsa* (renunciation) cremates all one's past and present relations. In the realm of feeling, *bhāva*s are private, contingent, context-roused sentiments, *vibhāva*s are determinant causes, *anubhāva*s the consequent expressions. But *rasa* is generalised, it is an essence. In the field of meaning, the temporal sequence of letters and phonemes, the syntactic chain of words, yields finally a *sphoṭa*, an explosion, a meaning which is beyond sequence and time.

In each of these the pattern is the same: a necessary sequence in time with strict rules of phase and context ending in a free state.

The last of the great Hindu anti-contextual notions, *bhakti*, is different from the above; it denies the very need for context. *Bhakti* defies all contextual structures: every pigeonhole of caste, ritual, gender, appropriate clothing and custom, stage of life, the whole system of homo hierarchicus ('everything in its place') is the target of its irony.

Did the breath of the mistress
have breasts and long hair?

Or did the master's breath
wear sacred thread?
Did the outcaste, last in line,
hold with his outgoing breath
the stick of his tribe?

What do the fools of this world know
of the snares you set,
O Rāmanātha?

Dāsimayya, 10th century
(Ramanujan 1973)

In European culture, one might mention Plato's rebellion against (even the limited) Athenian democracy. Or Blake in the technocratic democracy of the 19th century railing against egalitarianism, abstraction, and the dark Satanic mills, calling for 'minute particulars', declaring 'To generalize is to be an idiot' (generalising thereby); and framing the slogan of all context-sensitive systems: 'one law for the lion and the ox is oppression'. I would include the rise of minute realism in the 19th century novel, various 'indexical' movements of modern art in this counter-thrust towards particularism in the West.

Neither the unique, nor the universal, the two, often contradictory, concerns of western philosophy, art and polity, are the central concern of the Indian arts and sciences—except in the counter-cultures and modern attempts, which quickly get enlisted and remolded (witness the fate of *bhakti* movements) by the prevailing context-sensitive patterns.

VI

In conclusion, I would like to make a couple of observations about 'modernisation'. One might see 'modernisation' in India as a movement from the context-sensitive to the context-free in all realms: an erosion of contexts, at least in principle. Gandhi's watch (with its uniform autonomous time, governing his punctuality) replaced the almanac. Yet Gandhi quoted Emerson, that consistency was the hobgoblin of foolish minds. Print replaced palm-leaf manuscripts, making possible an open and egalitarian access to knowledge irrespective of caste. The Indian Constitution made the contexts of birth, region, sex and creed irrelevant, overthrowing Manu, though the battle is joined again and again. The new preferred names give no clue to birth-place, father's name, caste, sub-caste and sect, as all the traditional names did: I once found in a Kerala college roster, three 'Joseph Stalins' and one 'Karl Marx'. I have also heard of an Andhra named 'Bobbili Winston Churchill'.

In music, the *rāgas* can now be heard at all hours and seasons. Once the Venkaṭeśasuprabhātam, the wake-up chant for the Lord of Tirupati, could be heard only in Tirupati at a certain hour in the morning. Since M.S. Subbulakshmi in her devotion cut a record of the chants, it wakes up not only the Lord, but anyone who tunes in to All India Radio in faraway places.

Cultural borrowings from India to the West, or vice versa, also show interesting accommodations to the prevailing system. The highly contextualised Hindu systems are generalised into 'a Hindu view of life' by apologues like Radhakrishnan for the benefit of both the Western and modern Indian readers. The individual esoteric skills of meditation are freed from their contexts into a streamlined widely accessible technique. And when T.S. Eliot borrows the DA DA DA passage (quoted earlier) to end 'The wasteland' (1930), it becomes highly individual, introspective, as well as universal:

Then spoke the thunder
DA
dattā: what have we given?
My friend, blood shaking my heart
The awful daring of a moment's surrender
Which an age of prudence can never retract
By this, and this only, we have existed
Which is not to be found in our obituaries
Or in memories draped by the beneficent spider
Or under the seals broken by the lean solicitor
In our empty rooms
DA
dayādhvam: I have heard the key
Turn in the door once and turn once only
We think of the key, each in his prison
Thinking of the key, each confirms a prison
Only at nightfall, aetheral rumours
Revive for a moment a broken Coriolanus
DA
damyatā: The boat responded
Gaily, to the hand expert with sail and oar
The sea was calm, your heart would have responded
Gaily, when invited, beating obedient
To controlling hands

In reverse, Indian borrowings of Western cultural items have been converted and realigned to fit pre-existing context-sensitive needs. When

English is borrowed into (or imposed on) Indian contexts, it fits into the Sanskrit slot; it acquires many of the characteristics of Sanskrit, the older native Father-tongue, its pan-Indian elite character—as a medium of laws, science and administration, and its formulaic patterns; it becomes part of Indian multiple diglossia (a characteristic of context-sensitive societies). When Indians learn, quite expertly, modern science, business, or technology, they 'compartmentalize' these interests (Singer 1972: 320ff.); the new ways of thought and behaviour do not replace, but live along with older 'religious' ways. Computers and typewriters receive *ayudhapuja* ('worship of weapons') as weapons of war did once. The 'modern', the context-free, becomes one more context, though it is not easy to contain.

In modern thought, William James with his 'sub-universes', or Alfred Schutz with his 'finite provinces of reality' and 'relevance' as central concepts in any understanding, should be re-read in the light of what I have said about context-sensitive and context-free modes. The most recent kinds of science can hold together inconsistent systems of explanation—like wave and particle theories of light. The counter-movements in the West toward Schumacher's 'small is beautiful', appropriate technologies, and the attention paid to ethnicity rather than to a melting pot, though not yet successful, are straws in the wind—like the ethnography of communication in linguistics.

My purpose here is not to evaluate but to grope toward a description of the two kinds of emphases. Yet in each of these kinds of cultures, despite all the complexity and oscillation, there is a definite bias. The Buddha (who said 'When we see a man shot with a poisoned arrow, we cannot afford to ask what caste he or his enemy is') also told the following parable of the Raft: Once a man was drowning in a sudden flood. Just as he was about to drown, he found a raft. He clung to it, and it carried him safely to dry land. And he was so grateful to the raft that he carried it on his back for the rest of his life. Such was the Buddha's ironic comment on context-free systems.

REFERENCES

Burke, Kenneth. 1946. *A grammar of motives*. Berkeley: University of California Press.

Copleston, Frederick Charles. 1946. *A history of philosophy*, Vol. 6. London: Burns, Oates and Washbourne.

Daniel, E. Valentine. 1984. *Fluid signs: being a person the Tamil way*. Berkeley: University of California Press.

Daniel, Sheryl B. 1983. The tool-box approach of the Tamil to the issues of moral responsibility and human destiny. *In* Charles F. Keyes and E. Valentine Daniel, eds., *Karma: an anthropological inquiry*, pp. 27–62. Berkeley: University of California Press.

Dravid, Raja Ram. 1972. *The problem of universals in Indian philosophy*. Delhi: Motilal Banarsidass.

Dumont, Louis. 1970. *Homo hierarchicus: the caste system and its implications* (trans. Mark Sainsbury). Chicago: University of Chicago Press.

Egnor, Margaret Trawick. 1975. Principles of continuity in three Indian sciences. M.A. paper, Dept. of Anthropology, University of Chicago.

Eliot, Thomas Stearns. 1930. *The wasteland and other poems*. New York: Harcourt Brace.

Foster, Edward Morgan. 1952. *A passage to India*. New York: Harcourt Brace.

Geertz, Clifford. 1973. *The interpretation of cultures*. New York: Basic Books.

Harper, Edward B. 1959. A Hindu village pantheon. *Southwestern journal of anthropology* 15: 227–34.

Hegel, Georg Wilhelm Friedrich. *ca.* 1827. *Lectures on the philosophy of history*.

Inden, Ronald B. 1978. Ritual authority and cyclic time in Hindu kingship. *In* John F. Richards, ed., *Kingship and authority in South Asia*, pp. 28–73. Publication series, publication n. 3. Madison: South Asian Studies, University of Wisconsin.

Lévi-Strauss, Claude. 1962. *The savage mind*. Chicago: University of Chicago Press.

Lingat, Robert. 1973. *The classical law of India* (trans. D.M. Derrett). Berkeley: University of California Press.

Lyons, John. 1971. *Introduction to theoretical linguistics*. Cambridge: Cambridge University Press.

Mackie, John Leslie. 1977. *Ethics: inventing right and wrong*. Harmondsworth: Penguin Books.

Manu. 1886. *The laws of Manu* (trans. Georg Bühler). Sacred Books of the East, vol. 25. Oxford: Clarendon Press.

Marriott, McKim. 1976. Hindu transactions; diversity without dualism. *In* Bruce Kapferer, ed., *Transac.ion and meaning: directions in the anthropology of exchange and symbolic behavior*, pp. 109–42. Philadelphia: Institute for the Study of Human Issues.

———. 1980. The open Hindu person and interpersonal fluidity. Paper presented at the annual meeting of the Association for Asian Studies, Washington DC.

Müller, Friedrich Max. 1883. *India: what can it teach us*? London: Longmans Green.

Naipaul, V.S. 1977. *A wounded civilization*. New York: Random House.

Peirce, Charles Santiago Sanders. 1931–58. *Collected papers*. 7 vols. Cambridge MA: Harvard University Press.

Ramanujan, A.K., trans. 1967. *The interior landscape: Love poems from a classical Tamil anthology*. Bloomington: Indiana University Press.

———. 1973. *Speaking of Śiva*. Baltimore: Penguin.

———. 1980. *Hymns for the drowning*. Princeton: Princeton University Press.

———. 1986. *Second sight*. Delhi: Oxford University Press.

Renou, Louis. 1950a. Un thème litteraire en sanskrit: les saisons. *In* Louis Renou, *Sanskrit et culture*, pp. 145–54. Paris: Payot.

———. 1950b. Vedique *ṛtu*. *Archiv orientalni*, 18: 431–8.

Roland, Alan. 1979. *In search of the self in India and Japan: toward a cross-cultural psychology*. Princeton: Princeton University Press.

Said, Edward. 1978. *Orientalism*. New York: Pantheon.

Shweder, Richard. 1972. Semantic structures and personality assessment. Ph.D. dissertation. Harvard University.

Singer, Milton B. 1972. *When a great tradition modernizes*. New York: Praeger.

Zimmer, Heinrich Robert. 1946. *Myths and symbols in Indian art and civilization*. New York: Pantheon.

Zimmermann, Francis B. 1979. Remarks on the body in ayurvedic medicine. *South Asian digest of regional writing* 18: 10–26.

———. 1980. *Ṛtu-sâtmya*: the seasonal cycle and the principle of appropriateness. *Social science and medicine* 14B: 99–106.

3

The original caste: power, history and hierarchy in South Asia[1]

Nicholas B. Dirks

> Traditionally, power was what was seen, what was shown and what was manifested and, paradoxically, found the principle of its force in the movement by which it deployed that force. Those on whom it was exercised could remain in the shade; they received light only from that portion of power that was conceded to them, or from the reflection of it that for a moment they carried (Foucault 1979: 187).

The politics of caste

In pre-colonial Hindu India, the king—both as a historical figure and as a trope for the complex political dynamics underlying the Indian social order—was a central ordering factor in the social organisation of caste. This statement directly opposes the prevailing theories of comparative sociology, and in particular, the theoretical position of Louis Dumont (1980). As is well known, Dumont holds that the political and economic domains of social life in India are encompassed by the 'religious'. The religious principle becomes articulated in terms of the opposition of purity and impurity. For Dumont, the Brahman represents the religious principle, inasmuch as the Brahman represents the highest form of purity attainable by Hindus. The king, while important and powerful, represents the political domain, and is accordingly inferior to, and encompassed by, the Brahman.

There are in fact many textual confirmations of the view that Brahmans, and the spiritual authority (*brahma*) that they possess, are seen as higher,

[1] This paper summarises the argument of my book, *The hollow crown* (1987), and is based on research funded by Fulbright-Hays, the Social Science Research Council, the Danforth Foundation, and the American Institute of Indian Studies.

I am grateful to McKim Marriott for his careful reading of the final draft.

both relationally and ontologically, than kings, and the temporal authority (*kṣatra*) that is theirs. However, these same texts provide evidence as well of what has been called 'the central conundrum of Indian social ideology' (Trautmann 1981: 285; also see Heesterman 1978). At times the king is above the Brahman, as for example in the royal consecration ceremony. At other times the Brahman appears to be superior to the king, as for example in the Mānavadharmaśāstra, and in passages from the Mahābhārata. This conundrum is often addressed in terms of the postulation of two levels of truth, a higher level at which the Brahman is clearly pre-eminent, the source of everything else, and a lower level at which kings must protect and sponsor Brahmans in order for them to exist, as gods, on earth. Dumont's resolution of this conundrum extends the notion of higher and lower truths from a classically Indic epistemological contextuality to his well-known ontological separation of the religious from the political. The major development of political thought in India, he contends, is the secularisation of kingship, that is the separation of the magico-religious nature of kingship—preserved in the form of the royal chaplain in particular and in the function of Brahmans in the larger polity more generally—from the political aspects of kingship, depicted, inter alia, in the Machiavellian Arthaśāstra (Dumont 1962).

While Dumont is not wrong to insist on radical differences in the 'ideologies' of India and the West, the irony is that the way in which he postulates the difference is based on a fundamentally Western ideology, in which religion and politics must be separated. Dumont's position in many ways caricatures the Orientalist assumption that India is the spiritual East, devoid of history, untouched by the politics of Oriental despotisms. Critics of Dumont have often accepted his basic epistemological premises, but then reversed them. They take a materialist perspective and view social relations in India in terms of power, pure and simple (e.g., Berreman 1971). Recent work—often by those influenced by an ethnosociological approach to the study of India—has suggested that this separation of religion from politics, like many other dichotomies in Western social science, is inappropriate at the level of ideological (or cultural) analysis in Indian social thought (Appadurai 1981; Dirks 1982, 1987; Marriott and Inden 1977; McGilvray 1982). It is in this sense—and in particular in my analysis of the cultural poetics of power—that the following analysis is ethnosociological.

Not only is there no fundamental ontological separation of a 'religious' from a 'political' domain, but religious institutions and activities are fundamental features of what we describe here as the political system. Kings derive much of their power from worship, and bestow their emblems and privileges in a cultural atmosphere that is permeated by the language and attitudes of worship. Further, temples are key institutions in the formation of social communities (Appadurai and Breckenridge 1976), even while they reflect structures of power worked out both in and outside their own walls (Dirks 1987: 285–305, 358–83). In turn, temples represent the pre-eminent position of the king by granting him the highest honour in the temple, before even the learned (*śrōtriya*) Brahman. Religion does not encompass kingship any more than kingship encompasses religion. There are not two distinct forms of power, secular power had by kings and sacred power had by Brahmans. Kings and Brahmans are both privileged but by different forms of divinity in a world in which all beings were, however distantly, generated from the same ontological source. And power—whether defined as a constellation of cultural conceits or as an analytic concern—cannot be restricted to a single domain of Indian social life.

Dumont has suggested that caste is fundamentally religious, and that religious principles actualise themselves in the domain of purity and pollution. In my ethnohistorical study of a south Indian kingdom in which Kallars were the royal caste and Brahmans were heavily patronised according to scripturally mandated forms of royal gifting activity, I have found that purity and pollution are not the primary relational coordinates which endow hierarchy with its meaning and substance. Royal honour (*mariyātai, antastu*) combined with the notions of restriction, command, and order (*kaṭṭupāṭu, atikaram, oṛunku*) are the key discursive components which are embedded in, and productive of, the nature and order of hierarchical relations.

My analysis will, I hope, do more than simply contest Dumont over the issue of which key terms underlie the structural logic of hierarchy in South Asia. Indeed, I wish to reintroduce concerns with power, hegemony, and history into studies of culturally constructed structures of thought, whether structuralist or ethnosociological. The forms and relations of power in southern India efface social scientific distinctions of materialist etics from culturalist emics, for even an analysis of ritual action and language suggests the complex and conjunctural foundations of hierarchical relations. At least this is true among the Kallars of Pudukkottai, less affected perhaps than most other groups by colonialism and the demise of the old regime in the 19th century. For the concerns of comparative sociology are not only the products of a 19th century Orientalism, but also of the colonial intervention that removed the politics from society and created a contradictory form of civil society—with caste as its fundamental institution—in its place. It was not only convenient to render caste independent of political variables, but necessary to do so in order to rule an immensely complex society by a variety of indirect means. Colonial sociology represented the 18th century as decadent, and all legitimate Indian politics as past. Under colonialism, caste was appropriated, and in many respects reinvented, by the British (see Dirks 1989). However, the British were able to change caste because caste continued to be permeable to political influence. Ethnohistorical reconstruction is thus important not only for historians confronting new problems of data and analysis, but for anthropologists who confront in their fieldwork a social system that was decapitated by colonial rule.

Ethnohistory of an Indian kingdom

The Kallars, like the Maravars, settled in mixed economy zones (Ludden 1985) such as Pudukkottai on the borders of the central political and economic regions of the south. In these areas they quickly attained dominance in late medieval times by exercising rights of protection (*pāṭikkāval*) over local communities and institutions. The Kallars were successful in this role because their strong kin- and territory-based social structure and cultural valuation of heroism and honour were highly conducive to the corporate control of the means of violence and coercion. It was no accident that Kallars, like Maravars, were often, when not granted rights of protection, the very groups from which others sought protection.

The Tondaiman dynasty of Kallar kings wrested control over a significant swath of the Pudukkottai region in central Tamil Nadu in the last quarter of the 17th century. Whereas Kallars had been branded as thieves in much early Tamil literature and as criminals by the British under the Criminal Tribes Act, in Pudukkottai—a little kingdom that became the only Princely State in the Tamil-speaking region of southern India--they became the royal caste. Kallars controlled much of the land, occupied the greatest number of authoritative positions, particularly as village and locality headmen and as *mirācidārs*, and ran the most important temples as trustees. These temples were often their lineage, village, or sub-caste-territorial (*nāṭu*) temples, in which they received honours only after the king and Brahmans. In short, Kallars were dominant not only in terms of their numbers, but for economic, political and ritual reasons.

Pudukkottai, which at its most extensive did not exceed 1,200 square miles, was located in an exclusively rainfed agricultural zone right in the middle of the Tamil-speaking region of southern India, straddling the boundary between what had been the two great medieval Tamil kingdoms. Ruled by Kallar kings, it provides an excellent place to test many of the proposals of Dumont, who, before he shaped the concerns of much contemporary Indian anthropology in his general proposals and in *Homo hierarchicus*, portrayed Kallars in his major ethnographic work in India as a ritually marginal group that exemplified the Dravidian isolation of kinship from the influence of caste hierarchy. But in Pudukkottai, less than one hundred miles north of where Dumont conducted his fieldwork, Kallars were *kings*; they exercised every conceivable kind of dominance and their social organisation reflects this fact.

Pudukkottai rose, as did other little kingdoms throughout southern India, within the context of a late medieval Hindu political order. In both its emergence to and its maintenance of power, it exemplified the social and military vitality of certain productively marginal areas in the 17th and 18th centuries, a period that has commonly been characterised as one of decline and decadence. But the 18th century was not the 'black century': the decentralisation of political forms was neither a condemnation of the capabilities of the Indian state nor a natural prelude to British colonial rule (see Bayly 1983). The British conquest of the little kings in the south was anything but absentminded. and there are indications that not only was the economy buoyant in part because of the active court centres ruled by these little kings, but that small and local-level states were learning the political, military and administrative lessons that the French and the English were learning at the same time. But win the British did, and thus their version of the 18th century has collaborated with a subsequent neglect of the 17th and 18th centuries by Western and Indian historians to provide the grist for comparative sociology's Indian mill.

Colonialism purposefully preserved many of the forms of the old regime, nowhere more conspicuously than in the indirectly ruled Princely States. But these forms were frozen, and only the appearances of the old regime (without its vitally connected political and social processes) were saved. Colonialism changed things both more and less than has commonly been thought. While introducing new forms of civil society and separating these forms from the colonial state, colonialism also arrested some of the immediate disruptions of change by preserving many elements of the old regime. But by freezing the wolf in sheep's clothing it changed things fundamentally. Paradoxically, colonialism seems to have created much of what is now accepted as Indian 'tradition', including an autonomous caste structure with the Brahman clearly at the head, village-based systems of exchange, isolated ceremonial residues of the old regime state, and fetishistic competition for ritual goods that no longer played a vital role in the political system.

In my research on Pudukkottai, it took little study of local land records to uncover the most surprising historical characteristic of the political system: how little of the land was taxed (Dirks 1979). According to mid-19th century records, less than 30 per cent of the cultivated land was either taxed (9 per cent) or given out from year to year on a share basis (18 per cent) in which one-ninth of the produce was accorded to village servants and four-ninths each to the cultivator and the government. Seventy per cent of the cultivated land was *iṉām* or tax-free. This mid-19th century statistic was, if anything, far higher in the 18th century, when there were at the very least another 5,000 military *iṉāms*, i.e., 40 per cent more than the total number of *iṉāms* in the mid-19th century, before the gradual dismantlement of the military system of the state. Roughly 30 per cent of the *iṉāms* (numbers of *iṉām* units rather than acreage) were for military retainers, their chiefs, and for palace guards and servants; 25 per cent were for village officers, artisans and servants; and the remaining 45 per cent were for the support of temples, monasteries, rest and feeding houses for Brahman priests and pilgrims, and land grants to Brahman communities. In terms of acreage, roughly 19 per cent of the alienated land was for military retainers and others, 7 per cent for village officers, artisans and servants, 51 per cent for temples, monasteries, and charities, and 22 per cent for Brahmans. Remember that these statistics reflect a demilitarised political system, so that both the numbers and percentages had earlier been far higher for military categories. Remember also that this particular kingdom was ruled over by kings said by most observers to be an unclean caste, inappropriate for Hindu kingship, and therefore inappropriate donors for Sanskritic temples and Brahmans.

This structure of privileged landholding reflects the structure of political power and socio-cultural participation within state and village institutions. The chief landholders were the great Kallar Jagirdars and Cervaikarars. The former were collateral relations of the Raja. Jagir estates were created for the two brothers of the Raja after a succession dispute in 1730 severely threatened the stability of the state. These collateral families kept these estates intact until their settlement in the late 19th and early 20th century. The jagirs were, in effect, mini kingdoms in their own right, each containing a small court and a full set of *iṉām* grants, including 'military ones'. Importantly, however, the jagirs were not made up of contiguous villages and were therefore never geographically isolable units.

Just below the Jagirdars came the Cervaikarars. All but one of the Cervaikarars were of the same sub-caste as the Raja, and most had one or more affinal ties with the royal family. The Cervaikarars were given large grants of land, titles, honours, and emblems. Each of the Cervaikarars was awarded a specified number of retainers, or Amarakarars, to serve them at home, to go to battle with them abroad, and to carry their honours and emblems to ritual occasions in the royal court and in temples. Lesser chiefs, called Kurikarars, came from Kallar sub-castes other than the royal one. Lands and privileges throughout the state were also given to other Kallars, called in diminutive form Cervais, to keep watch over villages and localities not dominated by loyal Kallars (i.e., all groups other than the Vicenki Nattu Kallars who were only finally brought under nominal control in a series of wars in the late 18th century). The Cervais were mostly members of the royal sub-caste who had no affinal ties with the royal family.

The royal family and court was itself protected by Uriyakarars, all of whom were Akampatiyars, members of a non-Kallar caste which was aligned with the Kallars through membership in a special metacaste of three warrior groups along with the Maravars called the *mukkulattār*. These royal protectors in fact became a separate sub-caste marked off terminologically and affinally from other Akampatiyars in the region by virtue of their connection with and service to the Raja. A number of Uriyakarar chiefs had a prominent role in the kingdom. Like most of the lesser chiefs, these chiefs were given extensive lands but no formal group of military retainers under them.

In addition, within each village in the state, headmen were given lands in recognition of their rights of local authority as well as to render this representative of the state's power at large. These headmen came from the locally dominant castes. Kallars were dominant in the northern and eastern parts of the state. Maravars had a significant presence in the south. *Ampalams* (the title for headman, literally meaning the central common ground of the village, used by most of the castes in Pudukkottai) were also called *mirācidārs* after the mid-18th century. This new label, borrowed from Persian revenue terminology, was used in an attempt to render local authority as dependent as possible on recognition by the 'bureaucratic' state. Nonetheless, well into the 20th century these local headmen were often as powerful as small kings, with retinues and legends sufficient to cause their power to be felt over significant areas of the countryside.

Various village officials, artisans and servants were also given *iṉām* (more properly *māṉiyam*) lands by the state. In addition to this land, each village servant was also rewarded with shares of the village grain heap. Since the one-ninth share of the harvest that was owed to village servants was taken from the grain heap before its division into the Raja's and the village's share, this classic *jajmāni* payment was borne equally by the village and the Raja. Thus, the sets of relations usually characterised as *jajmāni*, that is as an institution of the village community alone, were sanctioned and underwritten not only by the community but also by the king both through *iṉām*s and the share system. *Māṉiyam*, the term used for many village grants, meant land that was held free of tax, as well as privilege in a more general sense. *Māṉiyam* derives from the Sanskrit word *manya*, which means honour and privilege. Many of the land grants to Brahmans were called *carvamāniyam*, meaning completely tax free and honourable. However, the term *māṉiyam* was not reserved for Brahmans, as British categories which separated 'religious' from 'non-religious' grants implied. Indeed, in its least marked form *māṉiyam* was sometimes used for *iṉām*s in general. *Māṉiyam* was also used in a marked sense for land grants given to village servants whose task was to maintain and operate irrigational facilities, to village officers or headmen, to the *pujārī*s or priests of small village temples or shrines, and to *iṉāmdār*s (holders of *iṉām*s) who had such variable responsibilities as blowing the conch for a village festival or tending a flower garden which produced garlands for the village deities. These *māṉiyam*s reveal that royal grants sustained the entire structure of local village ritual.

Even small locality temples were linked to the king through the *iṉām*. These local temples organised the ritual systems of villages, often constituting some of its fundamental cultural coordinates as well: they demarcated boundaries, centres, the relationships of social groups within the village, defining and internally ranking lineages, sub-castes and castes. Service to the temple was in many respects structurally equivalent to service to the village community, even as most village service *iṉām*s specified services to both temples and the village, as suggested for Sri Lanka as well in the work of Hocart (1950: 44), who saw each village service group as a priesthood, and thus saw caste as an institution that was simultaneously political and religious.

In addition to many *iṉām*s granted to village and local temples in the form of *māṉiyam*s to local priests and village servants, many *iṉām* grants were also made to Brahmans, temples, and charities of various sorts. As is well known, the principal sources for south Indian historiography are epigraphical records of such grants, publicaly proclaimed because of the merit which accrued to the donors from them and because of the centrality of these gifts to the ideology of kingship. One of the fundamental requirements of Indic kingship was that the king be a munificent provider of fertile lands for Brahmans who would study and chant the vedas, perform sacrifices and provide ritual services for the king so as to ensure and protect his prosperity and that of his kingdom; for temples which were the centres of worship and for festivals such as Dassara which renewed the sovereignty of the king and regenerated the kingdom; and for *cattiram*s (*chatram*s, also called *choultries*, which were feeding, sometimes lodging, houses for pilgrims) which provided sustenance and shelter for itinerant Brahmans and pilgrims. The merit (*puṇyam*) of the king who made the grant could be shared by all those who protected the gift, a duty enjoined upon all subsequent kings. In spite of Pudukkottai's marginal social and political position, it was well endowed with temples and Brahmanic institutions precisely because of the prevailing force of royal ideology.

The underlying political base of any little kingdom in the old regime was its military capacity. This capacity was in turn based on structures of alliance and command, which were articulated by gifts, privileges of varying kinds, and kinship. No little kingdom could survive if it did not have an efficient system of military mobilisation. These systems were organised around subordinate chieftains, connubial connections, and privileged landholding rather than a centralised or bureaucratically organised system of revenue collection and military rule. Royal grants helped to sustain military organisation as well as local village ritual and an impressive complex of larger temples and Brahmanic settlements. The political economy (by which I mean here the institution of kingship, the distribution of authority, and the nature and structure of resource allocation) was based on a logic of redistribution that penetrated far and wide.

The gift of land without onerous burdens of taxation, the occasional participation in wars in which honour and booty could be won, and the organisation of land and military rights in relations of ritual clientage to chiefly and kingly patrons resulted not only in a political system of great fluidity and dynamism, but one in which individuals could vie for relative distinction in a social system where honour was intimately tied up with rank through interpenetrating forms of political and ritual action. The valued constituents of sovereign authority were differentially and partially shared through the redistributive mechanisms of the gift. Service was offered as a way of entering this redistributive system. Kinship (a relatively open and inflected system) became the social base and expression of social and political relations. Honour—in particular the emblems and privileges that were given with each grant (itself a privilege), but also the honours in temples that were procured through worship and were ordered in relation to local and royal prerogatives—was both the mediation and the mechanism by and through which relations were established.

Thus I argue that the royal gift was basic to statecraft in all the kingdoms of the old order in southern India. All gifts were not the same; but they all shared one thing in common: they were given by the king. The substance of the gift (the land rights, titles, emblems, honours, and privileges of service, usufruct and command) was the partial sovereign substance of the king. Participation in the king's sovereignty was not, however, unranked, for the differential nature and contingent character of all these entitlements provided the basis for the creation of a political hierarchy. Ultimately, entitlements by their very nature constituted hierarchy through a logic of variable proximity to the king, to sovereignty itself. What Geertz has written about Bali is true of the old order in south India: 'The whole of the *negara* (court life, the traditions that organized it, the extractions that supported it, the privileges that accompanied it) was essentially directed toward defining what power was; and what power was what kings were' (Geertz 1980: 124).

My sense of the meaning of royal gifts was initially based not only on a reading of land records, which, though they gave histories of grants revealed a thick infrastructure of gifting and suggested that land rights were necessarily conjoined with other rights to privilege, service and honour, were themselves insufficiently explicit about the ideological content of the system to permit a full or satisfactory interpretation. Rather, I developed an understanding of kingly beneficence from textual sources that depicted the centrality of gifts and their various forms. Using 18th century texts (genealogies, chronicles, ballads) as cultural discourses, I found persistent motifs, events, narrative forms, tropes and images, and I read the parts they played in the poetics of power. I used this textualised discourse not only, as at first I thought was all I could do, to get a sense of how these Indians conceived their own past, but also to demarcate the key elements of my subsequent inquiry, to create a historiographical frame for understanding key structures, events, and their relations. I found that my textualised readings were indeed realised in historical processes. Thus,

I was able to identify and focus on the core conceptions of sovereignty; the interpenetrating transactions in gifts, service and kinship; the structure and form of political hegemony. I was able to understand what had previously been obscured in the colonial writing on the little kings, or *poligars* (*pāḷaiyakkārar*): that the adoption of Hindu forms of kingship by what were said to be low caste (later often defined as criminal castes under British rule) chiefs was not just an ideological ruse but rather, was reflected in the entire structure of the political system; that rights to landholding were political rights and reflected the structure of the little kingdom at the same time that they revealed the pervasive importance of royal honour; and that the states were not absolute failures because of their lack of emphasis on the bureaucratic demarcation of land rights and the collection of revenue, but successful, vital, and, to the British, highly threatening political systems because of the interplay of rights and privileges of land, service, kinship, honour and local resources.

The cultural poetics of power

But if kingship—and more generally the 'political'—was so important, how did it affect social relations in the little kingdom. Only after returning to Pudukkottai to do extensive fieldwork in 1981–82 was I able to find that the forms of clan and caste structures that the British had seen as organic growths from the Indian soil had in fact been vitally transformed by the political histories of local-level chiefs. First, through inquiries conducted in the field, I determined that the political hierarchy was also, with certain crucial exceptions, a social hierarchy. As I mentioned above, the Jagirdars were collateral chiefs, the Cervaikarars affinally connected warriors, the Kurikarars mostly Kallars but from sub-castes other than the royal sub-caste, and so on down the line. The Kallars themselves were, as Dumont also found for the Pramalai Kallar, territorially segmented, but in Pudukkottai the royal sub-caste occupied a uniquely important position, dominating all the other segments, or sub-castes. The internal organisation of the royal sub-caste, markedly different from all other sub-castes, itself reflected a systematic if sometimes paradoxical inflection by political forces. And the settlement of Kallar chiefs, both great and small, throughout areas of non-Kallar settlement, as well as in the area inhabited by a large and often unruly Kallar sub-caste, effected both the ideological and instrumental dominance of royalty. These Kallars often had royal retainers under them, privileged rights to local lands, and the right to receive first honours on behalf of the Pudukkottai Raja in all village and locality temples and festivals. The hierarchical force of royalty was expressed in many ways, not least through the comments of one of my principal informants, the titular head of the royal clan or *kuppam*. 'When we assumed our royal status (*antastu*)', this man told me, 'we became, as it were, a royal family. Hence, we, the five top lineages of the clan, began to have affinal relations only with royal families. So we became more elevated and dignified than the other groups and other clans. While the influence and glory of the Raja was high, the influence of those of us living in our group also went up accordingly. Others who do not have marriage ties with the five chief lineages also reside here but we classify them at a lower level.' All members of the royal sub-caste were loosely called *rājapantu*, meaning that they had a connection with the Raja. While this term was used to designate all members of the sub-caste in an unmarked sense, within the sub-caste itself there were multiple distinctions of rank, all of them, as it turned out, having to do with proximity to the king. In one particularly lucid discussion, my informant explained to me the logic of hierarchy in Pudukkottai.

> Why are we [meaning royal Kallars] superior? [he asked rhetorically.] Because we maintain control and order (*kaṭṭupāṭu*) in our community. We do not allow widow remarriage and we abide by the moral codes of our society strictly. Other Kallars may say that all Kallars are the same. It is popularly assumed that all Kallars are thieves. But we are not thieves. How can the ruling Kallars steal from others? Our Kallars are pillars of the community, chiefs, village leaders, politicians and nobles. We have to maintain law and order. How can we go off thieving. We decided that we should lead a life of order and restriction. Others are not like us. We live for honour and status. Our Kallars base our lives on the temple and on marriage relations. Only if the temple and the lineage are correct can we seek an alliance. Our honour is displayed in the palace and in temples. When honour is measured, in the same way the number of carats is measured in gold, will we like less dignified groups taking seats on a par with us. No, they are not fit to sit with us.

The pre-eminence of the royal sub-caste is thus explained not only through reference to the fact that the king hailed from this sub-caste, but by noting that this sub-caste has the most rigidly defined and maintained code of conduct of all sub-castes. These Kallars have the most order, and they enforced order through the set of restrictions which are implied by the term *kaṭṭupāṭu*. *Kaṭṭupāṭu*, which can be taken to mean code for conduct and discipline, literally means something more like restriction, or even constriction, deriving from the root *kaṭṭu*, meaning tied or knotted. The code for conduct includes rigidly defined kinship rules, some of which, like the Brahmanic prohibition of widow remarriage, mark the royal Kallars off from all other Kallars and suggest a kind of Sanskritisation. Others involve working one's way through the myriad gradations of upper Kallar society by trading political, social, and cultural capital back and forth, often through affinal transactions. *Kaṭṭupāṭu* is a term that is used frequently by all Kallar sub-castes and indeed all Pudukkottai castes, though only among

Kallars, and specifically within the royal sub-caste of Kallars, does it have the particular kind of inflection just described. For all these groups, though again most importantly for the royal sub-caste, *kaṭṭupāṭu* does not mean simply a code for conduct, but a set of authoritative procedures which renders this code enforceable within the community.

My informant's statements, and the general ideological orientation they reflect, reveal the continuation of concerns about the past reputation of Kallars as thieves, bandits, outlaws. The ethnographic discourse here shares much in common with the 18th century family histories that I mentioned earlier. In these texts as in the statements of Kallar informants, the acknowledged past becomes totally transformed by the attainment of kingship. Again, there is an implicit opposition between the representation of the activities of thieves and the activities of kings. In this case, the royal duty of protecting and subduing disorder is combined with an ideology of order and restriction which organises and becomes the sub-text of the social relations of the sub-caste.

The very word Kallar means thief in Tamil, and no one, at least none of my informants, disputes the fact that at certain places and times particular groups of Kallars engaged in predatory activity. In fact they constantly bring it up with a certain kind of relish, suggesting only partial embarrassment about their past. And as I and others have written elsewhere, this in itself is not necessarily a problem, since predation was often the principal means used to accumulate wealth by kings who were not so concerned about a regularised tax base as the British became when they began in the early 19th century to gain most of their profit from land revenue. In Pudukkottai, Kallars attained their position of royal authority in the first place by providing protection to local communities and institutions, and this is amply documented in inscriptions recording protection contracts from the 14th century on. Indeed, Kallars were given rights of protection because of their capacity to control, and to a very large extent monopolise, the means of violence, and there is much in Indian tradition to suggest that the opposition of bandit and king is a complementary opposition. But it is, culturally speaking, an opposition: the violence of the bandit is illegitimate, and it represents and causes the disorder that the legitimate violence of the king must control. Kings are not only legitimate, they define the realm of the legitimate. And the way in which the royal sub-caste organises its social relations makes it impossible that they could be thieves, or affected in any way by this general reputation. The royal sub-caste is headed by a king, and it provides almost all the royal nobles of the kingdom. The fundamental duty of these members of the elite is to subdue disorder, destroy lawlessness, and enforce law and order, both within the kingdom at large, and within the sub-caste itself. And of course, as kings, by virtue of defining what is orderly, they define disorder too.

But this is true in more than just the obvious, or for that matter the

Foucaultian, sense, as I discovered when doing fieldwork with other caste groups. For most castes, there is a steady decrease of order as one goes down the caste hierarchy, in the sense defined by my Kallar informants and assimilated with only minimal dissent by many non-Kallar informants. Maravars, for example, who in all fundamental respects were like Kallars except for the crucial fact that they were not kings, had found it impossible to organise their social relations in the larger territorial units, the *nāṭu*s, that Kallars had, and the Maravars lamented this loudly and frequently. Indeed, the Maravars themselves attributed this disorder not just to the general decline and fall of the world in general, but more particularly to their loss of political control. For other groups, there was not only a noticeable decline in order, and a laxness in defining and maintaining the *kaṭṭupāṭu*, but also a decline in the autonomy to define what order was. Untouchable groups, for example, took the locality, and sometimes the lineage, names of their dominant caste patrons. Whereas other groups had traditional rights called *kāṇiyāṭci* to land, honour, etc. Untouchables told me that for them *kāṇiyāṭci* only meant the right to serve their patrons. The fundamental structures of their social relations were inscribed by the hegemony of the dominant classes. Notions of honour, order, royalty, and command have been operationalised in the practices that produce and reproduce hierarchy. These practices (embedded as they are in cultural forms and historical processes) are themselves based on structures of power as well as on the hegemonic nature of cultural constructions of power.

If it be argued that my interpretation, though perhaps true for marginal regions like Pudukkottai, can hardly apply generally to south India, let alone to the subcontinent as a whole, I reply that it is precisely the marginality of Pudukkottai that makes it possible to detect the forces that were at work elsewhere. Because Pudukkottai was not brought under patrimonial control (neither that of the Islamic rulers in the south nor later that of the British), caste was never set completely loose from kingship. Many current theories of caste, particularly those emphasising Brahmanic obsessions concerning purity and impurity, but also those aspects of ethnosociological theory that stress the proper and improper mixing of substances, are in large parts artifacts of colonialism, referring to a situation in which the position of the king and the historical dynamic of royal power has been displaced, and sometimes destroyed. However much Dumont's theory is predicated on an a priori separation of what he describes as the domains of religion and politics, with the former encompassing the latter, he was also almost certainly influenced by an ethnographic reality in which kingship played only a very small, residual role. As for early ethnosociological proposals about caste, Inden has himself recently noted that his early work is largely derived from texts which were generated only after the demise of kingship as a powerful cultural institution (Inden 1986). The texts, he now says, reflected new traditions which attempted to deal with the problem of regulating caste interaction in an environment in which there was no longer a king.

The politics of hierarchy

Politics, as we define it here, has both to do with the processes by which authority is constituted at each level of representation and with the linkages of the constituent groups in society to the king (usually through the authoritative figures who represent their social groups). Politics has a territorial dimension, but is not exhausted by territorial forms. In the royal sub-caste of Kallars in Pudukkottai, the intervention of the king changed and reconstructed (as well as decomposed) the internal order of the system, affecting both social and territorial forms. Even in other sub-castes, less directly influenced by kingship, social organisation was only understandable within a framework which is fundamentally political, realised over time (*i.e.*, in history).

It is my argument here that structures of power play a central role in the social organisation of caste and kinship, that politics is fundamental to the process of hierarchialisation and the formation of units of identity. Dumont has great difficulty with the notion that kinship can be politicised. When he does see hierarchical tendencies develop in the domain of kinship, he blames them on the ideology of caste, which has to do not with politics but with purity and pollution. Dumont's elevation of alliance as the fundamental principle of south Indian kinship is in large part because alliance mitigates the asymmetrical effects of marriage relations through the generalised exchange of marriage partners within the endogamous group. Hierarchy creeps to the borders of the endogamous group, but only enters in the sense that it can bring about the creation of new endogamous subdivisions. Nonetheless, even though Dumont (1957, 1986) suggests the powerful role of political dominance in creating alliances and particular marriage patterns, he explains any such endogamous subdivisions by saying that they arise through bastardy or the differential status of wives in a polygynous marriage. Dumont maintains that new endogamous groups develop within larger endogamous groups only because of the lower status attached to marriages with women from outside the proper alliance group.

Politics not only occupies a subordinate position in Dumont's general theory, but is eclipsed on the one side by the pre-eminence of kinship, invaded by social bastardy and caste hierarchy, and on the other by caste, which elevates the Brahman and attendant principles of purity and pollution, above the king. Caste, and the hierarchical principle it entails, is fundamental because it is religious, and in Indian social thought, according to Dumont, the religious encompasses the social, the economic, and the political.

Dumont therefore sees caste authority and political autnority as fundamentally different. He writes that 'the notion of caste and of a superior caste exhausts all available transcendence. Properly speaking, a people's headman can only be someone of another caste. If the headman is one of their own, then to some degree they are all headmen' (Dumont 1986: 161). This is true in Pudukkottai in that headmen are at one level simply *primus inter pares* in their social group. However, by virtue of their connection to the king, they do also 'transcend' their own community. The king is himself simply a Kallar, and not the highest Kallar by his marriage or lineage. But by virtue of his connections to the entire kingdom—not caste transcendence—he is also the transcendent overlord.

Hierarchy in Pudukkottai concerns transcendence in the context of kingship, where the king is both a member of a segmentary lineage system and the overlord of the entire kingdom. What would seem contradictory to Dumont is the paradox upon which the entire caste system rests. Kinship is inflected, at its core, by politics; and politics is nothing more than the curious paradox of a king who transcends all even as he is one of his own metonyms. In the social and political world of the little kingdom, this meant that the king was an overlord, but one who was nonetheless always embroiled in the strategic concerns of kinship, status hierarchy, protection and warfare, and in the maximisation of his own honour and sovereign authority within the little kingdom and in a wider world of other kingdoms and greater overlords.

Part of Dumont's resistance to acknowledging the political inflection of caste and kinship may result from the political marginality of the Pramalai Kallars, a marginality rendering them far more similar to the unruly Vicenki Nattu Kallars who lived in the northwestern part of Pudukkottai state than to the royal sub-caste. With both the Pramalai Kallars and the Vicenki Nattu Kallars, the lack of well-developed affinal boundaries corresponding to discrete territorial units, as well as of a distinct sense of the hierarchy of groups, can perhaps be explained by their incomplete incorporation within (and therefore inflection by) the political system of a little kingdom. Everywhere in Tamil Nadu, the Kallars had highly developed notions of territory, but their sub-caste organisation achieved its particular level of territorial segmentation and hierarchical articulation in Pudukkottai alone. And only within the royal sub-caste of Pudukkottai did Kallars develop the pronounced and complex forms of territorial bounding and hierarchical marking that they did, and which I describe in great detail elsewhere (1987). Kingship does make a difference.

Some of Dumont's theoretical problems stem from the fact that he does not pursue an interest in the ethnohistorical reconstruction of the Pramalai Kallars. He is aware of the modern decline of headmanship, and that it no longer expresses itself as fully as it might once have done in the social logic of Pramalai organisation. Characteristically acute, he senses a correlation with recent political change: 'If authority rests on external sanction, it is to be expected that it cannot maintain itself without formal government recognition' (Dumont 1986: 159). Unfortunately, he does not consider the possibility that colonialism, and the attendant break down of the old regime, have much to do with the development of the separation of religion and politics which he has identified and reified into a timeless Indian social theory. A combination of theoretical programme, ethnographic 'accident', and historical disinterest have conspired to render Dumont's understanding of the Kallars, however powerful, limited in fundamental ways.

Here and elsewhere I have argued that the social relations that made up Indian society, far from being 'essentialist' structures predicated on the transcendence of a set of religious principles, were permeated by 'political' inflections, meanings and imperatives. Caste, as it is still portrayed in much current anthropological literature, is a colonial construction, reminiscent only in some ways of the social forms that preceded colonial intervention. The structural relations that made up the 'caste system' in Pudukkottai thus reflect—albeit with the distortions of ethnohistorical time—the ideological proposals of my informants. These ideological statements consistently referred to the historical means by and through which meaning was constructed and maintained. Caste, if ever it had an original form, was inscribed from the 'beginning' by the relations and conceits of power. And in medieval and early modern south India, it is clear that Geertz was indeed right: power was what kings were.

Ethnohistory and ethnosociology

'We need history, but not the way a spoiled loafer in the garden of knowledge needs it.'

Nietzsche, *Of the use and abuse of history*.

When I first began to use the term ethnohistory to describe the particular blend of history and anthropology that I sought to practise in my study of India, I thought that 'ethno' should do the same thing to history that it seemed to be doing to sociology. Of course the place was Chicago, the time the mid-1970s, and the word was culture. But even then, and despite the fact that in my work I sought to construct my sense of what it meant to do history in light of 'indigenous' historical texts, ethnohistory struggled against itself. Not only did ethnohistorians seem constantly to pose the questions about epistemological mediation that began only rather later to problematise the original assumptions of ethnosociology (questions such as, how does an outsider attain access to or re-present a culturally specific form of knowledge?), but culture as a domain was much more difficult to lock up (or off) as a separate area of inquiry. The injunction, 'Always historicise!', seemed always already there. But, then as now, it was not always clear what the injunction meant (see Jameson 1981).

Originally, ethnohistory meant the reconstruction of the history of an area and people who had no written history. As such, it was used to denote in particular the field of studies concerning the past of American Indians, and secondarily of other so-called primitive or pre-literate societies. But, as many have since demonstrated, ethnohistory cannot be restricted to the unwritten or oral sources of history in most parts of the world where texts and written sources exist, even if they do not seem to penetrate some sectors of society. In India, as in many other places, there are no pure oral traditions: texts have provided the basis for tradition as often as the other way round. Indeed, both texts and traditions relate not only to each other, but also to historical processes of production and social forms of contextualisation, interpretation and certification. Ethnohistory in India is clearly not about the history of primitive or preliterate people.

As suggested above, ethnohistory is also not simply a gloss for a cultural analysis of historical sensibilities in India, whether embodied in texts or traditions. However, part of the task of ethnohistory is to contest the dominant voice of history, which in India has always been a Western voice. This voice has always disparaged India, insisting that the relative absence of chronological political narrative and the unsettling presence of myth and fancy are indicative of an underdeveloped sense of history. Ethnohistory can therefore assist in the project of recuperating a multiplicity of historical voices, revealing for India an active, vital and integral historiographical industry. I have also argued that ethnohistory can help determine a culturally specific set of relevancies, moments and narrative forms to expand and alter the sense of how to think about India's past. But this past is never contained solely within the texts or traditions that would be used for this task. If ethnohistory is used to situate history, it is always itself seen as situated in history (see also Dening 1980: 38).

Thus, the difficulties in anthropologising history are not simply removed by the inverse call to historicise anthropology, for we never seem to reach explicit agreement about what history actually means. But if an investigation into the culture of history has both the strengths and the weaknesses of ethnosociology, an exploration of what is involved in the history of culture can assist in making a creative critique of culture theory, whether in ethnosociology or elsewhere. Not only has ethnosociology been insufficiently clear about the epistemological privilege it assumes in its claim to re-present indigenous forms of knowledge, it has excluded a wide range of historical questions, as also any consideration of the relations of knowledge and power beyond a restricted form of cultural analysis.

This is not the place, however, to summarise the arguments of Gramsci, Williams, Bakhtin, Bourdieu, Foucault, and other theorists who have helped specify and problematise the historicity of culture. It must suffice here to note that when culture is situated in history rather than opposed to it, the concept of culture inevitably unravels. I began by using culture as a method and conceit to privilege the discursive claims of my Kallar informants in relation to Dumont's proposals about the nature of hierarchy in India. That is to say, I began by participating in the ethnosociological claim that if you investigate native terms and meanings you will find that hierarchy is about x and not about y. However, the cultural statements of my informants subverted the autonomy of a presumed cultural domain, and in particular, the opposition between the political/historical and the cultural/religious. At the same time, the injunction to historicise, vague though it sometimes seemed, enticed me to enter the web of power, knowledge and history that constituted both the world of reference as well as the necessary conditions for contemporary cultural discourse. Culture, thus, was a conceit that deconstructed itself through its own historical reference, for culture distilled and displayed (and often displaced) the historical legacy of its own hegemonic ascendence.

The necessarily ambivalent position of history within any ethnohistorical project provides critical access to much of the current theoretical debate about culture. But ethnohistory should not simply disparage ethnosociology. For, in calling attention to the hegemony of Western social science, ethnosociology may both set some of the conditions for this kind of critique in Indian studies, and yet have the last laugh. The theoretical concerns about culture articulated here are as Western in their dominant figures and intellectual histories as the more positivist social science from which we tried to free ourselves in previous decades. However, if 'history' teaches us anything at all, it should at least help us dispose of the idea that culture can exist outside of history, however much this history—and I suspect any history—is always mediated through a multiplicity of cultural forms.

REFERENCES

APPADURAI, ARJUN. 1981. *Worship and conflict under colonial rule: a south Indian case.* Cambridge: Cambridge University Press.

APPADURAI, ARJUN, and CAROL BRECKENRIDGE. 1976. The south Indian temple: authority, honor and redistribution. *Contributions to Indian sociology* (n.s.) 10: 187–211.

BAYLY, C.A. 1983. *Rulers, townsmen and bazaars: north Indian society in the age of British expansion 1770–1870.* Cambridge: Cambridge University Press.

BERREMAN, GERALD D. 1971. The Brahmanical view of caste. *Contributions to Indian sociology* (n.s.) 5: 16–23.

DENING, G. 1980. *Islands and beaches: discourse on a silent land, Marquesas 1774–1880.* Melbourne: Melbourne University Press.

DIRKS, NICHOLAS B. 1979. The structure and meaning of political relations in a south Indian little kingdom. *Contributions to Indian sociology* (n.s.) 13: 169–204.

———. 1982. The pasts of a Palaiyakarar: the ethnohistory of a south Indian little king. *Journal of Asian studies* 41: 655–83.

DIRKS, NICHOLAS B. 1987. *The hollow crown: ethnohistory of an Indian kingdom*. Cambridge: Cambridge University Press.
———. 1989. The invention of caste: civil society in colonial India. *Social analysis* (forthcoming).
DUMONT, LOUIS. 1957. *Hierarchy and marriage alliance in south Indian kinship*. Occasional papers of the Royal Anthropological Institute, 12. London.
———. 1962. The conception of kingship in ancient India. *Contributions to Indian sociology* 6: 48–77.
———. 1980. *Homo hierarchicus: the caste system and its implications*. Chicago: University of Chicago Press.
———. 1986. *A south Indian subcaste*. Delhi: Oxford University Press.
FOUCAULT, MICHEL. 1979. *Discipline and punish* (trans. Alan Sheridan). New York: Vintage/Random House.
GEERTZ, CLIFFORD. 1980. *Negara: the theatre state in nineteenth century Bali*. Princeton: Princeton University Press.
HEESTERMAN, J.C. 1978. The conundrum of the king's authority. *In* J.F. Richards, ed., *Kingship and authority in South Asia*, pp. 1–27. Madison: University of Wisconsin Publications Series.
HOCART, A.M. 1950. *Caste: a comparative study*. London: Methuen.
INDEN, RONALD B. 1986. Orientalist constructions of India. *Modern Asian studies* 20: 401–46.
JAMESON, FREDRIC. 1981. *The political unconscious: narrative as a socially symbolic act*. Ithaca: Cornell University Press.
LUDDEN, DAVID E. 1985. *Peasant history in south India*. Princeton: Princeton University Press.
MARRIOTT, MCKIM, and RONALD INDEN. 1977. Toward an ethnosociology of caste systems. *In* Kenneth A. David, ed., *The new wind: changing identities in South Asia*, pp. 227–38. The Hague and Paris: Mouton.
MCGILVRAY, DENNIS. 1982. Mukkuvar vannimai: Tamil caste and matriclan ideology in Batticaloa, Sri Lanka. *In* D.B. McGilvray, ed., *Caste ideology and interaction*, pp. 34–97. Cambridge: Cambridge University Press.
TRAUTMANN, THOMAS R. 1981. *Dravidian kinship*. Cambridge: Cambridge University Press.

4

Centrality mutuality and hierarchy: shifting aspects of inter-caste relationships in north India[1]

Gloria Goodwin Raheja

The most pervasive and persistent Western view of Hindu society sees hierarchy as the sole ideology defining relations among castes. In this narrow view, caste is seen as focused on the Brahman value of purity, while the king and the dominant caste (which replicates the royal function at the level of the village) are taken to represent only a residual, devalued, and nonideological sphere of 'political' and 'economic' relations. In this paper, I offer an alternative view of caste and of Hindu society that focuses on the ritual aspects of the role of the dominant caste, particularly on prestation patterns and *jajmāni* relationships.

The deeply entrenched Western interpretation is set forth most starkly and most persuasively by Louis Dumont, but in fact most of its misapprehensions of the nature of caste and sovereignty were already found in 19th century European conceptions of India and in the colonial policies that mirrored these conceptions (Cohn 1968, 1983, 1984, 1985a, 1985b; Dirks 1987; Raheja 1988b). The elevation of Brahmanic textual formulations about *varṇa* and hierarchy to the level of unqualified hegemony over other traditions and other sets of values was accompanied by a radical misunderstanding of the nature of sovereignty, particularly insofar as royal gifts were concerned. Reducing a complex indigenous transactional logic to the raw instrumentalities of 'bribery', 'corruption', and 'profligacy' enabled

[1] This paper is based on fieldwork in Pahansu in 1977–79, funded by the Social Science Research Council and the American Institute of Indian Studies, and in 1988, funded by the Wenner-Gren Foundation for Anthropological Research. Details of the ethnographic data upon which the arguments of this paper are based may be found in my book *The poison in the gift: ritual, prestation, and the dominant caste in a north Indian village* (1988a).

the British colonial administrators as well as early theorists writing on caste to maintain their positions on the supposedly 'secular' power of Mughal and Hindu rulers, since the most significant aspects of kingship in both traditions had largely to do with the ritual implications of royal largesse (Appadurai 1978, 1981; Breckenridge 1978; Burghart 1987; Cohn 1983; Dirks 1976, 1987: 129–38; Gonda 1969: 62; Price 1979; Shulman 1985; Stein 1980).

Much the same view prevailed in 20th century ethnographic writing on village social systems. Focusing on the negative prohibitions and restrictions concerning marriage and commensality[2] perpetuated the view that inter-caste relations are, in all contexts, expressions of rank and purity. With few exceptions (e.g., Hocart 1950), the gifting engaged in by dominant castes was treated, if at all, as devoid of ritual significance, as in Dumont's 'shame-faced' Kṣatriya model of social relations (1980: 91). The privileging of marriage and commensal restrictions as modes of inter-caste relationships prevented anthropologists from perceiving the authoritative implications of ritual and gift-giving centred on the dominant caste. Nearly universally, the prestations made by such landholding castes to Brahmans and service castes were interpreted only as 'payments' for caste-related ritual and agricultural services. The possibility that such prestations carried more complex indigenous meanings and values related to village sovereignty was thus ignored.

The Dumontian assumption that Hindu society and Hindu ideology in general are ordered in terms of a single overarching principle, the opposition of the pure and impure, is predicated on a particular conception of a stable and seamless cultural 'whole' whose limitations and historically conditioned genesis in anthropological theory are only now beginning to be perceived (Appadurai 1986, 1988; Clifford 1988: 63–64). It is also predicated on a particular view of the relationship between 'ideology' and social life. For Dumont, 'ideology' is an internally coherent and logically organised set of ideas and values, a 'totality', a structured system that he opposes to the 'residual' phenomena of political and economic relations, power, property, territory, and so forth, the 'raw material' of behaviour and 'naked fact' that are knowable because of the ideas we have of them in western ideology and common sense (1980: 36–39). This opposition of an internally consistent ideological structure ordered by one 'simple principle of . . . thought' to a realm of behaviour that it either fully encompasses or leaves to itself as naked fact devoid of social value seems to be isomorphic

[2] As Census Commissioner for the 1901 Census of India, Herbert Risley was concerned, for example, with drawing up a classificatory scheme in which castes could be arranged in the order of their 'social precedence'. His classification, laid out in the 1901 Census Report for the Punjab, is constructed largely in terms of which castes could take *pakkā* food, *kaccā* food, or water from which other castes (Pedersen 1986: 22–23). The most influential anthropological representations of caste systems have likewise been constructed in terms of these commensal restrictions.

with Saussure's opposition of langue and parole, language as a structured grammar and semantic system opposed to, and distinct from, 'speech', the residual, non-socially constituted actualisation of language. Saussurean linguistics privileges the structure of language as code over the uses to which language is put in actual speech situations (Bourdieu 1977: 22–30) and over the multiplex and often ambiguous meanings that become apparent when signs, both linguistic and social, are seen in relation to the contexts in which they occur (Silverstein 1976). Dumontian anthropology privileges 'ideology' and defines it in such a way that it appears impervious to the circumstantiality of everyday life, in which relationships and ways of life are always open to multiple interpretations, indeterminacy and ambiguity.

Because of his view of social practice as either the enactment of a fixed and one-dimensional ideology or as 'naked fact', Dumont's interpretation of caste is incapable of comprehending the contextuality, circumstantiality and shifting emphases that characterise ongoing social life in India as elsewhere. His argument that hierarchy and the sole value of purity 'encompass' all aspects of inter-caste relationships has thus entailed a rejection of all other possible indigenous meanings and values in these relationships. He has, for example, criticised Hocart (1950) for deriving caste ranks from kingship and from kingly ritual in village caste systems (Dumont 1980: 213, 285; Dumont and Pocock 1958). He has also criticised Wiser's description of the 'reciprocity' or 'symmetry' involved in village *jajmānī* relationships. He dismisses these other aspects of inter-caste relationships precisely because he sees these alternate emphases and values as being incompatible with his postulation of a single encompassing ideology of hierarchy (Dumont 1980: 31, 101–02). In a similar fashion, Dumont and Pocock (1957) are compelled (against much evidence, partly summarised by Srinivas [1987]) to assert that the Indian village lacks an ideological unity and cohesiveness; the hierarchical ideology of caste, they argue, effectively precludes the development of an ideology of inter-caste unity within the village.

My argument in this paper is that there are several contextually shifting ideologies of inter-caste relationships apparent in everyday village social life. Meanings and values are foregrounded differently from context to context, and they implicate varying configurations of castes. Detailed data on prestation patterns and language use from the Gujar-dominated north Indian village of Pahansu[3] indicate that aspects of inter-caste relationships, that I shall call 'centrality' and 'mutuality', are distinguishable from the ranked aspect that is usually called 'hierarchy'. These various aspects of

[3] Pahansu is a relatively large village located in Saharanpur district, western Uttar Pradesh. Raheja (1988a) contains a detailed description of the history and demographic and land-holding situation in the village, and a discussion of the manner in which these particularities have shaped the social life and prestation patterns described in this paper.

relationships are differentially foregrounded in the giving and receiving of distinct types of prestations, and each is indexed by the occurrence of distinct terminological usages. Among these configurations of castes, both the ritual centrality of the dominant caste 'sacrificers' (*jajmāns*) and the mutuality among the castes of the village prove to be more significant in social intercourse than the hierarchical pre-eminence of priestly Brahmans.

The prestations made by *jajmāns* to Brahmans and service caste *kamīns* have generally been treated in the anthropological literature as undifferentiated 'payments' for ritual and agricultural services, with much of the debate focused on the issue of whether the amounts of grain and other items that are given constitute the system as exploitative or equitably integrative. (For discussion of this literature, see Parry 1979: 74–83.) Prestations made by the dominant caste Gujar *jajmāns* of Pahansu, however, do not comprise a single homogeneous type. Within the context of the giving and receiving (*len-den*) of *jajmānī* relationships, Gujars give two fundamentally different kinds of prestations to those who are attached to them in hereditary service arrangements, and these two types of prestations carry radically different meanings, pragmatic implications and ritual functions.

Rights to give, obligations to receive: **dān** *and the ritual centrality of the dominant caste in Pahansu*

For Gujar *jajmāns* in Pahansu, the most important prestations they make to their Brahmans and *kamīns* are those termed *dān* or *caṛhāpā*. As the par excellence *jajmāns* of the village, Gujars have the 'right' (*hak*) to give *dān* to these recipients, who, on their part, have an obligation (*pharmāya*) to accept it on many occasions throughout the yearly cycle of seasons and festivals, and throughout the life-course, as well as when specific afflictions and troubles have beset a family or the village as a whole. *Dān* is always given in the context of ritual actions that are said to promote the 'well-being [achieved through] gift-giving' (*khair-khairāt*) and auspiciousness (*śubh*) of the donor and the village, through the transferral of 'evil' (*pāp*), 'afflictions' (*kaṣṭ*), 'faults' (*doṣ*), and inauspiciousness more generally (*nāśubh*) from donor to recipient. Villagers say that *dān* is always given 'to move away inauspiciousness' (*nāśubh haṭāne ke lie*); through the giving of *dān* in the proper ritual contexts, these negative substances 'come out' (*utarnā*) of the donor, and may then have their effect on the recipient in the form of 'disease' (*rog*), madness, a diminishing of his 'power' (*śakti*) or his 'fiery energy' (*tej*), or in the form of a general decline of his family and lineage. The recipient must, as people in Pahansu put it, 'digest' (*pachnā*) the evil and inauspiciousness contained in the gift, or he must give it onward in the form of further prestations, often to wife-receiving affines, who are deemed to be the appropriate 'vessels' (*pātra*) for many types of *dān*. Brahmans, Barbers, Sweepers and the other service castes all have obligations to accept *dān* from Gujar *jajmāns*, and they all regard these obligations as problematic and dangerous.

Though the dangers inherent in the acceptance of *dān* have been noted by Heesterman (1959, 1964, 1985), Parry (1980, 1986), Shulman (1985), and Trautmann (1981), the significance of such prestations for an understanding of inter-caste relationships more generally has not been perceived. The evil and inauspiciousness transferred in *dān* cannot simply be a matter of the relative 'impurity' or the 'inferior essences' of the royal donor vis-à-vis hierarchically superior Brahman recipients, as Trautmann (1981: 287) and Heesterman (1964) have argued; hierarchy as an encompassing explanatory model of inter-caste relationships is thus called into question, because the acceptance of *dān* is dangerous for recipients of all castes. *Dān* prestations involve an enormous expenditure of material resources in the village; because they cannot be interpreted simply as 'payments' disbursed by a landed caste holding only 'temporal' power, the view that posits a split between religious ideology and temporal power is also incapable of elucidating the fundamental aspects of village ritual life that are enacted in the giving of *dān*.

From the point of view of most anthropological discussions of *jajmānī* relationships, the distribution of grain on the threshing floor is in many ways definitive of those relationships. Yet we have very few ethnographic reports detailing the manner in which such distributions are made and the ritual contexts of the disbursements. In Pahansu, the portion of the harvest given to the Brahman is distinguished from portions given to other castes by being called *sāvṛī* ('of the grain pile') or *dān*. The threshing floor disbursements made to other castes are not called *dān*, but *phaslānā* (from *phasal*, 'harvest'). But these other castes receive other *dān* prestations at the harvests, usually in the form of grain still on the stalks and still in the fields of the *jajmān*. *Sāvṛī* is given to the cultivator's Brahman not as a payment for services rendered in the course of the year, and not as a token of the Brahman's material dependence upon the *jajman*, as Dumont (1980: 294) would have it. Rather, the Brahman's portion of the grain is given to him as *dān* in the course of a sequence of ritual actions performed at the threshing floor for the 'increase' (*barkat*) of the grain: the Brahman removes the 'hindrances' (*bādhā*) that might otherwise diminish the grain or cause some other misfortune.

After threshing and winnowing his grain, the cultivator *jajmān* gathers it into piles. He places the winnowing basket at the south of the pile of grain. Facing north, he picks up the basket with his right hand, turns it on its side, and takes it around the bottom of the circular pile first in a clockwise direction, then counter-clockwise around the middle of the pile, and finally around the top of the pile in a clockwise direction. As he makes these circumambulations of the pile of grain, he makes small indentations in the grain pile with the winnowing basket. Then he repeats this procedure in reverse, this time beginning at the top of the pile and moving downward as he circles it with the winnowing basket. The *jajmān* then returns to the south of the pile, fills the winnowing basket with grain, and places it to the north of the pile. The basket of grain remains in that position until all the grain in the pile has been weighed, and then it is given as *dān* to the hereditary family priest, the *purohit*. These prestations from each pile of grain represent, in total, a very substantial amount of grain, and these winnowing baskets of rice or wheat are the only portions of the harvest that the Brahman receives at this time. The iconicity of the winnowing basket in this ritual is obvious: it removes the inauspicious 'chaff', as it were, from the auspicious grain that will be used by the *jajmān*. Winnowing baskets are used in a similar way in a number of other rituals preliminary to the giving of *dān*, even when actual winnowing operations are not being performed.

The Brahman is not the only recipient in Pahansu of prestations that ensure the *barkat* of the harvested grain. On each day of both the rice and wheat harvests, the family Barber goes to the fields of his *jajmān* to receive *muṭṭhī*, a 'handful' of the rice or wheat still on the stalks. This prestation, like the *sāvṛī*, is never weighed; nor is it ever referred to as *phaslānā*, the shares of the harvest that are given in exchange for the services that the Barber and other service castes perform for the cultivator during the course of the year. The similarity of the *sāvṛī* and the *muṭṭhī* prestations is explicit. Both are *dān* and thus it is the 'right' of the *jajmān* to give them and the 'obligation' of the Brahman and the Barber to accept. 'Brahmans receive *sāvṛī* and we receive *muṭṭhī*', a Pahansu Barber once said to me, and he went on to say that 'from giving [*dān*] to *kamīns* the grain increases.' Some Pahansu wives reported to me that in their natal villages *muṭṭhī* is also given to the Sweeper of the cultivator for the same reason, and some older informants recalled that this was once the case in Pahansu as well.

Further prestations are also made to ensure the auspiciousness of the harvested grain after it has been weighed and brought into the storage rooms of the house. At the conclusion of each of the harvests, the wife of the Gujar cultivator goes to the field shrines of the family ancestral deities, and along with the wife of the family's Brahman *purohit* she cooks some of the new rice or makes breads from the newly harvested wheat. The rice or the breads are offered to the ancestral deity and then given as *dān* to the Brahman *purohit*, thus removing any inauspiciousness that may be caused by the malevolent presence of the ancestral deities enshrined in the fields.

A similar ritual is performed by the wives of Gujar cultivators at the shrine of the village god Bhūmiyā ('the one of the land'), the 'protector of the village site' (*khetrapāl*). Wheat or rice offerings are made at the shrine to the north of the Pahansu habitation site, and these offerings are then given as *dān* to the Brahman *purohits*, for the auspiciousness of the village harvests.

While people of all castes in the village give *dān* at many times in the year, either to people of other castes or to particular kinsmen, the Gujar cultivators are the par excellence *jajmān*s and givers of *dān* in the village. Their ritual centrality is enacted with particular clarity in Pahansu at the yearly ritual for Bhūmiyā in which all castes of the village participate. Gujars have the ritual performed for the 'protection' and well-being of the village as a whole; they provide food for the offerings to Bhūmiyā and the feast that follows, and they give *dān* to Brahmans at the conclusion of the day-long ritual in the month of Bhādwe. Brahmans officiate in their capacity as priests and cook the food that is to be offered to the deity and the food for the feast. They are also obliged to accept the offerings in order to remove from the village any inauspiciousness occasioned by the presence of the deity. For the same ritual, Barbers make banana-leaf plates and clean the cooking vessels, Potters provide clay vessels, Sweepers beat on their drums, Water-carriers bring water for the ritual and for the feast, and so on. Gujars and the other castes of the village regard it as extremely significant that Gujars are the givers of *dān* at this ritual of the village deity. Their giving firmly establishes their ritual centrality in the village, as does the fact that among the castes of the village, only the Gujar never receives *dān* from any other caste. As *jajmān*s of the village and donors to all others, the Gujar cultivators stand at the conceptual centre of village ritual organisation; the Barber, the Sweeper, the Brahman, and many other castes of the village carry out virtually identical ritual roles insofar as they are recipients of *dān* from Gujar donors. It is this donative relationship that calls forth a central-peripheral configuration of castes in Pahansu.

The Brahmans and *kamīn*s of Gujar cultivators are also obligated to accept *dān* at numerous points in the cycles of lunar days and solar days, lunar months and *āyaṇā*s (the periods of time between the summer and the winter solstices) that constitute the year for Pahansu villagers. Evil and inauspiciousness are thought to be particularly fluid and likely to afflict one at certain astral junctions. Inauspiciousness is likely to be transmitted from the gods themselves during the *dakṣiṇāyana*, the six months of the year when the sun moves in a southward course, the 'night of the gods'. To remove and 'make far' (*dūr karnā*) such inauspiciousness and evil, Gujar *jajmān*s in Pahansu give *dān* to the Brahmans and *kamīn*s tied to them in hereditary service relationships, and again it is the obligation of the recipient to accept the *dān* and digest the inauspiciousness. The crucial and culminating point of all of the yearly festivals that occur during the *dakṣiṇāyaṇa* (and nearly all of the village festivals do occur during this period) is in fact the giving of *dān* to a Brahman or *kamīn* for the well-being of one's household and the village as a whole.

The rituals of the life-course too culminate in the giving of *dān*, and many of these are concerned almost exclusively with the making of such prestations. Birth, marriage and death are fraught with the possibility that inauspiciousness will erupt and this inauspiciousness is removed through the numerous *dān* prestations that are made at these times. Prestations to Brahmans and *kamīns* during these rituals have, in the ethnographic literature on *jajmānī* relationships, generally been thought of as payments for the ritual services required by the *jajmān* on these occasions. While it is indeed the case, as we shall see in the following section, that such 'payments' are made to ritual functionaries, the payments are incidental to the efficacy of the ritual, while the *dān* prestations that are made are quite separate from these, and are crucial to the outcome of the ritual and to the well-being and auspiciousness of the *jajmān* and his family. At a number of points in the course of the wedding rites, for example, the bride or the groom is seated over a design made with flour called a *ṭakkarpūrat* ('protection from harm'). These designs may be made by either a Brahman or a Barber woman, with flour supplied by the Gujar *jajmān*. The flour is said to absorb the inauspiciousness that may have afflicted the bride or groom, and it is then the 'obligation' (*pharmāyā*) of the Brahman or the Barber to accept the flour, and the inauspiciousness contained within it, as *dān*. Brahmans and Barbers are also called upon to accept similar prestations in the form of dishes of grain that have been circled over the heads of the bride or groom (*wārpher kā anāj*, 'the grain of the circling') in order to remove evil and inauspiciousness that may be clinging to them, and these prestations too are *dān*.

Death rituals are also occasions when numerous *dān* prestations are made. The family Barber is the recipient of several relatively minor *dān* prestations during the protracted series of funerary rituals, but the Brahman *purohit* of the dead man's family is obligated to accept the most dangerous and inauspicious of these prestations, those that are made on the thirteenth day after death. The *dān* prestation made on this day is called *karvā cūn* ('bitter flour') and it consists of a large quantity of uncooked foodstuff, a basket of grain, a full set of clothes, a staff, five brass pots and a pair of shoes. The giving of these items as *dān* to the Brahman *purohit* is said to remove the 'evil' (*pāp*), 'terror' (*ḍar*) and extreme inauspiciousness occasioned by the dead man's existence as a *pret*, a disembodied ghost, for thirteen days after death.

The intentionality implicit in the giving of *dān* in Pahansu, that is, the promotion of prosperity, well-being, and auspiciousness, is remarkably similar to the intentionality of the pre-classical Indic sacrifice as described by Hubert and Mauss (1964) and more particularly by Heesterman. As Heesterman so graphically demonstrates, the function of the Brahman recipient of sacrificial gifts was to accept the evil and death of the *yajamāna* by eating from the offerings; the recipient of the gift took upon himself the 'evil' (*pāpmān*) and thus ensured life and prosperity (*śrī*) for the donor.

This donative relationship between *yajamāna* and Brahman recipient[4]

Though it is a completely unexplored topic, Sanskrit textual traditions also describe the giving of prestations containing evil and sin not just to the Brahman (Gonda 1969: 222) but to other recipients as well. In the *rājasūya* sacrifice, for example, the king as sacrificer is circled that is depicted in the pre-classical ritual texts is replicated in Pahansu in the relationship between Gujar *jajmāns* and Brahman and *kamīn* recipients of *dān*. The persistence of this pattern in contemporary social life, and its significance in defining inter-caste relationships in north India, presents a critical problem for the conceptualisation of caste offered by Dumont and Heesterman.

Dumont's postulation of a radical separation of Brahmanic 'authority' and royal 'power' as the quintessential feature of caste, and his definition of kingship and dominance solely in terms of the 'shame-faced' Kṣatriya realm of force and material advantage is predicated in part upon a view of the gifts of a king or dominant caste as representing only the material dependence of the Brahman upon the royal donor (Dumont 1980: 294). Such a view of the gift is incompatible with the relationship between Brahman and royal *yajamāna* in the sacrificial texts elucidated by Heesterman: in giving ritual gifts the king ensured his own well-being and that of his realm by giving away evil in the gift. Because he subscribes to Dumont's view of the 'temporal' role of the king and the dominant caste in contemporary India, Heesterman has formulated a model of historical transformation in order to account for the obvious inconsistency between the depiction of the ritual function of the king in the texts and Dumont's depiction of sovereignty in India. Whereas, according to Heesterman, in the pre-classical ritual the ritual prestations passed on evil and death to the recipients, an 'axial breakthrough' in the interpretation of sacrifice and the gift brought about a situation in which the gift became simply a matter of a 'salary' or a 'fee' (Heesterman 1959: 258, 1985: 155, 212). Indeed, with what he calls the 'individualization' and interiorization' of the ritual, and the elaboration of the '*karma* doctrine', Heesterman views it as an impossibility that evil and death could be passed on to others. The sacrificer, he says, 'must digest it himself' (1964: 15). With this change, Heesterman postulates that the relationship between the Brahman and the king underwent a fundamental change, a change that he views as the transition to a 'caste society'. The interdependence of the sacrificial nexus, in which the king as sacrificer depended upon the Brahman to receive the gifts and take away the evil, gave way to a situation in which the spheres of the Brahman and the Kṣatriya are definitely split. The old pattern of social life in which the royal function was pre-eminently a ritual one came to an end, and the pattern of 'caste' came into being, in which the Brahman is the focus of the ritual order and the king represents only the realm of political and economic force.

---

with a copper razor, which is then given to a barber in order to remove 'danger' from the king: 'He throws away evil' as the texts put it (Heesterman 1957: 111–12). At the conclusion of an *aṣvamedha* sacrifice, evil is taken away by affinal relatives and by the rival (Heesterman 1985: 135). In Pahansu, too, a diverse list of recipients is necessary to maintain the auspiciousness and well-being of the village and to take upon themselves the many types of inauspiciousness that threaten this well-being.

In consonance with this postulation of a radical transformation in the meaning and significance of royal gifts, and with his understanding of contemporary Indian society as characterised by the Dumontian separation of the ritual order and the royal order, Heesterman views the prestations comprising *jajmānī* relationships as matters not of the ritual interdependence of castes and the maintenance of well-being and auspiciousness, but simply as material fact; the 'division of the grain heap' among village functionaries is in Heesterman's estimation a matter of 'rights and shares' (1985: 180–93) and not of ritual. It is not the sacrificial model that defines the giving and receiving, but a system of differential claims in relation to the 'secular' power of the king or the dominant caste (ibid.: 246–47, fn. 36).

When confronted with Hocart's argument that the king and the cultivator stand at the centre of an organisation for ritual in which 'priest, washerman and drummer are treated alike, for they are all priests' (1950: 44) and in which the royal function is a ritual function, Dumont also has been forced to posit a historical transformation in the meaning of sovereignty, on the basis not of historical evidence but simply because of his own assumptions. Dumont argues that the ritual centrality of the king as it is described by Hocart was a feature only of 'pre-Aryan' India and that the Indo-European disjunction of status and power brought about the transformation of this Hocartian pattern into a 'caste system' (Dumont 1980: 93, 213). In the Indic world of caste, he asserts, it is the Brahman priest, rather than the king or the cultivator, who is the ideological point of reference.

The patterns of the giving and receiving of *dān* in Pahansu inter-caste relationships are clearly articulated in a way that recalls the sacrificial model of the distribution and dispersal of evil and death and the Hocartian pattern of royal centrality. The Gujar *jajmān* stands at the centre of this configuration of castes as protector of the village in a capacity that is clearly not reducible to temporal power and force. The transformation in the nature of the gift and in the relationship between the Brahman and the king that Heesterman and Dumont have envisioned as the very starting point and defining feature of caste society seems not to have occurred at all in Pahansu.

Rights to receive and the mutuality of inter-caste relationships

The Gujar *jajmāns* who have the 'right', (*hak*) to give *dān* to Brahmans, Barbers, Sweepers, and others, who in turn have an 'obligation' to accept, are also involved in the giving and receiving of many specifically named prestations that do not transfer evil and inauspiciousness to the recipient. *Dān* is always given to those who are seen as 'other' (*dūsre*) precisely in order to 'move away' (*haṭānā*) the inauspiciousness afflicting the *jajmān*. Yet these same recipients are, in other contexts, said to be not 'other' but 'one's own people' (*apne ādmī*) and are given prestations that imply a mutuality of services rendered and payment received, or simply a 'sharing' that is deemed appropriate among 'one's own people' or 'tied together brothers' (*lagū-bandhū bhāī*) and 'sharers' (*hissedār*). Insofar as prestations of this type are concerned, it is the 'right' (*hak*) of the recipient to claim the gift, rather than the right of the donor to give it. Within the context of what are usually thought of as *jajmānī* relationships, such prestations are of two types: the *phaslānā* distribution of grain at the time of the harvests, and the *neg* and *lāg* prestations that are made for the performance of specific ritual services at calendrical and life-course rituals.

Of the castes that are represented in Pahansu, six derive their livelihood principally from distributions of grain at the harvests. Members of these castes are said to be 'attached' (*lage huē*) or 'joined' (*jore huē*) to their Gujar *jajmāns*; in exchange (*badle mē*) for their various services, these castes, other than the Brahmans who receive only *sāvṛī* from the grain piles, receive the *phaslānā* payments or 'shares' at the *sāvanī* harvest of rice and the *sāṛhī* harvest of wheat. The *phaslānā* prestations made by Telu Ram, a substantial Gujar landholder, are as follows:

Barber: The Barber's 'reckoning' (*hissāb*) is according to the number of men to be shaved in the *jajmān*'s household. For each man, he receives four *kaccā dhaṛīs*—about 20 kg—of grain at each harvest. For Telu Ram's household, this amounts to a total of sixteen *dhaṛīs* of grain per harvest. The Barber also receives at least three or four *dhaṛīs* of unrefined sugar at the time it is processed from the *jajmān*'s sugarcane harvest.

Washerman: The Washerman receives 80 kg of grain per harvest, as well as 20–30 kg of unrefined sugar from the sugarcane harvest, specifically for the work of washing clothes in the village pond.

Sweeper: For the Sweeper, the 'reckoning' is according to the number of ploughs in use by the *jajmān*'s household (according to the presumed connection between the number of bullock-pulled ploughs and the amount of dung to be collected). Telu Ram uses a tractor now, but prior to the purchase of the tractor his family had three ploughs in use, so they use this number in determining the *phaslānā* payment to their Sweeper. For each plough, 3½ *dhaṛīs* of grain are given at each harvest; the Sweeper of this family thus receives 'three ploughs of grain' (*tīn halō kā anāj*), or 10½ *dhaṛīs* per harvest. Just before the rainy season (usually in May), each Sweeper family also receives one *dhaṛī* of grain for constructing a *biṭaurā*, a thatch structure for storing cow-dung cakes during the rainy months that follow.

Carpenter: The primary responsibilities of the Carpenter to his *jajmān* involve the maintenance of ploughs and other agricultural implements. Thus, their *phaslānā* is also measured according to the number of ploughs used by the *jajmān*. For each harvest, Telu Ram's Carpenter receives 20 kg of grain per plough, and 10 to 15 kg of unrefined sugar at the sugarcane harvest.

Ironsmith: Also compensated according to the 'plough reckoning' (*hal kā hissāb*), the Ironsmith receives 20 kg of grain from each harvest for each plough.

Several points should be noted concerning this enumeration of the 'shares' of the harvest given by the Gujar *jajmān* to those he calls his *gharelūs*, those who are 'of the house' and who are nourished and sustained by the grain of his fields. First of all, these shares are simply weighed out and distributed, and this distribution is not a part of any ritual action. And it should be emphasised that these *phaslānā* payments are not given to *kamīns* for the performance of ritual services for the *jajmān*, but for the specific services involved in shaving and hair-cutting, laundering, sweeping and collecting cow-dung, carpentry, and ironsmithy. The relationship between these services and the amount of grain given in *phaslānā* is stressed in the indigenous view of these prestations, and this is evidenced particularly in the notion of *hal kā hissāb*.

People of three other castes in Pahansu—Potters, Bangle-sellers, and Goldsmiths—still adhere to their traditional craft specialities, but they do not have hereditary relationships with Gujar *jajmāns* and they do not receive *phaslānā*. They provide their pots, bangles, and ornaments to Gujars and others in the village and receive compensation on the spot, in grain, according to the specific quantities of goods they supply. Because people of these three castes are not involved in hereditary relationships with Gujar *jajmāns* and because they do not receive *phaslānā*, Gujars say that they do not have 'one's own' (*apne*) Potters, Bangle-sellers and Goldsmiths. But there are contexts in which the 'taking and giving' (*len-den*) between these castes and a Gujar household does foreground such an 'attachment' (*lagnā*). At the birth of a son in a Gujar household, for example, members of these three castes (as well as the *kamīns*, the *gharelūs* of the house) visit the Gujar family at the sixth-day ritual and present some *dūb* grass to the mother of the child; for this service they receive prestations called *lag* (from *lagnā*, 'to be attached', 'to be related') and are thought of as being in some ways, and in this limited context, 'one's own'.

For the performance of specific ritual services such as singing auspicious songs at the birth of a son, providing 'protective threads' for a newborn, playing drums, delivering wedding gifts, and so forth, Brahmans, Barbers, Sweepers, and others receive *lāg* or *neg* payments in the form of cash, cloth, grain or other items. The relationship between services rendered and payment received in these cases is not expressed in terms of a calculation of amount of services provided in relation to the amount of compensation, but primarily in the linguistic convention of designating the payment in the same terms as the service performed; thus, *gīt gavāī* means both 'singing songs' and the payment made for this service. Villagers characterise this type of prestation in terms that emphasise the culturally defined reciprocity and mutuality that is involved. Informants always stressed the fact that *neg* and *lāg* are forms of payment for 'labour' (*mazdūrī*) and that the word *neg* in particular means 'share', *hissā*. Now 'shares' of one's wealth or one's harvests are given, according to these same informants, only to those who are 'one's own people' (*apne ādmī*), those who are 'attached to us, joined to us' (*jo hamāre sāth lage hue haī, joṛe hue*); they would never be given to those who are 'other'. That *lāg* indeed is thought of as a 'share' as well as a payment is indicated by the fact that for the ritual services performed by Brahmans, Barbers, Sweepers, and Washermen at the wedding of a son, the *lāg* that is given is substantially larger than that which is given for the same ritual services performed at the wedding of a daughter. This is so because, it is said, a 'dowry' (*dahej*) comes into the house at the marriage of a son, and one's Brahman and those who receive *phaslānā* are 'sharers in the dowry' (*dahej mẽ hissedār*) precisely because they are 'attached' to the household and have a 'connection' (*sampark*) with it.

Whether conceived of primarily as a 'share' or as a 'payment', *neg* and *lāg* prestations are given to the recipient because he has a 'right' to claim it rather than an 'obligation' to accept. Indeed, the recipient may in some instances demand certain articles or amounts of grain as his or her *neg*, as the often repeated proverb 'everyone fights for their own *neg*' (*apne apne neg par sab jhagṛe*) implies.

As they receive *phaslānā, lāg* and *neg*, Brahmans and *kamīn*s are seen as 'one's own people' (*apne ādmī*) by their Gujar *jajmān*s and are referred to as *lagū-bandhū bhāī* ('tied together brother'), *gharelū* ('of the house'), or *dahej mẽ hissedār* ('sharer in the dowry'), all terms that emphasise the sharing aspect of these inter-caste relationships. As these same recipients are placed under an obligation to accept prestations that transfer inauspiciousness, on the other hand, the perspective undergoes a contextual shift and they are seen by Gujars as 'other' (*dūsrā*). In the context of the giving and receiving of *dān*, none of these terms—*lagū-bandhū bhāī, gharelū*, or *hissedār*—would ever occur; when *dān* is at issue, the recipients are referred to simply as *purohit* and *kamīn*. The two sets of relational terms function as pragmatic indices of the configuration of castes that is at issue in any given prestational context—the configuration that foregrounds mutuality and reciprocity in giving and receiving, or the configuration that foregrounds the ritual centrality of the dominant caste sacrificers and givers of *dān*, and the ritual equivalence of Brahmans and *kamīn*s as recipients of *dān* and the evil it contains.

Hierarchy and the gift

The importance of exchanges, particularly of food, water and grain, but also of bodily substances such as hair, menstrual blood, feces, and saliva in food leavings, has been extensively discussed by Marriott (1968, 1976) and Dumont (1980), with particular focus on food exchanges in various media (raw foods [*sīdhā*], foods cooked in water or breads cooked on a griddle [*kaccā*], foods cooked in oil or clarified butter [*pakkā*], and water) as constituted from (Dumont) or creative of (Marriott) a ranked order of *jātis*. For Dumont, the exchanges in these media simply reflected the distinction between the pure and the impure, although such exchanges are often, in his view, refracted through the nonideological residuum of the 'power' of the dominant caste.

In everyday village life in Pahansu, there is very little talk about these media of transactions, or the hierarchical considerations they implicate. When asked about considerations concerning the giving and receiving of *pakkā* and *kaccā* foods in interview situations, villagers inevitably responded that such considerations indicate 'dispositions about high and low' (*ūc-nīc kā bhav*) and '[considerations of] touching and not touching' (*chuāchūṭ*); when such considerations are at issue in a particular situation, the terminological usages that are implemented are those such as *ūcī jāti* ('high caste') and *nīcī jāti* ('low caste'), or the contrast between 'big castes' and 'little castes' (*baṛī jāti* and *choṭī jāti*).

The relationships characterised in these terms, high and low, little and big, and in which transactions are construed in terms of the media involved (i.e., *kaccā* and *pakkā* foods and so on) are not in fact those of giving and receiving (*len-den*) properly speaking. With respect to the concerns that are exemplified when villagers discuss the possible media in which various food transactions may occur, the question 'who did the cooking?' rather than 'who is the donor?' is the relevant one, as Blunt (1931: 89) and Dumont (1980: 142) have rightly pointed out. More generally speaking, the cook's and servers' bodily substances and their qualities, and their mixing with that which is cooked and served is what is involved here, and it is this that makes the eating of cooked food a matter of rank and hierarchy (Marriott 1976). But the particular relationship of donor and recipient, appearing in Pahansu as by far the most important one, remains unexplicated if we focus on this issue alone. Although there are hundreds of named prestations given in order to remove inauspiciousness or to maintain a mutuality among 'one's own' people in Pahansu, there are no situations in which a prestation is made precisely because of a hierarchical relationship. Hierarchical considerations and rank only partially structure the patterns of giving and receiving in the village; they provide only a limiting parameter or a presupposed set of assumptions concerning the media in which prestations are made, prestations that are culturally constructed primarily in terms of other concepts and concerns and which foreground aspects of relationships other than hierarchy.

If, for example, a particular *dān* prestation is to be made by a Gujar family to a Brahman, a prestation that involves the giving of a meal, the women of the Gujar household may prepare *pakkā* food, which a Brahman may properly accept from Gujars, or they may present the Brahman with the uncooked ingredients for a *kaccā* meal, and ask the Brahman to cook it himself, since hierarchical considerations generally prevent a Brahman from accepting prepared *kaccā* food from a Gujar cook. The hierarchical aspects of the relationship between Gujar and Brahman are thus made evident in the acts of giving and receiving, but they nevertheless tell us nothing of why the prestation had to be made to begin with; the donor-recipient relationship and the meaning of the prestation itself remain obscure if we attend only to the relative rank of the parties involved.

In the context of prestations made to remove inauspiciousness, and in the context of those given *badle mē*, 'in exchange', to 'one's own people', hierarchy is not a foregrounded aspect of the social relationship. The terms in which these two types of giving and receiving are understood provide alternative configurations of castes in the village, configurations that are indexed by the shifting terminological usages I have mentioned. These terms not only enter into propositional statements *about* particular persons, categories or events, but more importantly, they function as indicators of shifting, contextually appropriate and purposive foregroundings of the aspects of relationships—the oriented transfer of inauspiciousness and the ritual centrality of the dominant caste *jajmān*, or the mutuality among 'one's own people'—that may be at issue as the decisive social variables of the speech situation.

The elusive 'systematicity' of jajmānī *relationships*

Beginning with Dumont and Pocock's arguments that the prestations and counter-prestations comprising the so-called '*jajmānī* system' represented an empirically observable juxtaposition of the two antithetical realms of Brahmanical ritual authority and royal secular power, anthropological observers have debated the issue of whether these givings and receivings should be thought of as a self-contained 'system'. Fuller (1977) has argued that contemporary *jajmānī* relationships in the Indian village are only remnants of a much larger supra-local political and economic system for the allocation of shares of the agricultural produce of the land that was destroyed with the introduction of private property rights in the land. Fuller's argument presumes, with Heesterman, Pocock, and Dumont, that the prestations made by the dominant cultivators were primarily matters of the 'rights' of the recipients, and not of the ritual functions carried out, through gift-giving, by these donors in their capacity as *jajmāns*. More recently, Good (1982) has accepted Pocock's reasons for denying the existence of a '*jajmānī* system', and goes on to argue that *jajmān* and *jajmānī* are Hindi terms whose equivalents in the other Indian languages, or at least in Tamil, are not much used and to speak therefore of a '*jajmānī* system' outside of the Hindi-speaking region is to impose an alien interpretation on the data. The presence or absence of a specific linguistic

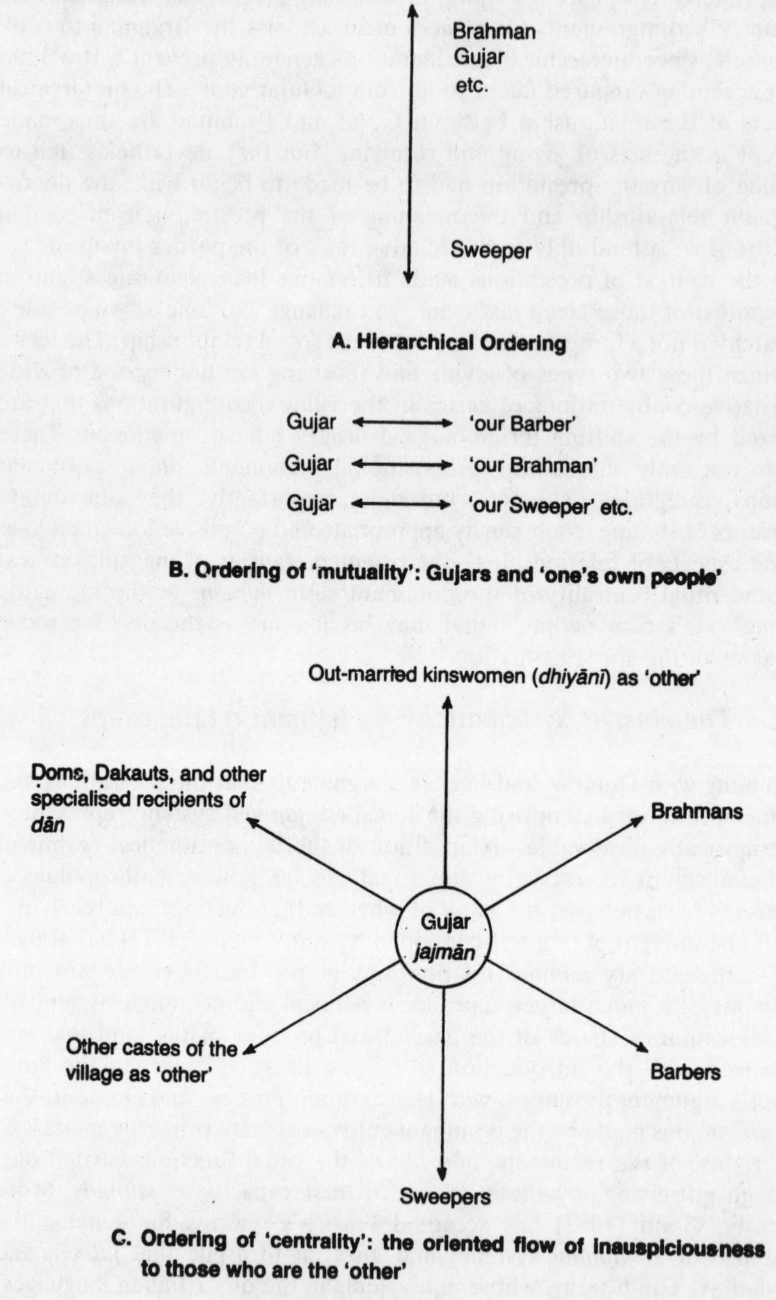

Figure 1: Configuration of castes in Pahansu

terminology notwithstanding, the demographic configuration of the villages that Good studied, villages in which there is no one dominant caste (1982: 39, fn. 16) that holds most of the land or acts as par excellence *jajmān*, may have presented a situation in which the salience of the ritual 'centrality' of the *jajmān* as donor is less evident and harder to discern as the fulcrum of a 'system', than is the case in Pahansu. (This is a point that I will return to in the final section of this paper.)

Good raises another point concerning the definition of a '*jajmānī* system' that is of great relevance for our understanding of giving and receiving in Pahansu. As in the three Tamil villages that Good studied, many of the same sorts of prestations that are given to Brahmans and *kamīn*s are also given to one's kinsmen in Pahansu. Studies of the so-called '*jajmānī* system' have generally been limited to a consideration of inter-caste prestations, and anthropologists have failed to recognise the fact that the same categories of prestations that are given to Brahmans, Barbers, Sweepers, and others by the dominant *jajmān*s are given by people of these castes to certain specified kinsmen. Within one's caste, *dān* prestations, because they must always be given to those who are 'other', are without exception given to one's wife-taking affines. *Neg* and *lāg* prestations on the other hand, which are thought of as 'shares' that are given to 'one's own people', may be given mutually or reciprocally to the people of one's own lineage or to one's affines, who are in those contexts not referred to as 'other' but as 'one's own'.

That *dān* prestations, when they become matters of intra-caste giving and receiving, should be given to one's wife-taking affines is not surprising. Marriage itself, in north India, is conceived of as a *dān* (*kanyādān*, 'the gift of a virgin') and through the acceptance of the *kanyādān* and the many accompanying prestations, the groom and his family are said to take upon themselves a load of sin and evil from the bride's natal kin. Such evil can only be removed by passing it onward (*āge denā*) to the Brahman *purohit* of the groom's family; during the course of the wedding rites, the groom makes several *dān* prestations to his own *purohit* in order, it is said, 'to remove the faults occasioned by the acceptance of a wife'. Having once served as the 'vessel' (*pātra*) for the inauspiciousness of his wife's natal kin, the groom then has the 'obligation' (*pharmāyā*), in all castes except the Gujar *jāti*,[5] to accept many more prestations of the same sort, prestations that Gujars themselves give to their Brahmans and *kamīn*s.

[5] Gujars as well as the other castes of the village regard it as extremely significant for the Gujar position as the pivot of the central-peripheral configuration of castes that they give no *dān* prestations to the husbands of their married daughters and sisters after the actual wedding prestations have been concluded. Gujars do, however, give many *dān* and *caṛhāpā* prestations to their married daughters and sisters, their *dhiyānī*. These prestations and their implications for a contextualised understanding of north Indian kinship are discussed in detail elsewhere (Raheja 1988a, 1988c).

That prestations comprising *jajmānī* giving and receiving are often given to one's wife-taking affines should also not be surprising if indeed we take seriously the persistence of the sacrificial model of the disbursement of evil through prestation in contemporary village life. In the textual materials on sacrifice, it is the wife-taking affines who are often called upon to accept the sacrificial gifts. In the *aśvamedha* sacrifice, for example, evil (*pāpman*) is taken away from the sacrificer by affinal relatives, particularly the son of a younger sister of the *yajamāna* (Heesterman 1985: 135; O'Flaherty 1976: 141).

If, then, we look for the 'systematicity' of *jajmānī* giving and receiving in a single domain (inter-caste prestations) of our own devising, we will surely fail to find it. If, however, we see the sacrifice and its accompanying prestations as the model for the giving and receiving of *dān*, as we are forced to do if we take seriously the indigenous view of Pahansu villagers concerning the removal of sin and evil through the gift (and not dismiss it as an 'absurd theological interpretation' as Mauss [1967] did in *The gift*), we may find in these *jajmānī* prestations a coherent view of social relations as ritual relations mobilised for well-being and prosperity with the dominant caste as donors acting in a 'royal' capacity as the chief sacrificers and protectors of the village.

Towards a reinterpretation of dominance

For Dumont, the ordering of the *varṇa*s in Indic texts and Indic society is founded precisely on what he sees as the disjunction between hierarchy and power, priesthood and royalty, the encompassing Brahmanic ideology of the pure and the impure and a 'shame-faced Kṣatriya model' of naked force. The anthropological literature on dominance in South Asia has reflected this disjunctive vision; the pivotal position of the dominant caste in village life and in *jajmānī* relationships in particular has almost without exception been interpreted as a nonideological and nonreligious aspect of Indian society. The Brahman *varṇa*, in this view, represents the priestly and ritual function, and the Kṣatriya *varṇa* the encompassed royal function, the exercise of power and force. As I have tried to show, the ethnographic evidence from Pahansu suggests that other readings of the royal function and the role of the dominant caste are indeed possible. Such is also the case with regard to the interpretation of Sanskritic and popular vernacular textual traditions that concern themselves with kingship and the relations between the Brahman and the Kṣatriya.

In the very first verses of the Laws of Manu, for example, it is declared that the purpose of the text is to set forth the *dharma*s of the four *varṇa*s. By way of introduction to the description of these *dharma*s, Manu asserts that in the first age of the cycle of four *yuga*s, the chief duty of mankind is the performance of austerities, in the second it is knowledge, in the third sacrifice, and in the fourth age, in which all of history has in fact been played out, it is the giving of *dān* that is the central sustaining value. *Dān*, then, is said to characterise the present era, but in order to 'protect the universe' differential *dharmas* are appropriate to the four *varṇas*. It is the *dharma* of the Kṣatriya to give *dān* for the protection of the universe and the people of his realm, and it is the *dharma* of the Brahman to accept *dān*.

It is not only in Manu that the giving of *dān* is seen as constitutive of kingship and Kṣatriyahood. When I arrived in Pahansu for the first time and announced that I had come in order to study the place of the Gujar caste in village social life, among the first things that I was encouraged to record in my notebooks were stories of kings who are said to be the progenitors of the Gujar *jāti* and its various clans (*gots*). I was told time and time again the story of King Harishchandra (who is said to be an ancestor of the Gujars of Pahansu) who, when pressed by the Brahman Vishvamitra to give everything he owned in *dān*, gave even himself, his wife and his son to be sold by the rapacious Brahman. Not only are many Gujars able to recite a version of this very old and well-known story, but it is also heard in the form of a song sung by Gujar women at the birth of a son, as if in proclamation that it is Harishchandra himself that a new member of the Gujar *jāti* should hold as a model for the conduct of his life in the village.

Pahansu Gujars of the Khūbaṛ *got* assert that the people of their clan are descended from one Jagdev Singh Panwar. The stories they tell of him concern his munificence as a giver of *dān*. The greatness of kings is measured, in these stories, in terms of the greatness of the *dān* prestations that they are able to make, and Jagdev surpasses all other kings in his willingness to give even his own head in *dān*. As Gujars recounted these stories to me, I was reminded more than once of the relation between Jagdev's great capacity to give *dān* and the gifts given by Gujars in Pahansu. As one Gujar man said to me as he concluded his rendition of the story: 'We too are such givers of *dān*, the Khūbaṛs of today'. And I would be told, in such situations, of the many *dān* prestations that they make to their Brahmans, Barbers, Sweepers, and others, because they are the *jajmāns* and the protectors of the village.

These legendary ancestors of Pahansu Gujars are also praised as munificent givers of *dān* by the hereditary bards and genealogists who come to Pahansu to serve their Gujar *jajmāns*. Genealogists of the Bhāṭ caste and the bards of the Ḍom and Bādi castes visit the village periodically to sing and recite the stories of Harishchandra and Jagdev. They also remember the more proximate ancestors of specific Gujar families; their names too are recited, and the magnitude of their 'royal' largesse is extolled as the source of their honour and fame, and of the renown of Pahansu among the eighty-four villages of the Khūbaṛ *got*.

As a caste, then, Gujars define their own position in the configuration of castes precisely in terms of their ritual centrality and the *dān* prestations that they make. This is not to say that the giving and receiving of *dān* and this ritual centrality will necessarily have the same salience and the same significance in all Indian villages in which *jajmānī*-like relationships are extant.

In Pahansu, Gujar dominance is absolute. They comprise slightly more than one-half of the total population, but they hold virtually all of the land. They are regarded as the *jajmān*s not only with respect to their own domestic and agricultural rituals, but also in relation to the ritual life of the village as a unit at the annual ritual for Bhūmiyā and at many other times throughout the year. In many of the villages that have provided data for the analysis of *jajmānī* relationships, however, landholding is more dispersed and it is less clearly defined as a matter of caste. In Karimpur, for example, when Wiser studied the village in the 1920s, Brahmans comprised approximately one-fourth of the total population. There were forty-one Brahman households, of which thirty-eight gained their livelihood as farmers and landholders and three families engaged in priestly work (Wiser 1936: 19, 22). In 1969, when Wadley conducted fieldwork in the same village, Brahmans again comprised roughly one-fourth of the population and held 54 per cent of the land (Wadley 1975: 19–21). Though Brahmans in Karimpur understand themselves and are understood by others to hold the decisive balance of political and economic power in the village, the existence of a caste of 'traditional' farmers (the Kacchis) who have sizeable landholdings (Wiser 1936: 33–34; Wadley 1975: 20–21) has perhaps mitigated the salience of a central-peripheral model of inter-caste relationships, with the result that landholding does not define the Brahmans as a caste in the way that landholding and their status as *jajmān*s defines the position of Gujars in Pahansu.

A similar situation exists in Kishan Garhi, the Uttar Pradesh village studied by Marriot. Most of the land there was held by Brahmans as tenants of Jats whose ancestors had seized the village in the 17th century. In 1952, after the implementation of the Uttar Pradesh Zamindari Abolition and Land Reform Act, Brahmans paid slightly more than one-half of the land revenues that were due from the village (Marriott 1968: 135). Jats—givers of *dān* like Gujars—are a minority there, and Kishan Garhi was said to be a Brahman village just as Pahansu is said to be a Gujar village.

The demographic situation and patterns of landholding in Karimpur and Kishan Garhi may have given a Brahman bias to previous views of *jajmānī* relationships, and prevented the recognition of the ritual centrality of the dominant caste (as distinguished from its hierarchical position, and from the so-called 'secular' aspects of dominance) for several reasons. 'Centrality' may be less obvious to the observer of village life, and less salient to villagers themselves, when no one landholding caste is defining itself, in opposition to all others, as *jajmān*s and givers of *dān*. Second, when Brahmans are the principal landholders, and some members of the caste act as *purohit*s for the village (as they do in both Karimpur and Kishan Garhi), several conflicting models, conflicting *dharmas* as it were, come into play. Brahmans are at once the 'highest' caste in a hierarchic configuration, some are called to act as *purohit*s and recipients of *dān*, and some are *jajmān*s and the givers of *dān*. In such a situation, one may find that *dān* is indeed given to remove evil and inauspiciousness, but the giving of *dān* would not have there the significance that it has in Pahansu in defining caste identity and relations among castes as such. Data from villages like Pahansu in which Brahmans depend mostly on their priestly occupations and in which the landholders are drawn almost exclusively from a caste identified with the 'royal' Kṣatriya *varṇa* allow us to see more clearly the multiple and shifting configurations of castes, particularly that configuration focused on the ritual centrality of the dominant caste.

With respect to the prestation patterns found in Pahansu and other such villages in northern India, dominance is not simply a matter of a caste's numerical preponderance or the 'temporal' aspects of landholding. Though landholding and numerical preponderance may in fact, as I have tried to suggest, be necessary conditions for the foregrounding of centrality as a phenomenon of caste, it is the sacrificial function, the giving away and dispersal of evil and inauspiciousness for the well-being and prosperity of the village, that is seen by all castes in Pahansu as the fulcrum of dominance and of *jajmānī* relationships in the village.

REFERENCES

APPADURAI, ARJUN. 1978. Kings, sects and temples in south India, 1350–1700 A.D. *In* B. Stein, ed., *South Indian temples*, pp. 47–73. New Delhi: Vikas.

———. 1981. *Worship and conflict under colonial rule*. Cambridge: Cambridge University Press.

———. 1986. Is Homo hierarchicus? *American ethnologist* 13: 745–61.

———. 1988. Putting hierarchy in its place. *Cultural anthropology* 3: 36–49.

BLUNT, E.A.H. 1931. *The caste system of northern India with special reference to the United Provinces of Agra and Oudh*. London: Oxford University Press.

BOURDIEU, PIERRE. 1977. *Outline of a theory of practice*. Cambridge: Cambridge University Press.

BRECKENRIDGE, CAROL. 1978. From protector to litigant: changing relations between Hindu temples and the Raja of Ramnad. *In* Burton Stein, ed., *South Indian temples*, pp. 75–106. Delhi: Vikas.

BURGHART, RICHARD. 1987. Gifts to the gods: power, property and ceremonial in Nepal. *In* D. Cannadine and S. Price, eds., *Rituals of royalty: power and ceremonial in traditional societies*, pp. 237–70. Cambridge: Cambridge University Press.

CLIFFORD, JAMES. 1988. *The predicament of culture: twentieth century ethnography, literature, and art*. Cambridge, Mass.: Harvard University Press.

COHN, BERNARD S. 1968. Notes on the history of the study of Indian culture and society. *In* M. Singer and B.S. Cohn, eds., *Structure and change in Indian society*, pp. 3–28. Chicago: Aldine.

———. 1983. Representing authority in Victorian India. *In* E. Hobsbawm and T. Ranger, eds., *The invention of tradition*, pp. 165–209. Cambridge: Cambridge University Press.

———. 1984. The census, social structure and objectification in South Asia. *Folk* 26: 25–49.

Cohn, Bernard S. 1985a. The command of language and the language of command. *In* R. Guha, ed., *Writings on South Asian history and society*, Subaltern Studies, vol. 4, pp. 276–329. Delhi: Oxford University Press.

———. 1985b. Law and the colonial state in India. Wenner-Gren symposium, Ethnohistorical Models for the Evolution of Law in Specific Societies, Bellagio, Italy, August 1985.

Dirks, Nicholas B. 1976. Political authority and structural change in early south Indian history. *Indian economic and social history review* 13: 125–57.

———. 1987. *The hollow crown: ethnohistory of an Indian kingdom*. Cambridge: Cambridge University Press.

Dumont, Louis. 1980. *Homo hierarchicus* (trans. M. Sainsbury, L. Dumont, and B. Gulati). Chicago: University of Chicago Press.

Dumont, Louis and Pocock, David. 1957. Village studies. *Contributions to Indian sociology* 1: 23–41.

———. 1958. A.M. Hocart on caste—religion and power. *Contributions to Indian sociology* 2: 45–63.

Fuller, C.J. 1977. British India or traditional India? An anthropological problem. *Ethnos* 3–4: 95–121.

Gonda, J. 1969. *Ancient Indian kingship from the religious point of view*. Leiden: E.J. Brill.

Good, Anthony. 1982. The actor and the act: categories of prestation in south India. *Man* (n.s.) 17, 1: 23–41.

Heesterman, J.C. 1957. *The ancient Indian royal consecration*. The Hague: Mouton.

———. 1959. Reflections on the significance of *dakṣiṇā*. *Indo-Iranian journal* 3: 241–58.

———. 1964. Brahmin, ritual, and renouncer. *Wiener Zeitschrift fur die Kunde Sud- und Ost-Asiens* 8: 1–31.

———. 1985. *The inner conflict of tradition: essays in Indian ritual, kingship, and society*. Chicago: University of Chicago Press.

Hocart, A.M. 1950. *Caste: a comparative study*. London: Methuen.

Hubert, Henri and Mauss, Marcel. 1964. *Sacrifice: its nature and function* (trans. W.D. Halls). Chicago: University of Chicago Press.

Marriott, McKim. 1968. Caste ranking and food transactions: a matrix analysis. *In* M. Singer and B. Cohn, eds., *Structure and change in Indian society*, pp. 133–71. Chicago: Aldine.

———. 1976. Hindu transactions: diversity without dualism. *In* B. Kapferer, ed., *Transaction and meaning*, pp. 109–42 Philadelphia: Institute for the Study of Human Issues.

Mauss, Marcel. 1967. *The gift* (trans. I. Cunnison). New York: W.W. Norton.

O'Flaherty, Wendy. 1976. *The origins of evil in Hindu mythology*. Berkeley: University of California Press.

Parry, Jonathan. 1979. *Caste and kinship in Kangra*. London: Routledge and Kegan Paul.

———. 1980. Ghosts, greed, and sin: the occupational identity of the Benares funeral priests. *Man* (n.s.) 15: 88–111.

———. 1986. *The gift*, the Indian gift, and the 'Indian gift'. *Man* (n.s.) 21: 453–73.

Pedersen, Poul. 1986. Khatri: Vaishya or Kshatriya, an essay on colonial administration and cultural identity. *Folk* 28: 19–31.

Price, P. 1979. Raja-dharma in 19th century South India: land, litigation, and largess in Ramnad Zamindari. *Contributions to Indian sociology* (n.s.) 13: 207–40.

Raheja, Gloria Goodwin. 1988a. *The poison in the gift: ritual, prestation, and the dominant caste in a north Indian village*. Chicago: University of Chicago Press.

———. 1988b. India: caste, kingship, and dominance reconsidered. *Annual review of anthropology* 17: 497–522.

———. 1988c. Ironies of the self: gift-giving, double relationships, and women's ritual songs in north India. Manuscript.

SHULMAN, DAVID. 1985. Kingship and prestation in south Indian myth and epic. *Asian and African studies* 19: 36–79.

SILVERSTEIN, MICHAEL. 1976. Shifters, linguistic categories, and cultural description. *In* Keith H. Basso and Henry A. Selby, eds., *Meaning in anthropology*, pp. 11–55. Albuquerque: University of New Mexico Press.

SRINIVAS, M.N. 1987. The Indian village: myth and reality. *In* M.N. Srinivas, *The dominant caste and other essays*, pp. 20–59. Delhi: Oxford University Press.

STEIN, BURTON. 1980. *Peasant, state, and society in medieval south India*. Delhi: Oxford University Press.

TRAUTMANN, THOMAS R. 1981. *Dravidian kinship*. Cambridge: Cambridge University Press.

WADLEY, SUSAN S. 1975. *Shakti: power in the conceptual structure of Karimpur religion*. Chicago: University of Chicago Studies in Anthropology, Series in Social, Cultural, and Linguistic Anthropology 2.

WISER, WILLIAM. 1936. *The Hindu jajmani system*. Lucknow: Lucknow Publishing House.

5

Hindu periods of death 'impurity'[1]

Diane Paull Mines

A Hindu dies. From the moment when the "spirit" or "life" (*jīva*)[2] leaves the body, certain survivors are said to become temporarily "impure" and are thus "incapacitated" (*āśauca*)[3] for performing certain ordinary duties. By ancient textual formulas, some of which continue to be widely quoted, the periods of heavy "incapacity" are said to vary from one day to a month. Periods vary according to the survivor's "occupational class" (*varṇa*), "life stage" (*āśrama*), place of residence, and other relations to the deceased. Such states of incapacity restrict the survivor's contacts with other persons and variously require abstention from cooking, from salted food, from usual bodily care, etc.; they require the completion of certain rituals, especially feedings and waterings of the departed spirit, that provide it with a new body; and they end with the survivor's bathing. The texts do not attempt to explain (*i*) how the survivor's incapacity is caused or ended, nor

[1] This paper's numerical problems were first posed for me by E.V. Daniel, its Hindu issues by a Bengali example (Nicholas 1982). I am grateful to Terence S. Turner for suggesting a productive theoretical approach, and to McKim Marriott for his overall advice and editing. The paper is based on a Master's thesis (Mines 1985) which I wrote while holding a fellowship from the National Science Foundation.

[2] To assist the reader in distinguishing between Indian and non-Indian concepts, I use single quotation marks when I quote non-Indian words, double when I gloss Indian words.

[3] *Āśauca*'s literal meaning is "not pure", and the word is commonly glossed as "impure" by Kane (1953: 267–333) and other indologists. However, Kane and other authors of *dharmaśāstra* define *āśauca* specifically as 'impurity on birth and death'. They describe it as a particular time-defined 'ritual incapacity' that can affect other persons and that is ended by ritual performances. Other words used in some texts and regions interchangeably with *āśauca* are *agha* (a kind of "sin") and *sūtaka* (implying connection through the female genital [Veena Das, personal communication]). Neither *āśauca* nor any of its synonyms is used for everyday "impurities" which are described by different words (*aśuddha*, etc.), and do not affect related persons. To avoid confusion with such broader notions of "impurity", I shall henceforth generally translate *āśauca* as "incapacity".

(*ii*) why periods of incapacity vary as they do. The task of this essay is to develop such explanations.

Explanations have been offered before, but to the extent that they rest on presuming that Hindu death observances express a hygienic wish to avoid decaying flesh or the Western religious value of separating spirit from bodily substance, they remain at odds with many Hindu data. I attempt here to develop more accurate explanations by adopting the Hindu assumption that spirit is difficult to separate from substance, and by attending to the greater and more immediate Hindu concern with managing their continued union.

Dharmaśāstra texts do not expound any general theory as to how death causes incapacities or how they are cured. After years of research, Kane writes:

> A question arises why . . . death should cause impurity to members of the family or to relatives. Only few texts have to say anything on this question. Haritas says: 'the family incurs death impurity, because by death the family feels overwhelmed (or frustrated) . . .' (1953: 269–70).

Death may be shocking, but its effects are ordered in precise textual formulations whose rationale remains to be stated.

Writing on the lesser number of days of 'impurity' ascribed to persons of higher *varṇa*, whose presumed 'purity' he would expect to be more injured by the organic contamination of death, Dumont writes in apparent puzzlement:

> either we have not yet managed to enter the spirit of the system, or else the Brahmans have here transformed into privilege what ought to be a greater incapacity (1970: 70).

Tambiah (1973: 208–18) and Marglin (1977: 255–67) agree with Dumont that shortened periods of 'impurity' may reflect the Brahman authors' self-interested desire to minimise the 'austerities' imposed upon themselves as survivors. However, Manu (5.84) and other law-givers criticise lengthy periods of incapacity as escapes from Brahmans' more urgent and onerous duties, such as vedic study and maintaining everyday "purity" (*śuddhi*); they advocate minimising the definition and duration of death-caused incapacity as ways of controlling "laziness" (Kane 1953: 268–69, 271, 299–300, 308). Suggestions like the above that privilege or exploitation may explain the different durations of incapacity leave in place the dubious general assumption that 'impurity' is incurred by connecting one's spirit with 'organic' substance; they also leave otherwise undisturbed the antiorganic explanations of periods of death-caused incapacity detailed by the late Henry Orenstein (1970a, 1970b).

Without subscribing to utilitarian hypotheses of Brahmanical bias, Orenstein attempts by positing an antiorganic value-preference to explain both the general Hindu reasoning behind the phenomenon of death 'impurity' and the logic underlying the scheme of particular periods, including exceptions to this scheme. He is apparently the only scholar to have made such a comprehensive attempt, and with minor modifications his efforts continue to be widely cited (e.g., by Kolenda 1978: 165; Marglin 1977: 255–60; Parry 1979: 140–42; Tambiah 1973: 208–11). As I shall show below, however, his general and particular explanations fail both ethnographically and logically.

In this paper I offer new attempts at explaining both the general and the particular logics of death-caused incapacity. First I present the puzzling formulas in their numerical specificity. Second, I summarise the model of 'spiritual purity' which Orenstein attributes to Hindus and I criticise both its results and its weak theoretical bases. The latter consist of the structuralist principles forwarded by Dumont (1970) and Dumont and Pocock (1959), along with the so-called 'functionalist' perspective that these authors and others borrow from Hertz (1960). In the third part I present an alternative general Hindu ethnosociological model of "impurity" and "incapacity" drawn largely from recent ethnography. Using the terms of this model, in the fourth part I outline Hindu funeral rites, a topic surprisingly omitted by Orenstein from his 'functional' analysis. I place these rites within the larger set of birth, marriage and other family rites, since funerals would not otherwise be comprehensible. In the fifth part, taking account of the preceding general model and rituals, I offer new explanations of the durations of incapacity specified by the texts.

I
The numerical problems

The table below displays the numbers of days for which surviving *sapiṇḍa*s are said to become "incapable" (*āśauca*) upon a fellow-*sapiṇḍa*'s death. A *sapiṇḍa* is a person who has "similar particles" with an ascendant and with that ascendant's other descendants through continually giving water to and feeding the ascendant's spirit with rice "balls" (*piṇḍa*s) and/or through having received "particles" (*piṇḍa*s) of his own "body" (also *piṇḍa*) from the ascendant. *Sapiṇḍa*s are reckoned by some Hindus as far as the seventh ascending generation through the father and the fifth generation through the mother.

The numbers in the table are common ones selected from somewhat variable texts of *dharma* (Kane 1953: 267–74, 288). They are those cited by Orenstein (1970a: 1367) and many others. Days of incapacity are stated here by *varṇa* "classes",[4] listed here in their conventional order of rank. The numbers 10, 12, 15, 30 in cells along what mathematicians call the 'main diagonal' of the table's matrix (the line from upper left to lower right) pertain to decedents and survivors who are of the same *varṇa*. The numbers in the rest of the cells, where the rows and columns of different *varṇa*s intersect, pertain to mixed cases where decedents and their related survivors are of different *varṇa*s, presumably because of previous mixed-*varṇa* marriages. Higher-decedent-over-lower-survivor combinations (*anuloma*s, "with the [slope] of the hair") are found in the upper right triangle, lower-over-higher (*pratiloma*s, "against the [slope of the] hair") in the lower left triangle.

Days of Surviving *Sapiṇḍa*'s Incapacity, by *Varṇa*

Varṇa of deceased		*Varṇa* of survivor			
		B	K	V	S
	Brahman	10	10	10	10
	Kṣatriya	6	12	12	12
	Vaiśya	3	6	15	15
	Sudra	1	3	6	30

The rising numbers of days along the main diagonal represent periods of incapacity that may actually be observed by persons of some *jāti*s that are identified with the specified *varṇa*s,[5] but the numbers in the rest of the table may seem to represent little reality, since they appear to concern only survivors descended from inter-*varṇa* marriages, which have probably always been few. However, the numbers' implications are much wider. While they refer only to *sapiṇḍa* relatives and are tabulated here only according to the *varṇa*s of those relatives, they form a paradigm whose general form recurs in notions regarding non-*sapiṇḍa* survivors who are in other ways substantially connected with and otherwise ordered in relation to the deceased. Thus, students are said to incur incapacity at the deaths of their gurus (Kane 1953: 281), servants at the deaths of their masters (Srinivas 1952: 111), and subjects at the deaths of their kings (Manu 5.82); but no incapacity is said to be incurred by gurus at the deaths of their

[4] The four *varṇa*s are occupational "classes"—learned Brahmans (B), warrior Kṣatriyas (K), farming Vaiśyas (V), and serving Śudras (S). They are said (in *Rg Veda* 10.10) to have been born from the primordial sacrifice and division of *puruṣa*, the original "Man". Some present 'castes' or "genera" (*jāti*s) are identified with certain *varṇa*s or mixtures of *varṇa*s.

[5] Systematic research on actual usages, past and present, remains to be done.

students, masters at the deaths of their servants, or kings at the deaths of their subjects. As in the table above, the upper right (*anuloma*) triangles of such students' and servants' (and many other connected survivors') matrices will thus show some duration of incapacity, while the lower left (*pratiloma*) triangles will show little or none. The numbers in such other matrices may differ, but since the general form of variation in this *sapiṇḍa-varṇa* matrix appears to model many other relations in Hindu society, its underlying logics merit an effort at greater understanding.

Modifications of the above matrix for certain *sapiṇḍa*s are many in *dharmaśāstra*: reduced abstentions and reduced periods of incapacity are calculated for the survivors of young children, students, renouncers, persons dying away from home, and others (Kane 1953: 296–306). I propose explanations for some of the exceptions after dealing with the main formal features of the matrix, which are those of the *sapiṇḍa-varṇa* scheme.

Four formal features of the above matrix beg for explanation: (*i*) an inverse relationship between declining rank and the rising numbers along the main diagonal—10, 12, 15 and 30 days; (*ii*) uniformity of numbers in rows to the right of the main diagonal, where survivors who rank lower than the deceased incur incapacity for periods identical with those incurred by survivors who are of the same rank as the deceased; (*iii*) declining numbers in columns to the left of the main diagonal, where survivors who rank above the deceased incur incapacity for fewer days than survivors who rank equal to or lower than the deceased; (*iv*) the asymmetry in rates of reduction for *sapiṇḍa*s of different *varṇa*s: a Brahman's incapacity reduces from ten days for the death of a *varṇa*-equal to only one day for the death of a Śudra *sapiṇḍa*—a reduction of 90 per cent; but a Śudra, who observes thirty days of incapacity upon the death of an equal, observes ten days for the death of a Brahman *sapiṇḍa*—a reduction of only two-thirds.

II
Orenstein's analysis

Orenstein claims that his 'structural-functional' analysis of death reveals the logic not only of the different periods of 'impurity', but also of the ways in which Hindus understand death, impurity, rank, and kinship in general. In this section I summarise his analysis. I offer a criticism of the theoretical premises on which it is based and of the findings that result from it.

Rank as 'spiritual impurity'

According to Orenstein's postulation, the Hindus of the *dharma* texts perceive all living things to be ranked as relatively 'impure', 'polluted', or 'defiled' (words that he uses synonymously) because they are 'worldly', 'biological' and 'organic'. He asserts, for example, that *varṇa* ranks are determined by levels of 'normal impurity', such that 'low castes were conceived as naturally more deeply implicated with life substance and process than high ones', who are presumed to be more 'spiritual' (1970a: 1359).

Orenstein's antiorganic value-postulation has deep roots, both Western and Indian. Like many 19th century and earlier European scholars, he supposes that Hindus, like Europeans, have been centrally concerned with a conflict between nonworldly and worldly values. He assumes a neoplatonic Western philosophic position which dichotomises and prefers nonworldly spirit, culture, form and law on the one hand, over flesh, materiality, substance and worldly action, on the other. In so doing, he also follows an upaniṣadic and advaita-vedantic Indian tradition which values "renunciation" (*saṃnyāsa*) and eventual "release" (*mokṣa*) as the only way to pure "truth" (*brāhman*), and which speaks of the "coherent" (*dhārmika*),"material" (*bhautika*) world as "illusory" and "impure" (O'Flaherty 1980: 4–5).

Orenstein's assertions on *varṇa* ranking follow directly from an essay by H.N.C. Stevenson (1954: 49–52), who posits a 'Hindu Pollution Concept' (referring to the 'forces of nature' and ritual impropriety) as the negative criterion against which Hindu persons measure their status and guide their behaviour. Orenstein further follows Dumont and Pocock (1959), who like Dumont (1970: 42–3, 47), posit a 'priestly' (Brahmanic) or 'hierarchical' opposition of 'the pure' (spiritual) and 'the impure' (worldly, biological) as the single value of the caste system. 'Impurity' for these authors (and for Douglas [1966]) as well as for Orenstein originates from 'irruptions' of, or contact with, 'organic' life, while 'purity' can be developed only by separation from it. Such views are partly confirmed for Orenstein in ethnographies by Srinivas (1952) and Harper (1964), who describe certain Hindus as living normally in states of moderate impurity (of caste and person) that are subject to alterations toward more and less 'impure' states.

Following Lévi-Strauss' methods, Orenstein attempts to construct his model solely by binary operations. Elaborating on his initial postulation, he defines *varṇa* ranks by repetitions of a single symmetrical contrast (a 'difference' of 'pure' and 'impure'), rather than by any sort of asymmetrical relationship, such as sequential ordering or inclusion. Indeed, he explicitly presumes that only Euclidean 'equivalence relations' (symmetry, reflexivity, transitivity) can provide a contradiction-free set of axioms to explain the logically 'congruent . . . structures' with which he deals (1970b: 22–23).

Kinship as 'spiritual impurity'

Applying his initial postulation once more, Orenstein (1970a: 1358) defines Hindu 'kinship' as a mutual fleshly or organic involvement of the spirit. He thus assimilates it to what popular usage in the West calls 'blood'. In practice, since his *dharmaśāstra* texts do not discuss 'blood kinship', he limits his discussion of Hindu relatedness to a genetic interpretation of the Hindu communities called *sapiṇḍa*s (defined above) and *samanodaka*s.[6] In conformity with Western genetics, Orenstein does not discuss conjugal, ordinary nutritive, residential, educational, political, or other ritual relatedness as Hindu 'kinship', even though these connections are said to entail some periods of death incapacity.

Death for Hindus, Orenstein asserts, is an extremely biological and intrusive event. It multiplies 'impurity' and spreads it among all those who are unfortunate enough to share genetic particles. Time is needed for them to wash away their defilement and to attenuate their kinship with the decedent.

Periods of 'impurity'

According to Orenstein, as death defiles, it acts as a constant multiplier on the various multiplicands of 'normal impurity'. Thus he sees the numbers of days along the matrix's main diagonal as products of the 'impurity' normally carried by persons of each *varṇa*, increased several times over by death. He posits a multiplicand for each *varṇa*, but regards all these numbers as arbitrary and unworthy of detailed consideration.

Two other operations—a 'premise' and a 'bias'—are Orenstein's ways of accounting for the reduced numbers that fill some other cells of the matrix. These two operations also reduce the scope of kinship from his previous definition.

His 'proximity of kinship premise' (1970a: 1363), itself another symmetrical relation, states that differences of 'normal impurity' weaken kinship connections among kinsmen: the greater the difference of *varṇa* either way, the fewer the particles shared between them and the less influence 'death impurity' can have on the differing kin of the deceased. Although not documented ethnographically or textually, such a premise could account for reductions of periods of incapacity away from the main diagonal in certain cells, although it could not account for any particular configuration of reductions, or for the lack of reductions in other cells.

A more specific 'bias'—implicitly an asymmetrical, directional relationship—is then finally postulated by Orenstein to account for the disproportional *varṇa* rates of 'pollution'—reduction (the fourth feature of the matrix noted above). Orenstein here ascribes greater receptive capacity to lower *varṇa*s' kinship connections than to higher.

The lower position is thought to be more intimately involved with

[6] *Samanodaka*s are more remote relatives who are enjoined to give water, but not food, to the same ancestral spirits, and who incur only briefer periods of impurity at each others' deaths.

> biological process and substance than the higher; hence there exists a tendency for a man of lower *varṇa* to be thought of as more intimately akin to his high caste *sapiṇḍa* than was the latter to the former (1970a: 1368).

Thus, after having presumed by the foregoing 'premise' that their mutual biological differences symmetrically reduce the capacity of *both* higher and lower *varṇa*s to affect each other, Orenstein negates half of the effect of that premise by supposing that the lower *varṇa* can still be more affected than the higher. He allows asymmetry to creep in here only as a 'result' of this 'bias', not as an underlying assumption of Hindu thought (1970a: 1367).

In application to each of the exceptional cases that Orenstein addresses—the deaths of children, students, hermits, renouncers and women—his model fails again logically, or empirically, and/or requires some further, awkward amendment.

When young children die, they produce little or no incapacity for their survivors. Orenstein (1970a: 1364–65, 1368–69) reasons about this fact from his 'proximity premise', supposing that infants must be polluted by the biological charge of birth, have not yet been ritually debiologised, and therefore cannot communicate 'impurity' as equals of adults. An empirical difficulty here is that young children, far from being considered "impure" (*aśuddha*) are treated in many *dharmaśāstra* passages as being outside the reckoning of "impurity". If children were reckoned to be especially "impure", as Orenstein supposes, his proximity premise would predict that children incur longer periods of incapacity upon the deaths of related and equally "impure" children—a prediction which is clearly false, since there are no textual statements of such incapacity at all. Here Orenstein offers a 'flexibility' principle and suggests the possibility of textual error—escapes which allow anomalies wherever the analyst's logic proves to be inadequate.

Full periods of incapacity are said by most texts to be caused only by the deaths of adult persons of the "householder" (*gṛhastha*), or second of the four stages. Incapacity is cancelled or reduced for the deaths of males in the first stage—"religious studentship" (*brahmacārya*)—as well as for those in the final two stages—those of "forest-dwelling" (*vānaprastha*) hermitage and of "renunciation" (*saṃnyāsa*). Orenstein argues that persons in these stages must be considered as again different—not as less 'pure' (like children), but as 'purer' than their householder *sapiṇḍa*s, who are in 'normal states of impurity': because they are themselves less organic, their deaths do not produce as great an organic effect. Because they are less organic, such decedents are also less capable of kinship, so that any organic increase at their deaths could not spread (1970a: 1363, 1365). Orenstein points to the separate residences of such nonhouseholders as proof of their reduced genetic kinship. He plausibly refers to their common practice of 'asceticism' (*tapas*) as the means by which their organic natures might be reduced, but does not detail the physiology.

Orenstein recognises that his analysis produces one large anomaly for his proximity premise. In some *dharmaśāstra* texts, married women are bracketed with the Śudra *varṇa* as less "pure", and Orenstein presumes that this is because women are more deeply involved with organic substances than men. If this is so, then by the logic of his proximity premise, the death of a woman, like that of a child or a person of lower *varṇa*, ought not to cause a full period of incapacity for her purer male *sapiṇḍas*. However, this proves not to be the case: women's deaths generate the full periods of incapacity for their male as well as female surviving relatives. Orenstein maintains that this discrepancy with his premise results from an overriding necessity of Hindu kinship systems: regardless of their natures, wives must have purity ranks and kinship capacities equal to their husbands', 'for . . . it is through their bodies that caste purity is maintained' (1970a: 1366).

Potentially the largest, but unrecognised failing of Orenstein's model is its contradiction to Hindu treatments of marriage and fertility, which he ignores. If 'organic involvement' constitutes 'impurity', then like death, the explicitly organic rites of Hindu marriage and procreation (for example, in Bengal as described by Inden and Nicholas [1977: 48–55]), should generate extensive periods of ritual incapacity. In fact, according to *dharmaśāstra*, Hindu marriage and the subsequent reproductive rites entail no "impurity" or "incapacity" for any related persons. Similarly, the relatively slight incapacities occasioned by birth and by, for instance, Tamil girls' puberty rites (Pfaffenberger 1982: 200–06)—two events also ritually recognised as major organic 'irruptions'—seem discrepant with the central understanding of 'impurity' on which Orenstein's model is constructed.

The functions of funerals

Orenstein adopts a holistic and static reflectionism in his 'functionalist' approach to the meaning of death as well as that of 'impurity'. He acknowledges his debt to the 1907 functionalism of Hertz (1960), who in consonance with the early French sociological tradition, posits a reified social consciousness that refutes internal discontinuity:

> society imparts its own character of permanence to the individuals who compose it: because it feels itself immortalized and wants to be so, it cannot normally believe that its members . . . should be fated to die (Hertz 1960: 77).

Orenstein similarly asserts that funeral rites and practices constitute a reaction by a [nonorganic] society to the 'shock' that the organic intrusion of death deals to social continuity. These rites and practices simply 'contribute to the persistence and solidarity of society' (Orenstein 1970a: 1372).

The same sort of functionalism, strongly revived by Berger (1969), recurs in some recent writings on death in Hindu culture. Das (1982: 120–21) and Kaushik (1976: 265–67) both subscribe to this view. Kaushik says in this vein that 'the rituals associated with death try to place the whole event within a wider, all-encompassing reality of the cosmic world, thereby validating the social world which . . . is threatened by the event of death' (1976: 266). Adding such a universal function to his model, Orenstein offers his effort as a complete structural and functional exploration of Hindu 'death impurity'. However, the functionalism that he espouses is a broad and static reflectionism that adds nothing by way of explanation. It tells nothing of *how* the elapse of various numbers of days of incapacity can effect social 'solidarity' and 'continuity'.

Bloch and Parry (1982: 6) suggest that Hertz's reflectionist functionalism may as well be turned on its head, since 'if we can speak of a reassertion of the social order at the time of death, this social order is a *product* of funeral rituals of the kind we consider rather than their cause.' Theirs is a functionalism that does not simply rationalise funeral practices, but rather invites an exploration of the creative or reproductive processes triggered by death. Bloch and Parry's creative functionalism so well fits the explicit intentions of Hindu funeral rites that I undertake such an exploration in the alternative model that follows.

In summary, both the structuralist and functionalist positions forwarded by Orenstein fall short of the complete analysis he claims to be constructing. The structural framework that he would build from a single Western spirit-flesh contrast seems ill-suited to what Hindus take as realities, and therefore to the kind of 'semantic' analysis he wishes to make. Concerns with 'pure and impure' may be conceived to be, in Dumont's (1970: 60) words, 'like an immense umbrella' held over the entire semantic space of Hindu life; but umbrellas are not good tools for differentiating the complexities of meaning. If Hindu terms for "impurity" are to be used as analytic concepts, they themselves require semantic analysis, and if Western concepts like 'purity', 'ranks' and 'kinship' are to be used, they require adaptation to Hindu realities—tasks to which I now turn.

III
An alternative model of rank, kinship and impurity

In this section, I replace Orenstein's alien definitions of Hindu rank, kinship and purity with definitions developed from what may be called an implicit substantive sociology of the Hindus themselves. This sociology may be inferred and constructed from other texts and from recent ethnographies.

Rank and "purity" as three qualities

Hindu ranking defines and may be defined by the qualities of substance, among which the three *guṇa*s (literally "strands") are the metaconceptual terms most widely perceived and used. The three *guṇa* qualities are themselves stated in an order that proceeds from (*i*) *sattva*, meaning among other things, "essentiality" or "goodness", to (*ii*) *rajas*, meaning "passion", "energy", external "activity", to (*iii*) *tamas*, meaning "darkness", "inertia" and "disorder".[7] The *guṇa*s are said to have coexisted originally in an undifferentiated or perfectly balanced state in "nature" (*prakṛti*), according to the Bhagavad Gītā (13.19, 21), or in the person of a primordial deity, according to Viṣṇu Purāṇa (1.2.4) and other texts, and also according to Tamil villagers (Daniel 1984: 4–5). Once disturbed, all agree, the *guṇa*s became distinct, and once distinct, they combined and recombined to produce varied entities and states of flux.

Bhagavad Gītā, Viṣṇu Purāṇa, and later texts generally treat the three *guṇa*s as ubiquitous, independently variable, and intersecting. Beings differ and change because their actions manifest the *guṇa* qualities in varying proportions. Thus, some residents of one Bengali village say that *sattva* predominates in most deities, *rajas* in demons and *tamas* in plants. They say that all substances and entities of the human world—"genera" (*jātis*), "classes" (*varṇa*s), persons, etc.—are constituted by the three *guṇa*s as (*i*) more or less godlike, that is, superior and pervasive (= having more or less of *sattva*); and as (*ii*) more or less externally "active" or "energetic" (= having more or less of *rajas*); and as (*iii*) more or less negative—"ignorant", "veiled", "stupid", or "fearful" (= having more or less of *tamas*) (Davis 1983: 48–49, 51–52). Other common socially evaluative words in the village—"high" versus "low", "big" versus "small", "not good" versus "good" (Davis 1983: 64)—appear also to signal the greater or lesser predominance of the same three *guṇa*s—respectively, *sattva, rajas* and *tamas*.

According to Marriott's (1989) correlations, the *guṇa*s attributed to persons and groups commonly implicate the three principal "aims", "goals", or "concerns" of life (*puruṣārtha*s): (*i*) *sāttvik* action leads to the goal of relative "advantage" (*artha*); (*ii*) *rājasik* action promotes open, hot "attachment" (*kāma*); and (*iii*) disorderly and separative *tāmasik* action opposes the aim of *dharma*, or "appropriateness", "coherence", "union". The intersecting triads of strands and aims together indicate a three-dimensional property-space.

Of special relevance in the present analysis is the ability of the same three scales to distinguish three intersecting meanings of "impure"

[7] Das (1985: 187, 204 fn. 5) points out that while *tamas* refers to sloth and torpor in many classical texts, it often refers to riotous and uncontrolled movement in puranic and popular usage.

(*aśuddha*): (*i*) "low" impurity (which is non-*sāttvik*, or in Marriott's terminology, the 'marked', or receiving end of an asymmetric relationship); (*ii*) "attached" impurity (which is *rājasik*, describing what Marriott identifies as an irreflexive or 'mixing' relationship); (*iii*) and "inappropriate" (*asātmya*) impurity (which is *tāmasik* and thus "incoherent" or *adhārmik*—Marriott's 'unmatching', intransitive relationship).[8]

The "impurity" word *āśauca* and its synonyms are used only for type (*iii*) states of 'unmatching' which are caused by bodily separations at birth and death. These are states of incoherence with consequences for all persons who are part of that body (the *sapiṇḍa*s) and for any others who are sustained by it.

Aśuddha, which is probably the commonest and broadest "impurity" word, may refer to states of (*i*) 'marking'—down-ranking and devaluation; (*ii*) 'mixing'—attachment, heat and heterogeneity of substance; and (*iii*) other kinds of 'unmatching', such as excretions, and 'mismatchings', such as inappropriate timings or locations. Such impurities continually occur in everyday life. They are troublesome, and are especially at issue in rituals, including funerals, but do not separate bodies and do not spread among relatives.[9]

"Purity" (*śuddha*) is definable as the contrary of each of the above—as (*i*) "high" (unmarked), (*ii*) "nonattached", or "homogeneous" (unmixed), and (*iii*) "appropriate" (matched)—and also as none of the above, but as (*iv*) the possibility of transcending the whole property-space and all such substance-linked qualities (Carman 1985: 109–16). The last, nonqualitative kind of "purity" may characterise the highest deity (Davis 1983: 70) or the state of human spiritual "release" (*mokṣa*) that is most like the one definition of 'purity' on which Orenstein unsuccessfully attempts to build his model. While such transcendence helps to define the metaphysical parameters of Hindu life, it is peripheral to most of the concerns of *dharmaśāstra* and to understandings of the rituals reported in most texts and ethnographies.[10]

Estimates of the "qualitative" (*saguṇa*) "purity" (*śuddha*) scalings of *varṇa*s and *āśrama*s, which have been implicitly at issue in Orenstein's discussions of 'death impurity', appear to make use of the whole three-dimensional quality-space sketched above (Davis 1983: 70). Thus, the

[8] The intersecting relations of such diverse meanings of "purity" are depicted in Marriott's (1989) cubical Figure 2.

[9] Orenstein does not distinguish *āśauca* from general *aśuddha* by any Sanskrit nomenclature—he calls them both "impurities". He does, however, take note of this difference by distinguishing (*a*) 'relational pollution' caused by death and birth, which 'spreads' among 'kinsmen', from (*b*) 'act' pollution which results from personal behaviour and does not spread.

[10] Gold (1988: 287–98) details the views of Rajasthani villagers on the near-impossibility of attaining the purity of absolute transcendence and also records some of their many compromises with this view. Few other ethnographies mention "release" as more than a remote ideal.

Bengali villagers reported by Davis say that the Brahman *varṇa* is "high" and most "pure" because *sattva* alone predominates in it, while the Śudra *varṇa* is "low" and "fearful" because it is dominated by *tamas* alone. They say that the Kṣatriya *varṇa* is less "pure", being both "active" and "high", because it is dominated by *rājasik* as well as by *sāttvik* qualities;[11] and the Vaiśya *varṇa* (here apparently thought of in classical terms more as farmers and herdsmen than as traders) is still less "pure", being both "fearful" and "active" because it is dominated by *tamas* as well as *rajas*.[12] Since both Kṣatriyas and Vaiśyas are here strongly characterised by "activity", the middle-ranking *guṇa*, this pair of *varṇa*s can be called "lower" and less "pure" than Brahmans, but "purer" than Śudras (Davis 1983: 51).

Such scalings of the *varṇa*s may affect and be affected by the adequacy of the *saṁskāra* rituals (sketched in Part IV below) by which they process their members. So it appears from correlations like those between *jāti*s' ranks and their numbers of rituals, shown for one village by Davis (1983: 64, 91–92).

The rankings and purities of *āśrama*s similarly involve all three dimensions of the *guṇa* property-space (Davis 1983: 84–87). A beginner in the student *āśrama* is likely to be relatively deficient in *sattva*—he is a receiver, not a giver of truth—and is thus low on that scale of "purity", while the forest-dwelling hermit and the renouncer have climbed to high *āśrama*s on the same scale and the householder to a rung between them—so it is among Kashmiri Pandits (Madan 1987: 10). These Pandits—Brahmans but themselves householders—agree that householders should be able to balance their takings and givings and moderate their activities; but they may also be less "pure" on the *rajas* scale, due to their attachments and to their necessary and appropriate engagements in external interaction (Madan 1987: 32–33). Potentially less "impure" in this *rājasik* sense than the householder are hermits, students and renouncers, who all have less external control, but practise the powerful discipline of "internalising heat" (*tapasyā*). The renouncer is properly a virtuoso of internalisation, and if successful, may be "purer" on the *rajas* scale. The purity comparison between householder and renouncer is thus in general a draw. But along the *tamas-dharma* scale, the renouncer must be rated as the least "pure", indifferent as he is to personal and social coherence; the hermit and student are respectively moving out of and into states of personal and

[11] Viṣṇu Purāṇa (1.6.1–2) differs from these village opinions slightly by holding that the Kṣatriya *varṇa* is dominated by *rajas* alone.

[12] Ethnographic evidence from elsewhere, such as Moreno and Marriott's (1989) report on Ceṭṭiyars in this volume, indicates that the traders (who are more likely to be identified as "Vaiśyas" today) are generally thought of as "cooler" in temperament and less open in their transactions with others, hence as less *rājasik* than Śudras or Kṣatriyas, rather than more; and that Śudras who are agriculturists and herdsmen have inherited the occupation-linked reputations for *rajas* that Davis' informants attribute to Vaiśyas.

social coherence and thus must be rated somewhere between renouncer and householder. Householders (like kings and other *jajmāns* [Raheja 1989]) are potentially the least *tāmasik* and most *dhārmik*, and on this scale have to be rated the best and "purest" (Madan 1987: 30–31).

Reckoned along any of these *guṇa* scales, a person's or group's qualities are not fixed. They are changed by the performance of *saṁskāra* rituals and change with the person's *āśrama*, as above. They are altered by all other activities (Marriott 1976: 111), summarised by the term *karma*, whose full operation is beyond knowing. A person may activate or reduce tendencies toward "purity" (a more *sāttvik*, less *rājasik* and *tāmasik* condition) or "impurity" (a less *sāttvik*, more *rājasik*, and *tāmasik* condition). The qualities produced by action (*karma*) may be more or less consistent with *svadharmas*—the behavioural tendencies already inherent in the substances of particular persons, *varṇas* and *jātis* (Davis 1983: 50)—and if inconsistent may alter those *svadharmas* (ibid.: 69–70).

The qualities of persons of various *varṇas*, *āśramas* and *jātis* are also interactive, that is, they may affect each other through transactions of substances bearing those qualities (Marriott 1976: 111–12; Marriott and Inden 1977). Clearly, the more transactors resemble one another, the less likely they are to alter each other through interpersonal transactions. Thus, members of a single *jāti* may transact substances more freely and openly (with more *rajas*) among themselves than with members of different *jātis*. What makes the members of a *jāti* alike may be in part their repeated mutual transactions.

Because qualities of a giver may be in a thing given and taken, any differences of qualities between givers and takers are important considerations in the exchange of substances. Thus, a Brahman's wastes or leftovers—substances which are impure for him—may be readily received by a person of lower rank because some "goodness" of the giver will be transferred through those substances to the receiver. Substances that originate with lower-ranked persons, on the other hand, may be less "good" and therefore "unsuitable" (*adhārmik*) to persons of higher rank; thus only "purer" (more *sāttvik*, less *rājasik* and *tāmasik*) substances tend to be transferred upwards. Such asymmetrical movements of substantial qualities are what constitute and continually reconstitute the 'rank' or "purity" of relative highness, whether of persons or classes (Marriott 1968, 1976).

Finally, those whose greater control of resources gives them centrality in the distribution of substances and in ritual are able to define and continually redefine "cohesive", "appropriate" (*dhārmik*) organisation as their own achievement, while attributing its lack (and by implication, more *tāmasik* qualities) to their peripheral, non-controlling receivers (Pfaffenberger 1982; Raheja 1988, 1989).

Hindu transactions thus generally bring about and model the same three-dimensional quality-space that is anticipated by the *guṇa* theory of substantive qualities and the triad of aims.

'Kinship' and relatedness

A substance-transactional theory based on such Hindu realities also challenges the notion that persons are related solely through common ancestral bodily substance. Even the sharing of vital "particles" with deceased ancestors requires maintenance through repeated offerings, while cohesion (*dharma*) among living relatives requires continued intensive (*rājasik*) exchanges of the other substances that are necessary for bodily existence.

Transactional practice both emerges from (either confirming or opposing) previous relationships and serves to generate further relatedness. For example, the transactions occurring through sharing the same living space may be sufficient to create a relatedness much like Western 'kinship' among Bengali persons (Inden and Nicholas 1977: 32). Daniel furthermore finds among Tamils that houses, like persons, have natures defined by *guṇa*s and that houses are perceived as sharing and exchanging substances with inhabitants (1984: 140, 161). Co-residents thus come to share in one another's substances not only through direct exchanges among themselves, but also indirectly through their parity relationships to a house. Similarly, many *dharma* texts refer to the "incapacity" not only of persons, but also of houses where a death has occurred (Kane 1953: 321–22). Whole villages may work the same way (Anantha Murthy 1976; Daniel 1984: 101; Inden and Nicholas 1977: 32–33).

In Mahābhārata, as in such ethnography, Hindu relatedness is similarly affected by transactions in media of many kinds (Clay n.d.). It is closest where transactions are primary (*sāttvik*), intensive (*rājasik*) and appropriately sustained (*dhārmik*). Initially through birth, paternal seed constitutes the bones and other more enduring foetal parts; maternal blood constitutes the flesh and softer parts. Once born, the child's body requires mother's milk, sharings of food, water, words, and a unified living place to maintain its natal relatedness. It requires ritual processing as well. Each of these media also provides opportunities for forming relationships with persons other than the parents. Conversely, Hindu relatedness may be reduced or ended for persons who are cut off from the flow of substantial transactions.

Such conceptualisations of purity, rank and relatedness are applied in the following summary of ritual transactions and in the subsequent reinterpretation of periods of impurity.

IV
Unions and separations in domestic ritual

Orenstein represents Hindu death as a regretted organic intrusion into a preferably spiritual life and as an unwanted change in a preferably static personal and social structure. In this section, I will show rather that the Hindu domestic rituals called "*saṁskāras*" treat death as a problematic break in a desired substantial, but dynamic continuity and as an opportunity, like that provided by birth and other domestic rituals, for reshaping personal and social relations. Since all these rituals are understood to reshape interpersonal relations over time, I return through them to the durations of death-caused incapacity and its numerical scheme.

A *saṁskāra* is a kind of action intended to "effect purification" (*śuddhi*), to "refine", "prepare", or "polish" persons, that is, to "form [them] well". The word refers to ways of doing common daily actions such as bathing, feeding and worshipping, as well as to major rites of transition in the lives of certain family members (Davis 1983: 91–92; Inden and Nicholas 1977: 37; Kane 1941: 192–98). Such refinements are intended, say the texts, to remove any "defects" (*dośas*) or "inappropriate" (*adhārmik*) attributes that may otherwise mar the qualities of a person's genetic composition. Daily rites reduce the "adventitious" (*rājasik*) influx of "negative" (*tāmasik*) substances and wash them away, while major rites of initiation, marriage and death attempt to craft a figure or form that is finer, more *sāttvik*, overall.

Saṁskāras are symbolically rich in their dealings with all kinds of "impurity", but here I concentrate on (*tāmasik*) themes of separation and on (*dhārmik*) themes of union, themes that are particularly developed in the *saṁskāras* of birth and death.

Most separations are gradual and inconclusive. As people are modified through the *saṁskāras* and move through the first three *āśramas*, they diminish their intakes of the processed and marked substances of others. But they do not cease to transact. Instead, they become givers rather than receivers, moving "up" from more passive, patient relations in the network of exchange to more active, agentive ones (Rudolph and Rudolph 1976). The "subtle body" (*sukṣma śārīra*) of one who through interpersonal transactions fully achieves the refinements appropriate to a present birth becomes ready for a better rebirth—for a new composition whose refinements can lead through death to yet other births in a continuing cycle of redeaths and rebirths called *saṃsāra* (Inden and Nicholas 1977: 37; Madan 1987: 35–36).

Death effects a three-fold separation. It separates the "spirit" (*jīva*, subtle body, and/or *ātman* soul) from the "gross body" (*sthūla śārīra*), the gross body of the person from the family, and sometimes families from each other. But the spirit can be united with a new subtle body made for it by the living, and then, through this body, can join the "ancestors" (*pitṛs*) and later take rebirth in another earthly gross body, unless released from further rebirth through dwelling beside the deity or merging with the bodiless *brāhman*. The former family body continues without the deceased, modifying its networks of transactions, possibly splitting apart (especially upon the death of the head of an extended household), yet in so doing often reforming its constituents to accommodate new marriages and new births.

The disunities or unmatching separations occurring at birth, like those at death, provide material for combinations that will emerge later as new personal and familial bodies. Hindu ritual treatments of death and birth are notably similar in that both entail periods of "incapacity" (*āśauca*) following the separations of parts of an entity that continue until the resulting new bodies are made viable and reconnected.

Marriage. Hindu ritual treatments of marriage are similar in their concerns for making viable bodies. Marriage rites work to unite two persons into one, and to make substantial connections among families. Bride and groom are prepared: they are bathed, they have their hair cut, they fast in order that each may carry no extraneous markings and may be readily mixed and merged with the substances to be received from the other (Inden and Nicholas 1977: 41). The bride's departure creates a crisis of partial separation for her natal family, but a climax of union or incorporation for the groom and his family. At a high caste Bengali marriage, the priest, with his hands over the groom and the bride, 'seals the gift and acceptance by pouring water over their joined hands' (ibid.: 43), at which juncture the groom's hands are placed above the bride's. When the bride begins to reside with her husband's family, more rites of union are performed. Most important among these is the husband's family's sharing of boiled rice cooked by the bride. The bride here moves close to the *dhārmik* centre of her new family.

Reproduction. Concern with promoting fertility—with the "auspicious" (*śubha*), productive merger of bodies and the "purity" of their well-matched, *dhārmik* union—predominates in the rituals of marriage. Marriage rituals ignore the "impure" (*aśuddha*) situation created by the intentionally warm or *rājasik* mixing and the *tāmasik* separations of sexual substances, which they also necessarily encourage (Madan 1987: 60). Sexual union makes openings for growth, as a plough opens the earth for seed and fruitfulness (Egnor 1978: 197–98). Marriage is on the whole "pure" and "auspicious" because it appropriately and desirably expands the family body.

Inside the woman, male and female fluids mix by *rājasik* processes that create a united, *dhārmik* body for a new life's habitation. The rites of conception are directed to 'the union and fertility of the husband and wife'. Once conceived, the embryo forms a continuing unity with the mother who contains it (Inden and Nicholas 1977: 55).

Birth. Rites of parturition begin a division of this intensely organic union, but always with provisions for substantial continuity. After the Bengali father offers food to the ancestors, he 'cleanses' the baby's tongue with rice powder, gold and ghee; he chants *mantra*s into the ears of a son. Only then is the umbilical cord cut. At this body-separative moment, the household enters a period of "incapacity" that is slight for all except mother and child, who have separated, and who are restricted for ten days while the bodies of both are healed and made ready for wider interactions (Inden and Nicholas 1977: 55–56).

Childhood. Egnor (1978: 87) notes that among Tamils, "birth" means not just parturition, which is a separation, but also the beginning of a union between the child and the larger world. The child is introduced slowly to this world. On the tenth night after birth, the child is named and begins receiving other verbal transactions from other members of the household.

After five to eight months, the mother's brother opens a channel to maternal kin, who usually reside elsewhere, by feeding the child its first boiled rice. Then the child is displayed to the neighbourhood or village, its name announced, and its inclusion in the male descent line formalised (Davis 1983: 96; Inden and Nicholas 1977: 56–58).

Later saṁskāras. The subsequent *saṁskāras* are sex-differentiated. Boys receive more elaborate *saṁskāras* and a greater number of them than their sisters. With each *saṁskāra*, more unions are made, more intersections with more persons, and more inclusions in wider spheres of transactions (Davis 1983: 106; Madan 1987: 35).

At death, incorporation is once more achieved. The subtle body of the deceased is made to join slowly with ancestors and is thus prepared for rebirth. I trace parallels between birth and death in greater detail below. Periods of impurity in both death and birth prove to be not empty times for psychological adjustment but are rather active occasions for rearranging substantial and especially bodily relations.

Funeral rites

Death and birth both begin with separations that cause "incapacity" and both are ended through ritual incorporations.[13] Death causes more incapacity than birth, but not because it is treated as a reversal or a negation of birth. A baby at birth can be particulately related only to ancestors, parents and collaterals, so that the birth separation creates relatively little incapacity. But decedent adults are likely to have transacted particles with many others—with spouses, with those to whom they have given birth, with those for whom they have provided sustenance, and so on. The incapacities caused by separations at an adult's death therefore ramify and descend to a wider body of related persons.

Separations begin.[14] Prior to a death, if possible, gifts are made by the family to an unrelated Brahman on behalf of their dying member. Recommended gifts vary, but may include land, sesame, gold, ghee,

[13] Tamil rituals treat the deceased first as a lifeless body—exterior, unfruitful, hard and dry—but later emphasise union, interiority, fruitfulness, openness and wetness (Egnor 1978: 75, 196). These contrary ritual phases seem thus formally to take account of, while opposing in their sequence, the ambivalent emotional tendencies noted by Das (1986: 197).

[14] This composite description draws repeatedly on the following sources: Das 1977, 1982, 1986; Dumont 1986; Kane 1953; Kaushik 1976; Madan 1987; Moffatt 1968; Pandey 1969; Parry 1982a, 1982b; Raheja 1988; S. Stevenson 1920. Only unique data and some other sources are specifically cited in the text.

grains, clothing, salt and silver (Kane 1953: 182–83). Important also is the gift of a cow, thought to help the deceased pass from this world to that of the ancestors. Gifts such as these are also means of ridding the dying person and the survivors of the inauspiciousness and sense of sin or guilt resulting from death (Khare 1976: 177; Madan 1987: 60, 134–35; Raheja 1988: 147–56). The variety of gifts made at funerals also affirms the continuity of social organisation in the family and larger communities (Das 1986: 195, 202; Vatuk 1975).

Inside the house, family members move the dying person to a place on the earth near the exit (Kaushik 1976: 271; Moffatt 1968: 36; Kane 1953: 182). This place is itself made "pure" (*śuddha*) with water, a new mat, or *darbha* grass so that the dying person will be free of any clinging particles of inappropriate substance that could mar the best possible rebirth (Madan 1987: 120–26). Whispered in the ear of a dying person, *mantra*s or other sacred words—high, *sāttvik* substances—may be said to wash away low and scattered thoughts, focusing the dying person's attention on future union with what is superior and also central, appropriately cohesive, *dhārmik*.

When news of the death reaches relatives who are at meals, they stop eating their normal food because of the broken, "incapacitated" state of their shared body. Cooking at the regular family hearths is suspended and only saltless (nonuniting) food is eaten while the incapacity lasts. The widow breaks the glass marriage bangles from her arms: she has lost part of her outer-bodily self.

In preparation for the cremation, attention is lavished on the corpse, which is laid with head pointing south, toward the *dhārmik* abode of Yama, god of the dead. Still sheltering the subtle body or soul of the person, the corpse is shaved and bathed to wash away any loose bodily particles: moist, cool and integral, it is made as "pure" (*śuddha*) in all senses—as *sāttvik* and as non-*rājasik* and non-*tāmasik* as possible. The more elaborate and Brahmanical variants of funeral rites include cleaning and blocking all bodily orifices with cotton and ghee against influx or outflow of substance (Kaushik 1976: 277). The vulnerable and disordered body is thus brought to a state of closure and separation from the world's usual exchanges.

The corpse is then dressed in new clothing and covered with a shroud. A deceased female is dressed according to her marital status: an unmarried girl is dressed as a bride; a wife is dressed in a red (for fertility) saree with ornaments, and a widow in plain white. The corpse is garlanded. Rice and gold, reminiscent of a father's first gifts to his child, are placed in the corpse's mouth.

The cremation site is typically located outside and to the south of any residential place. The ground, the mourners and especially the chief mourner are made "pure" (*śuddha*), the last with shaving, manicure, and new clothing, like the corpse.

Before setting out, members of the funeral procession circumambulate the corpse in an auspicious, incorporative and honorific manner, that is, with their right sides turned toward it. The principal agnates shoulder the bier, thus assisting the deceased's journey ahead, but first touch the bier with their left shoulder; they thus assume a newly inauspicious, separative relationship (Das 1986: 190). Their own path ahead sprinkled with water, they may be followed by others bearing fire for the cremation from the house's ancestral altar. The procession moves to successively more exterior places, pausing at any threshold or boundary to leave balls of cooked rice for unembodied, possibly hungry, peripheral spirits.

Both funeral pyre and corpse are treated finally with "pure" (unmarked, unmixed, matched) substances such as gold, sesame seed, ghee and water. Rice balls for its sustenance during the journey may be placed upon the corpse.

So far the funeral rituals emphasise the closure of a personal, bodily life and its honoured exit from within a continuing social organisation. They contrast with the emphasis on opening and entering in the *saṁskāras* up to and including marriage.

Cremation: further separations. Before lighting the fire, the chief mourner circumambulates the pyre with his left side toward the corpse, separating himself from it. Midway through the burning, he may crack the skull to allow an appropriate escape for the "ghost", (*preta*) or subtle body. The elements of the gross body are separated by the cremation fire. While the fire still smoulders, the chief mourner again circumambulates the fire to the left, this time dripping water "to cool the fire" from a perforated earthen pot, which is finally smashed near the head of the charred corpse (Kaushik 1976: 272, 278; Kane 1941: 214; Moffatt 1968: 50–51). All present at the cremation separate themselves from the scene by bathing before returning home.

Left are a disembodied ghost, a family body in a state of "incapacity" because it has lost some vital part, and a pile of ash and bone. On the third day (or earlier in some versions) the chief mourner returns to the cremation site, further cools the site with water and milk, then gathers remnants of the bones and ashes for immersion in a river. At this point the tasks of reforming all entities and relationships begin.[15]

New unions and reunions. Destructive separation (*pralaya*) is a prelude to constructive reunion and regeneration in many Hindu cosmic myths (Parry 1982b: 76; Shulman 1980: 90) and it is so in the funeral rituals as well.

The regenerative phase is the most complex and time-consuming. For twelve or thirteen days, the high caste family performs daily *śrāddha* feedings and waterings of the ghost to assist its reembodiment and prepare

[15] In the Rajasthani ethnography by Gold (1988: 241–60), the water in which the bones are immersed is directly taken home as a substance promoting future family fertility. Here the completion of separation and the beginning of reunification are almost simultaneous.

it for a year-long passage toward a full union with the "ancestors" (*pitṛs*). The "ghost" ultimately forms union on potentially three planes: as ancestor dwelling in the "world of the ancestors" (*pitṛlok*), collectively represented in the family altar; as resident of a world called "heaven" (*svarga*) that is populated by gods; and as the "life force" (*jīva*) of a new foetus born into this world.

According to some views, the spirit or soul of a person whose refinement transcends embodiments like the above may alternatively achieve release from rebirth and redeath. Universal expectation of such transcendence would support Orenstein's antiorganic model, but ethnographers testify that release is regarded as difficult and rare, if it is desired at all (e.g., Gold 1988: 287–98; Pfaffenberger 1982: 103–04).

For ten days, the ghost hovers near its surviving family members, perhaps as unwilling as they are to maintain the recent separation (Das 1986: 193, 198; Gold 1988: 63–79). It receives water, milk and rice balls (*piṇḍa*s) from the family. While keeping open a channel of nourishment between the living and the deceased, these feedings create a new subtle body for the ghost. On the tenth day, the ghost's bodily viability apart from its previous life-world is complete. Its ultimate union as an ancestor with previous ancestors is anticipated by a merging of rice-ball bodies in the *sapiṇḍī-karaṇa* ("the making of a *sapiṇḍa*") ritual, which is conducted either then or later.

The ghost-feeding channel is also one of bodily life, since eating these rice balls after their uses as offerings is thought to help a pregnant woman grow her foetus. The ten days of feeding are analogous to the ten lunar months counted for a pregnancy. The rice balls of the twelfth day, which represent the united ancestors, may be eaten after the ritual by a childless woman who wishes to conceive (Knipe 1977; Parry 1982b: 85).

Survivors who have observed the most complete restrictions may bathe, shave and cut their nails after offering the tenth day's *piṇḍa*s. Some consider that their incapacity ends then, others at the thirteenth day, and still others wait for a full thirty days.[16] The end of their incapacity and separation is marked with a communal feast given by the deceased's family and with a subsequent resumption of ordinary activities and transactions.

The ghost's full passage southward to the abode of the ancestors takes one year and is aided by a schedule of subsequent *śrāddha* feedings. On reaching its goal and merging with previous ancestors, it simultaneously attains a place in the home's interior altar. Just short of its ancestral goal, it must cross over a river of blood and foul substance, a passage that Parry likens to that of birth (1982b: 85).

In sum, death is made into several kinds of birth. The separations that death introduces into family continuity are resolved into new unities. Once

[16] See note 4.

the separations of death occur, new unions of the deceased's constituents are actively sought. The family helps the ghost to become an ancestor and thus, albeit in a new and subtle form, to be again part of the family body; and the family once more enters the community of transactions from which death had separated them by making their family body temporarily "incapable"—disunited, *tāmasik*.

V
A reanalysis of periods of incapacity

Assuming the gross and subtle bodies postulated by Hindus and interpreting the funeral as a ten-day period of gestation for a new subtle body, I can now attempt a reanalysis of the incapacities caused by death. The different periods with their variants and exceptions respond to three substantial and transactional variables that are real for Hindus:

(*a*) Persons and families whose bodies are constituted of relatively cohesive (*dhārmik* and non-*tāmasik*) substance—those who are more central in their transactional networks—are more resistant to the shocks of death and more able to disperse those *tāmasik* influences appropriately to their peripheries. Their periods of incapacity should be shorter. Persons of less cohesive substance—transactionally peripheral people—are more susceptible to the separations of death, more likely to receive, and less able to disperse them. They and those sharing their greater disturbance will need longer periods to reunite them.

(*b*) Persons of superior (*sāttvik*) substance—those who subordinate others through their channels for asymmetrical transactions—act with greater knowledge and influence. They have themselves more comprehensive grasp and, like those who are more *dhārmik*, can avoid and dispose more easily of unwanted influences. They conduct and/or command more effective domestic rituals which can transform incoherence into coherence. They should thus require relatively few days to repair an incapacity caused by death. Persons lower in *sattva* must obey and more often receive incapacitating influences from above; they will need more time to regain a broken capacity.

(*c*) Persons and families of more energetic or "externally active" (*rājasik*) natures—those who have larger and more active transactional networks—are potentially more vulnerable to and productive of bodily disruption, but are also able to act with greater vigour to deal with it externally. Persons with less external and more "internal activity" (*tapasyā*) are on the other hand both less open to receiving and more capable of disposing of problems internally. The average net effect of greater "external activity" should thus be intermediate upon the period of incapacity. The diminution of external activity is, however, a diminution of relatedness.

Numerical problems. If these three qualitative and transactional variables have been cogently stated, then the table of periods of incapacity for *sapiṇḍa* relatives by *varṇa* should be explicable from them. The explicanda that I take up first are the four formal features of the table that were noted in Part I, beginning with the rising sequence of numbers—10, 12, 15 and 30—along the main diagonal. Here the effects of all three factors are evidently seen in combination.

1. The Brahman *varṇa* with 10 days and Kṣatriya with 12 evidently suffers the least incapacity from death. Their relatively rapid recoveries from such incapacity can be anticipated, since these *varṇa*s are first and second in general "purity" and are much alike. Both are said to have much *sattva* and little *tamas* in their natal substance, and both command a great number of domestic rituals to maintain these superior and cohesive properties. Both have self-elevating, self-centralising patterns of transaction with other *varṇa*s. Qualitatively, Kṣatriyas are generally said to be slightly behind Brahmans in general purity, being less wholly dominated by *sattva*, since *rajas* is also a dominant quality of their substance.

Vaiśyas with 15 days of incapacity follow closely behind the two top *varṇa*s. They are said to follow in general purity as well. Peripheral and subordinate to Brahmans and Kṣatriyas transactionally, Vaiśyas are labelled as lower in *sattva* and as more *tāmasik*. But Vaiśyas command refining rituals along with higher *varṇa*s, most notably the ritual of "second birth", and enjoy (along with Kṣatriyas) a predominance of *rajas*, the giving and taking of energy. With this mixture of purifying and possibly polluting properties and processes, Vaiśyas need, as might be predicted, an intermediate number of days to recover from their incapacity at death—half the number of days needed by the Śudra *varṇa*.

Sudras in all respects appear most capable of causing and least capable of repairing death's disruptions. They have more strongly *tāmasik* natures than all the others, are deficient in both *rajas* and *sattva*, and lack the domestic rituals for their own refinement. Transactionally they can be described as restrained, subordinated and peripheralised as controllees and dependants of the other *varṇa*s. Thirty days—the longest period of death-caused incapacity—is expectable for them.

Away from the main diagonal, formal features (2), (3), and (4) are all approximately predictable if one assumes—as the pervasive quality of "superiority" (*sattva*) and the universal seeking of "advantage" (*artha*) assert—the general (but not total) prevalence of asymmetrical relations: everything is more or less up and whatever is more up tends more to come down. Higher persons influence lower more than lower influence higher. The matrix's asymmetrical features follow accordingly.

2. In the upper right (*anuloma*) triangle of the table's matrix, relatives of lower *varṇa* are shown to be pervaded fully by any incoherence caused by the death of a higher relative. These relatives are incapacitated for identical numbers of days as their superior relative. The downward force of *sattva* is here complete.

3. In the lower left (*pratiloma*) triangle, relatives of higher *varṇa* are affected only partially by deaths among their lower relatives. The table registers the otherwise common ethnographic fact that constraints are placed on upward transactions: higher persons maintain their own superior substance by reducing their acceptances of substance from inferior persons. Asymmetry is still evident.

4. Here the explicandum is the uneven extent to which survivors in one *varṇa* incur incapacity from decedent relatives in other *varṇas*, compared with the incapacity incurred from relatives of their own *varṇa*. The explanation is again supplied by the assumption of a pervasive asymmetry (implied by *sattva*): higher persons are perceived to give more of value, lower to receive more; those who have received more are affected proportionally more when transactions are terminated by death.

Exceptions. A further test for this model lies in the ease with which it accounts for what Orenstein considers anomalies in his analysis as well as for other exceptions that he does not address.

The full and equal participation of wives and husbands in causing and incurring incapacity (an 'anomaly' for Orenstein) is no anomaly for a transactional model, since spouses are the most intimate and intensive (read *rājasik*) of mutual transactors. A wife cooks food for her husband who, by eating, consumes particles of her; in return she eats his leftovers, consuming particles of him. They mix and unite so profoundly in each other's bodily substance that they are treated in some rituals as a single person. Yet each also has many other distinct relationships.

When young children die they produce only brief periods of incapacity as a logical consequence of their slight previous differentiation. Their "coherence" (*dharma*) with their surviving parents is so nearly complete that their deaths are more like minor injuries to that body than like its breakage. Only later in life when they develop capacities as distinct transactors do children qualify as relatives. Only then do their deaths generate full periods of incapacity for their survivors.

Persons in life stages other than that of householders logically generate little or no incapacity by their deaths because of their minimal external "activity" (*rajas*). The vedic student, the hermit, and the renouncer (especially the latter) attempt to close themselves off from ordinary transactions. Without exchanges of vital substance, previous relatedness atrophies. Moreover, the renouncer has already "died" (separated from his relatives) at the time of his renunciation and has no more incapacity to affect his survivors.

'Non-kin'. Once it is realised that for the Hindus of *dharmaśāstra* vital relatedness is not limited to genetic bodily substance, then the incapacities incurred by survivors who are not related by descent become intelligible. Students classically receive shelter, food and education—mental substance—from their guru. Servants receive and absorb sustenance from their master.

Subjects may receive protective shelter and punishment from their king. Incapacity can descend to all these dependants at the death of their *sāttvik* source.

VI
Conclusions

The assumption that Hindus share the Western valuation of 'pure' spirit over 'impure' flesh and are mainly motivated by a quest for spiritual release from this world seems to have led Orenstein and others to misunderstand Hindu concerns with ranking and purity as antiorganic and to misinterpret Hindu death rituals as efforts by the survivors to reduce their bodily involvement and their kinship with the deceased.

Adopting Hindu assumptions and terms of analysis I have counter-proposed a model of rank and relatedness that recognises as "impure" (*aśuddha*) whatever degrades the three main qualities of substance and as "incapacitating" (*āśauca*) whatever disrupts the continuity of bodily life. By this model, rank, purity and kinship are all constructed from transactions of substance among bodies. Periods of incapacity at death are times for reconstructing bodies and reviving bodily relations, and the periods' differing durations are derived logically from the model's three dimensions of relationships.

Such a pragmatic model may well replace the antiorganic models and reflectionist functional interpretations which have hitherto been taken as authoritative. Continuing to interpret periods of death-caused incapacity as spiritual and/or emotional paralysis resulting from organic intrusion would be inaccurate and would obscure understanding of the pragmatic operations of death rituals. Members' deaths may indeed disrupt a family body, but domestic ritual treats such disruptions as occasions for refining the substance and spirit of the decedent and for promoting the continuity of the family. Birth, growth and rebirth are principal concerns of Hindu funerals.

Further applications of this substantial, transactional, pragmatic model are possible and desirable. Ethnographies and the books of *dharmaśāstra* abound with other variants requiring interpretation, and new field data will be needed for further tests of the model's deductions. Until such data raise insurmountable contradictions, the present model should serve. By reasoning from Hindu realities, it accounts with ease for differences among periods of incapacity at death.

REFERENCES

Anantha Murthy, U.R 1976. *Saṁskāara: a rite for a dead man* (trans. A.K. Ramanujan). Delhi: Oxford University Press.

BERGER, PETER L. 1969. *The social reality of religion*. London: Faber and Faber.

BHAGAVAD GĪTĀ. 1969. *The Bhagavad-gītā* (trans. R.C. Zaehner). London: Oxford University Press.

BLOCH, MAURICE, and JONATHAN PARRY. 1982. *Death and the regeneration of life*. Cambridge: Cambridge University Press.

CARMAN, JOHN B. 1985. Conclusion: axes of value in Hindu society. *In* John B. Carman and Frederique Apffel Marglin, eds., *Purity and auspiciousness in Indian society*, pp. 109–20. Leiden: E. J. Brill.

CLAY, THOMAS WHARTON. n.d. Person and family as units of kinship in the Mahabharata. Unpublished Master's paper. Chicago: Department of Anthropology, University of Chicago.

DANIEL, E. VALENTINE. 1984. *Fluid signs: being a person the Tamil way*. Berkeley: University of California Press.

DAS, VEENA. 1977. On the categorization of space in Hindu ritual. *In* R.K. Jain, ed., *Text and context: the social anthropology of tradition*, pp. 9–27. Philadelphia: Institute for the Study of Human Issues.

———. 1982. *Structure and cognition: aspects of Hindu caste and ritual*. 2nd ed. Delhi: Oxford University Press.

———. 1985. Paradigms of body symbolism: an analysis of selected themes in Hindu culture. *In* Richard Burghart and Audrey Cantlie, eds., *Indian religion*, pp. 180–207. London: Curzon Press.

———. 1986. The work of mourning: death in a Punjabi family. *In* Merry I. White and Susan Pollok, eds., *The cultural transition*, pp. 179–210. Boston, Routledge and Kegan Paul.

DAVIS, MARVIN G. 1983. *Rank and rivalry: the politics of inequality in rural West Bengal*. Cambridge: Cambridge University Press.

DOUGLAS, MARY. 1966. *Purity and danger: an analysis of concepts of pollution and taboo*. London: Routledge and Kegan Paul.

DUMONT, LOUIS. 1970. *Homo hierarchicus: the caste system and its implications* (trans. Mark Sainsbury). Chicago: University of Chicago Press.

———. 1986. *A south Indian subcaste: social organization and religion of the Pramalai Kallar* (trans. Michael Moffatt and L. and A. Morton). Delhi: Oxford University Press.

DUMONT, LOUIS, and DAVID POCOCK. 1959. Pure and impure. *Contributions to Indian sociology* 3: 9–39.

EGNOR, MARGARET TRAWICK. 1978. The sacred spell and other conceptions of life in Tamil culture. Ph. D. dissertation, Anthropology. Chicago: University of Chicago Library.

GOLD, ANN GRODZINS. 1988. *Fruitful journeys: the ways of Rajasthani pilgrims*. Berkeley: University of California Press.

HARPER, EDWARD B. 1964. Ritual pollution as an integrator of caste and religion. *In* Edward B. Harper, ed., *Religion in South Asia*, pp. 151–96. Seattle: University of Washington Press.

HERTZ, ROBERT. 1960. *Death and the right hand* (trans. Rodney and Claudia Needham). Aberdeen: University Press.

INDEN, RONALD B., and RALPH W. NICHOLAS. 1977. *Kinship in Bengali culture*. Chicago: University of Chicago Press.

KANE, PANDURANG VAMAN. 1941. *History of dharmasastra, Vol. II*. Poona: Bhandarkar Oriental Research Institute.

———. 1953. *History of dharmasastra, Vol. IV*. Poona: Bhandarkar Oriental Research Institute.

KAUSHIK, MEENA. 1976. The symbolic representation of death. *Contributions to Indian sociology* (n.s.) 10: 265–92.

KHARE, RAVINDRA SAHAI. 1976. *The Hindu hearth and home*. New Delhi: Vikas Publishing House.

Knipe, David M. 1977. Sapiṇḍīkāraṇa: the Hindu rite of entry into heaven. *In* Frank E. Reynolds and Earle H. Waugh, eds., *Religious encounters with death: insights from the history and anthropology of religions*, pp. 111–24. University Park PA: Pennsylvania State University Press.

Kolenda, Pauline. 1978. *Caste in contemporary India: beyond organic solidarity*. Menlo Park CA: Benjamin/Cummings.

Madan, Triloki Nath. 1987. *Non-renunciation: themes and interpretations of Hindu culture*. Delhi: Oxford University Press.

Manu. 1886. *The laws of Mānu* (trans. Georg Bühler). Sacred books of the East, vol. 25. Oxford: Clarendon Press.

Marglin, Frédérique Apffel. 1977. Power, purity, and pollution: aspects of the caste system reconsidered. *Contributions to Indian sociology* (n.s.) 11: 245–79.

Marriott, McKim. 1968. Caste ranking and food transactions: a matrix analysis. *In* Milton Singer and Bernard S. Cohn, eds., *Structure and change in Indian society*, pp. 133–71. Chicago: Aldine.

———. 1976. Hindu transactions: diversity without dualism. *In* Bruce Kapferer, ed., *Transaction and meaning: directions in the anthropology of exchange and symbolic behavior*, pp. 109–42. Philadelphia: Institute for the Study of Human Issues.

———. 1989. Constructing an Indian ethnosociology. *In* this volume.

Marriott, McKim, and Ronald Inden. 1977. Toward an ethnosociology of South Asian caste systems. *In* Kenneth David, ed., *The new wind: changing identities in South Asia*, pp. 227–38. The Hague: Mouton Publishers.

Mines, Diane Paull. 1985. Remaking the dead and ranking the survivors; an analysis of Hindu periods of death impurity. Unpublished Master's paper, Department of Anthropology, University of Chicago.

Moffatt, Michael. 1968. The funeral in south India. Unpublished B. Litt. thesis in Social Anthropology, Oxford University.

Nicholas, Ralph W. 1982. Sraddha, impurity, and relations between the living and the dead. *In* T.N. Madan, ed., *Way of life: king, householder, renouncer*, pp. 366–79. Delhi: Vikas Publishing House.

———. 1980. Karma and rebirth in the vedas and puranas. *In* Wendy O'Flaherty, ed., *Karma and rebirth in classical Indian traditions*, pp. 3–37. Berkeley: University of California Press.

Orenstein, Henry. 1970a. Death and kinship in Hinduism: structural and functional interpretations. *American anthropologist* 72: 1357–77.

———. 1970b. Logical congruence in Hindu sacred law: another interpretation. *Contributions to Indian sociology* (n.s.) 4: 22–35.

Pandey, Raj Bali. 1969. *Hindu saṁskāras: Socio-religious study of the Hindu sacraments*. Delhi: Motilal Banarsidass.

Parry, Jonathan P. 1979. *Caste and kinship in Kangra*. London: Routledge and Kegan Paul.

———. 1982a. Death and cosmogony in Kashi. *In* T.N. Madan, ed., *Way of life: king, householder, renouncer*. Delhi: Vikas Publishing House.

———. 1982b. Sacrificial death and the necrophagous ascetic. *In* Maurice Bloch and Jonathan Parry, eds., *Death and the regeneration of life*, pp. 74–110. Cambridge: Cambridge University Press.

Pfaffenberger, Bryan. 1982. *Caste in Tamil culture: the religious foundations of Sudra domination in Tamil Sri Lanka*. Syracuse: Maxwell School of Citizenship and Public Affairs.

Raheja, Gloria Goodwin. 1988. *The poison in the gift: ritual, prestation, and the dominant caste in a north Indian village*. Chicago: University of Chicago Press.

———. 1989. Centrality, mutuality, and hierarchy: shifting aspects of inter-caste relationships in north India. *In* this volume.

Ramanujan, A.K. 1989. Is there an Indian way of thinking? *In* this volume.
Rudolph, Susanne H., and Lloyd I. Rudolph. 1976. Rajput adulthood: reflections on the Amar Singh diary. *Daedalus* 102: 145–67.
Shulman, David Dean. 1980. *Tamil temple myths: sacrifice and divine marriage in the south Indian Śaiva tradition*. Princeton: Princeton University Press.
Srinivas, M.N. 1952. *Religion and society among the Coorgs of south India*. Oxford: Clarendon Press.
Stevenson, H.N.C. 1954. Status evaluation in the Hindu caste system. *Journal of the royal anthropological institute* 84: 45–65.
Stevenson, Mrs. Sinclair. 1920. *The rites of the twice-born*. London: Humphrey Miford, Oxford University Press.
Tambiah, Stanley J. 1973. From varna to caste through mixed unions. *In* Jack Goody, ed., *The character of kinship*, pp. 191–229. Cambridge: Cambridge University Press.
Vatuk, Sylvia. 1975. Gifts and affines in north India. *Contributions to Indian sociology* (n.s) 9: 155–96.
Viṣṇu Purāṇa. 1972. *The Viṣṇu purāna, a system of Hindu mythology and tradition* (trans. H.H. Wilson). Calcutta: Punthi Pustak.

6

Eating sins in Karimpur

Susan S. Wadley and Bruce W. Derr

Translation of an article that appeared in *Amar ujala* (Agra), 30 April 1984, page 7.

Mainpuri 29 April. About 11 km. from Mainpuri, in Kuraoli Thana, in village Karimpur,[1] about 8:45 at night there was a big fire. We received information that many lives and possessions were destroyed by the fire.

In this event three ladies and three children burned and died. Thirty-one houses were destroyed and a large number of cattle died in the fire.

We learned that there was a big dust storm [*āndhī*] about 8:45 pm in the village. At the same time the *chaupar* [thatch over the verandah] of Pandit Ramchandra Pandey caught fire. Because of the wind, the fire spread very quickly and immediately destroyed thirty-one houses. These people died in the fire: three ladies—Smt. Sheila Devi (23 years), Smt. Saroj Devi (33 years), Radha Devi (50 years), Sheila Devi's one and a half year old son, and Saroj Devi's 12 year old Raghubar and 3 year old Guddu. They burned and died tragically. Four horses, two water buffaloes, one donkey, and one water buffalo calf of villager Girish *dhobī* also died. Other than this, some cattle of Mahesh also died in the fire.

[1] Pseudonym used by the authors for this community. All names of villagers used in the text of the paper are also pseudonyms and correspond to those used in other writings on Karimpur by the Wisers (1971) and ourselves. Research on which this paper is based was carried out in 1983–84 by the authors, with the assistance of Monisha Behal, Umesh Chandra Pandey and Nanhe Khan. Research was funded by a Faculty Research Grant from the US Department of Education and by a Special Foreign Currency Fund Project Grant from the Smithsonian Institution. We thank these agencies for their support. To our many friends in Karimpur who suffered in greater and lesser degrees from the events described here, we send our thanks for their aid in explicating their understanding of this tragedy. Unfortunately, nothing we write can compensate for the losses incurred in the fire.

With this fire, Rajju of the same village had currency notes of Rs 23,000 burn and become ash. These he had kept to use in his daughter's marriage. In addition, thousands of rupees of wealth of Munsilal Dixit, Krishna Lal, Mohan, Mahesh Dube, Ramlal, Daya Ram, Shri Krishna, and Bed Ram were destroyed.

Some bags of urea were burned from the Cooperative Godown's 20,000 bags.

As soon as information came of this incident, the fire brigade, under H.S. Malik, controlled the enormous fire within one hour after much hard work. As soon as they received information of the fire, District Magistrate Shri Rajendra Bhonwal, and police chief SSP Shri Karam Vir Singh inspected the site of this tragedy. And they met with those people who were affected. MLA Shri Lalu Singh Chauhan and Social Services Officer, Shri Anand Swarup Aggrawal also visited the village and met the suffering families. MLA Shri Chauhan described this accident to the Government. He asked the Government to give aid very quickly to the suffering families. According to Chauhan, 'everything these families owned has been destroyed. It is a great problem for those families who have suffered.'

With, in actuality, twenty houses seriously burned, plus six humans and twelve animals dead, the village known as Karimpur faced a crisis. Initially, the village responded as a unit, with the sensed disaster shared by all, whether burned out or not.

> Impressive was the quick reaction of the emergency squads . . . the official attention today, and the spirit of *communitas* in the village today. It will be interesting to see how long it lasts.
>
> –Field notes, BWD, 29 April.

Within hours, explanations emerged to explain this enormously tragic event and the ensuing governmental response.

> The villagers say that Sanīcar is the god who brings 12 years of bad times upon people, the fire occurred on *sanīcar*[2] (Saturday) and it has certainly brought 12 years of bad luck on those families affected.
>
> –Field notes, BWD, 29 April.

Not surprisingly, the mutual commiseration expressed early on 29 April was quickly eroded by the scramble to gain from the government's largesse: the disaster originally perceived as public and general was reassessed to

[2] The day of *sanīcar* is noted for its potential problems, ruled as it is by the god, Sanīcar. The twelve years of *okhā*, troubles caused by Sanīcar, are well known in village religious tales. They are prominent in the very popular epic known as Ḍholā, commonly sung in the vi[llage]

justify compensations claimed for varying degrees of private mental and financial distress. Moreover, generalised explanations in terms of the sorrows of Sanīcar were also particularised, as a rationale was developed to explain the specific losses of each family. The fire's path was erratic: it demolished some houses, jumped another, while stopping on the doorsteps of yet others. Through the pathways of their own cultural system explaining sorrow and disaster, Karimpur's residents sought and found explanations for this erratic path.[3]

The early communal explanations disintegrated along caste and factional lines defined by the political economy of the community and by the government's response (so the villagers believed) to caste and factional ties. Explanations of the fire's path were based in part on this understood political history, especially the role of past village leaders who wrote a bad fate for the whole community. Other explanations ignored caste and political alliances to focus on the sins of each family that had caused the gods (no longer Sanīcar alone) to bring such sorrows to them. Thus, both political fragmentation and moral tensions helped to bring forth the full intricacy of a system of religious and metaphysical explanation that was rarely evident in more everyday circumstances.

The fire

As a physical entity, Karimpur is a farming village of some 350 closely packed mud and brick houses surrounded by several thousand acres of fields. Narrow lanes separate the houses, which are often connected to one another by walls and roofs. Each house has a thatch roof over its cooking area, located in a corner of the women's courtyard (or in the corner of the verandah if the family is too poor to have a courtyard). Thatch roofs also provide shade over many verandahs and often cover sections of the courtyard to shelter the women. In late April, the roofs of most houses are piled with dried sticks, salvaged from the harvest and stored as fuel, while stacks of cow-dung cakes dot the village to guarantee supplies of fuel for the coming rainy season. Although the houses themselves are of mud or brick, roof rafters are made of wood (usually tree trunks or large branches), as are doors and door frames. The house of Mahesh and Girish *dhobī*, whose wives and children died in the fire, is typical of Karimpur housing.

The fire started in the thatch over a small cooking hearth, used by a group of old men to light their pipes, on the verandah of a house across and down the lane from Mahesh's house (see Figure 2). The fierce winds of the dust storm immediately lifted lighted sticks and embers from the initial fire (House 7) into a neighbour's house (House 6) and hence to Mahesh's

[3] Explanations concerned only houses in the path of the fire. Houses at greater distances were ignored.

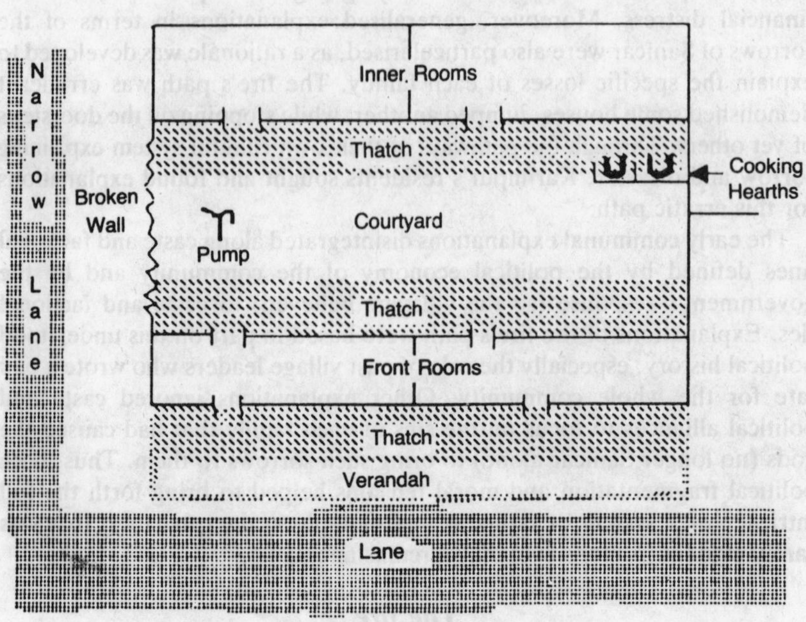

Figure 1: Diagram of the *Ḍhobī* House

(House 11). Mahesh, his brother and their wives and children were eating their evening meal near the hearth. As they realised there was a fire, the two men grabbed three of the children (aged 9, 5 and 1) and leapt over the broken courtyard wall away from the fire. The wives, with two smaller children and one 12 year old, tried to leave through the front room and doorway to the lane. But by then the thatch over the outer verandah was on fire. As it collapsed and the rest of the thatch in the courtyard caught fire, the women were trapped inside their front room. Their bodies were burned beyond recognition.

The winds swept the fire rapidly from house to house, so that within five minutes twenty houses were engulfed and the village appeared to be a sea of flames.[4] The owner of House 21 later claimed to have seen the fire start (at House 7) and immediately ran to his own house only to find that the fire had arrived first. The wind storm sent burning embers flying into the fields as well, with a large rocket-like ball of flame (as it was later described) setting fire to a harvest floor (*khāliyan*) one-quarter mile from the village. Cultivators worried about their own harvest piles, as the spring wheat

[4] Some four miles away, the Superintendent of Police and his wife saw the orange glow in the sky and debated whether it was a fire. The arrival of the anthropologists in their car (the only motorised vehicle in the village) to call the fire brigade was the first they knew of what had happened and where.

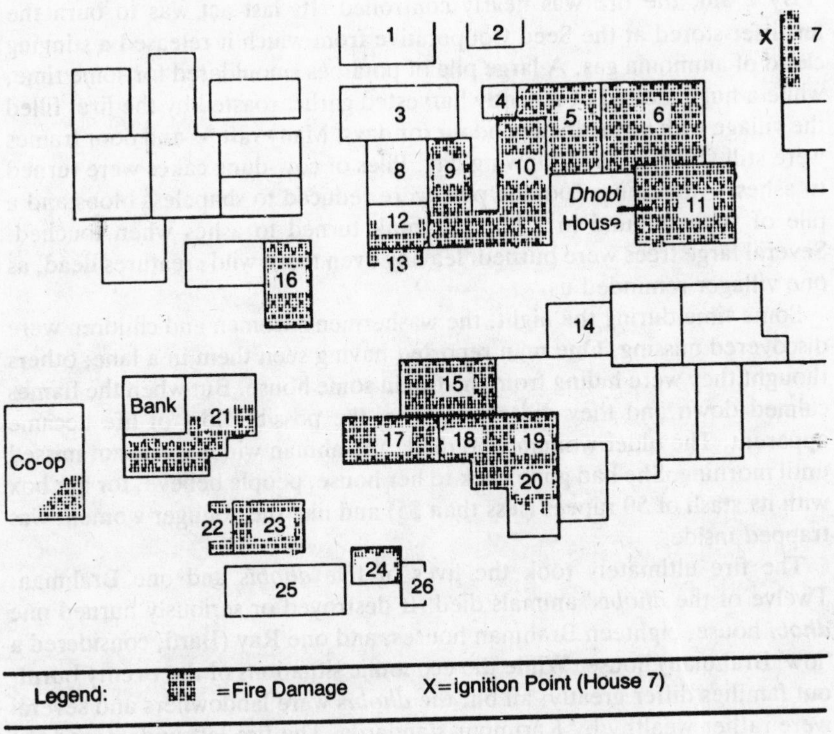

Figure 2: Map of Fire-affected Area

harvest awaited threshing on all sides of the village. Some families thought to send men with buckets to guard their harvests; others simply awaited their fate. But in the end, the only wheat destroyed was that belonging to the old men whose unwatched hearth had started the fire.

As the fire swept through the village, people thought to unfasten their livestock[5] and the lanes leading out from the village were filled with swirling embers, weeping and distraught humans, and panic-stricken animals.

Within forty-five minutes, the fire brigade arrived from the nearby district town and everyone worked to contain the flames. The thatch roofs of dwellings near the fire were knocked down to prevent further spread and the stores of inflammable goods on roofs were tossed to the ground, where they could be doused with buckets of water if a fire started. After the first five minutes, the fire did not spread to new houses, but quietly devoured the possessions of its initial victims.

[5] The only animals killed were those of the *dhobi*s, whose house went in the first minute of the fire.

By 2 am, the fire was nearly controlled. Its last act was to burn the fertiliser stored at the Seed Cooperative from which it released a stinging cloud of ammonia gas. A large pile of potatoes smouldered for some time, while a huge mound of recently harvested garlic, roasted by the fire, filled the village with its distinctive odour for days. Many rafters and door frames were still smoking the following day. Piles of cow-dung cakes were turned to ashes. Aluminium cooking pots were reduced to shapeless blobs and a pile of rupees found in a burned trunk turned to ashes when touched. Several large trees were burned, leaving even more wild creatures dead, as one villager reminded us.

Some time during the night, the washermen's women and children were discovered missing. One man reported having seen them in a lane; others thought they were hiding from the fire in some house. But when the flames calmed down and they did not appear, the possible loss of life became apparent. The older woman who died, a Brahman widow, was not missed until morning. She had gone back to her house, people believe, for her box with its stash of 50 rupees (less than $5) and like the younger women, was trapped inside.[6]

The fire ultimately took the lives of five *dhobīs* and one Brahman. Twelve of the *dhobīs*' animals died. It destroyed or seriously burned one *dhobī* house, eighteen Brahman houses, and one Ray (Bard, considered a 'low' Brahman) house. While the economic situations of the twenty burnt-out families differ greatly, all but the *dhobīs* were landowners and several were rather wealthy by Karimpur standards. The fire left undamaged the poorer and more densely populated sections of the village, where the devastation and loss of life would have been more extreme.

The village response

For thirteen generations, the village of Karimpur has been dominated economically and politically by its Brahman landowners, although the economic strength of the Brahmans has been eroded in recent years by loss of land (in 1925 they owned 75 per cent of the village land while in 1975 their share was only 50 per cent); by the gradual rise in influence of other communities due in part to population increases that reduced Brahman numerical rule; by educational advances, allowing lower castes to avoid relying on their Brahman patrons in various dealings; and by the 'green revolution' which has freed the smaller landholders from Brahman control of water and other agricultural inputs and resources. Various government programmes, for example, have been directed at the rural poor, who are usually not Brahman in Karimpur. Karimpur's traditional dominance by a

[6] A more likely possibility is that she had been in the back of her house and was merely trapped there by the quickly spreading fire. But the native explanation was firm in pointing to her greed for an insignificant sum. They also said that the washermen's wives had also returned for money, though some did question, 'what money?' What was notable here was the search for some human error, rather than nonhuman causes.

strong Brahman group is thus presently more precarious, and speculation is rife within the village about when and by what means some noticeable shift will occur. The headman (*pradhān*) of the village council is, and has been since the 1950s, a Brahman, and control of this position has been targeted by the politically motivated lower castes as crucial to shifting the power structure of the village. The Brahmanness of the village and of the victims became key components in the villagers' interpretations of the responses of government and private benefactors. Moreover, the leadership given the village by the Brahman community for many generations became a factor in their understanding of the initial cause of the fire.

With this background, let us now turn to the events following the fire and village interpretations of them. Within hours of the fire, the District Magistrate and Superintendent of Police visited the bereaved families and checked the extent of the damage. Lists of losses were compiled. Food was made available morning and night for three days to those burned out of their homes. Service clubs in the nearby district town provided clothing and beds, while the government gave five steel pots, rice and flour to each family with enormous losses.

But there was a problem: most of those hurt by the fire were Brahmans and this was a village known to be ruled by Brahmans. The government had been seen as championing the rights of the low castes and the landless, hence villagers expected its response to be minimal. This view was reinforced by the extent of reparation given the two washermen whose wives had died. Within days, they had a load of bricks, wood and doorframes to build a new dwelling. Although the *pradhān* was told that each ruined family would be given a load of bricks by the local brick industry, these never materialised. Wood for rafters was also promised but never appeared.

The Brahman–non-Brahman problem deepened. Some said that Brahmans, other than those directly threatened, did not help to put out the fire. And when a local doctor brought volunteers from town two days after the fire to help clean up, he found no one from the village willing to pitch in. After an angry showdown with the headman, he left.

Since the fire had swept through several Brahman factions, fights over reparations immediately became factional fights. Karimpur Brahmans are divided into two major factions, each descended from one of the sons of the village founder. The fire destroyed houses from both factions. No one would help someone belonging to the other faction. Those who were not already close allies wished to avoid the obvious declaration that helping in a particular house would make. So each house was able to call upon only its own members and whatever labourers were bound to it through share-cropping or *jajmānī*.[7] Moreover, the leaders of the two factions whose

[7] The *jajmānī* system in Karimpur has attenuated greatly since Wiser (1958) wrote on its workings as seen in the 1930s. However, it still functions enough to allow servants to be called upon in instances such as this.

houses were burned were seen as particularly degenerate—one group because they were blatantly involved in women, drink and robbery, and the other because its leader had recently been an especially corrupt and self-serving headman. The enmity toward these families from the non-Brahman community is enormous. The grand cooperative clean-up envisioned by the city service clubs was not to be.

Also contributing to the lack of cooperation that developed was the expectation that no one would receive full restitution for actual losses. Yes, the washermen received a new and better house and clothes, but no wives, children or animals. Others would never get their stores of rice and lentils replaced, let alone the money that had been hidden in the rafters. All knew that relief goods were in limited supply and could not be had without a fight. The carefully constructed lists of the headman would never be adhered to in actuality.

Meanwhile, a consensus developed about the cause of the fire, a consensus that attributed blame to the Brahman community generally and to its corrupt leadership more specifically. A year later, a visiting friend of ours asked two young non-Brahman men from the village about the fire, while deploring the losses. 'But they sinned', was their vehement response.

Merit and sin as explanations of disaster

In Karimpur understanding, *karma* changes one's body substance, and hence one's future. *Karma*, derived from the verbal root *kar-*, 'to do, to make', is first of all purposeful action, including mental acts such as desire, faith and compassion (Potter n.d.). These actions are continuous in life (one is, after all, always acting) but are categorised as either *pāp* (sin, evil) or *punya* (merit). Because of the fire, *pāp* was used to explain *karma*. If one does *pāp* (*pāp kartā hai*), one reaps the fruits (*phal*) of that action. Sins are most widely defined as causing sorrow for others (*kisī ko dukh denā to pāp hai*, 'If [you] give sorrow to others, then it is sin'). A person can sin because of an overt intention or because it is fated—in one's *bhāgy*, fate written at birth on one's forehead. Thus sins, leading to bad fruits, come from one's activities (*pāp apne kām se ātā hai*—'sin comes from one's own work') and then adheres or pervades one's body—'he sinned previously, now sin adheres to him' (*vah pāp kiyā pahle to us ko pāp lag gāī*). To complete the circle, 'sin adheres to him, therefore he finds its punishment' (*us ko pāp lag gāī is liye us kī sajā milī*). The sins of individuals living in Karimpur have adhered to them and caused the fire.[8] Since house and village share in that personal substance, they too burned.

There is one final twist to *karma*: those who suffer from their own (or

[8] Material in this paragraph comes from an interview in July 1985, fifteen months after the fire.

others') sins have eaten the fruits of those sins. One Farmer told of a Brahman landlord and money-lender who died several decades ago. This man so terrorised the poor that when he came near, people were as frightened as when the wind (a spirit) came to attack a child. This landlord liked it, they say, when someone's bullock died, for then he could benefit by giving loans. But then the landlord died a horrible death, with maggots eating away his body. And all his friends too died slowly and painfully—one of cancer, one with worms. Thus, these people who had initially gained from eating the earnings of sin (*pāp ke kamāī khāt hai*), i.e., from enjoying the profits of immorally gained wealth, were now suffering from it. The fruits of their making were eaten in agonising deaths. Likewise, one of the houses destroyed by the fire belonged to the nephew of the ex-headman who was so hated by the poor. Here we were told, 'However much sin his uncle has, hasn't he too eaten it?' The fire was seen as just retribution, for worse than sinning is eating the earnings of sin. Even more critical though, is the fact that 'to eat the earnings of one's sins' carries a second connotation: in some contexts it means to eat the fruits of one's *karma*, that is to receive retribution, good or bad, for one's previous actions.[9] People eat the fruits that they have earned, either in this life or the next.

Karma, *pāp* and *puṇya* are closely linked to *dharma*. Like *karma, pap* and *puṇya*, *dharma* is both a thing and an action. As one elderly Brahman said, 'It has no colour nor has anyone seen it. Yet it is known in all three worlds, by the whole earth, and nature. Both *pāp* and *dharma* are present from before.' *Dharma* is a kind of work—to dig a well, to feed the poor, to build a *dharmśālā*. It is also *puṇya*, merit. To steal, look at another woman or refuse to feed a beggar is *adharma* or *pāp*. One does *dharma* or *adharma*, defined by one's own principles or tradition, and thus does acts of merit or sin. A person should do his/her own *dharma*. 'Each [man or woman] should do his/her respective works which give *dharma*.' *Dharma* is something which a person has and does; it defines their actions (*karma*) as good or bad, giving a person *puṇya* or *pāp* as fruits.

Note that this core understanding of *karma* and *pāp* does not depend upon a theory of transmigration. Whether one's karmic fruits are the results of actions in this life or a previous one is not necessarily distinguished or known. In fact, the emphasis is on immediacy since the sin at once adheres to the sinner. Moreover, one does bear personal responsibility for one's actions: as we were repeatedly told, 'whatever work you do, you will get its fruits.' This view of *karma* runs contrary to much of the literature where *karma* is seen first as a theory of transmigration and second as an abdication of moral responsibility (see Keyes 1983).

Karma in Hindu philosophical writings is a presupposition of theories of

[9] As Raheja (1988) has shown, inauspiciousness can be given away to be digested by others. Here the makers of sin were digesting it themselves and hence suffering.

transmigration. *Karma*, or action, in previous lives is seen as a determinant of one's current life situation. The gods or their representatives tally up one's good and bad actions and fix one's future in immutable headwriting (lines on one's forehead that contain one's fate, as defined by *karma*).[10] What is written is unchangeable. A view of past *karma* as fixing some unknown aspects of one's fate in this life removes the possibility of placing full moral responsibility on any given individual. Keyes states,

> one's karmic legacy is seen as the consequence of moral actions in a previous existence. In practice, karmic explanation of present misfortunes carries, both for Buddhists and for Hindus, few if any connotations of personal responsibility (1983: 15).

This potential lack of full moral responsibility in one's actions, because anything that happens in one's life may be due to *karma*, is further augmented by the fact that an individual can suffer the karmic consequences of another's *karma*. A father's *karma* may require that a son die at 12 years of age; a woman's *karma* to be a youthful widow will require that her husband die young. Somehow, of course, the gods' accountants supposedly have matched the *karmas* of these various individuals, so that a man fated to die young is married to a woman fated to be a youthful widow. Hence, the living individual has limited opportunity for actions of free will and, in this life, limited moral responsibility.

Some interpreters of *karma* heard in Karimpur recognise its implications for transmigration. An elderly Brahman said,

> And whatsoever is your earning from previous birth, that you are consuming. Penances, sacrifices, pilgrimage, wealth, money, whatever there is—descendants, offspring—all is because of the earnings of your previous birth. In this birth you are consuming it.[11]

A man of lower caste concurred, in a separate interview: '*karma* works like this—that you get the fruits of your own actions. Whatever you do you get the fruits of that work—forever.' Later he added, 'Who does wickedness in a previous birth, *his body* will suffer in this birth as many sins as he has done in previous birth' (emphasis added). Later he tried to explain his own handicap—malformed upper arms from an injury received as an infant:

[10] Although I have no direct evidence from Karimpur that headwriting is *karma*, other evidence from north India affirms that it is (Wadley 1967: 28).

[11] Interviews for this and the next paragraph were held early in 1984, months before the fire, and covered a variety of topics. Other quotations in this paper are from the two weeks immediately following the fire.

> At the beginning I was a child. In this life, I hadn't done any actions (*karam*). But in my previous life, I did such actions (*karam*) . . . [SSW: Sc you have the fruits of your previous birth?] Yes, those very fruits

Yet he quickly contradicted a purely transmigrational scheme by saying, 'If there are few sins, those are excused by bathing in the Ganges' (which alters one's bodily state by, to use the common Hindu phrase, washing away one's sins). His final statement was equivocable with reference to *karma* as destiny from acts in a prior life or this one: 'I have told you before: Whatever work you do, you will get its fruits' (*jaise karam kariyo teseĩ phal miliye*).

The intent of this final statement recurred in various forms, in explanations of the fire. But the works and their fruits were primarily actions and results realised in this current life. For, in fact, in Karimpur as in many other parts of India, *karma* is not merely a theory of transmigration. As Babb notes, the essential idea of karmic theory is 'that of action determining the subsequent destiny of the actor' (1983: 165). Some informants, such as the Jats quoted by Lewis (1965) insist that the results of one's actions are realised in this life, not another. When the this-life effects of *karma* are realised, responsibility for them may be attributed to specific persons.

After the fire, the explanations sought by Karimpur natives took into account the possible personal moral responsibility of those afflicted. Sin and merit, bad and good actions, accounted for the fire: a karmic explanation was sought, but it was firmly an explanation placed in this life. Unlike Babb's Chattisgarhi informants or Sharma's (1973) Punjabis, the people of Karimpur in this particular instance sought to explain misfortune through the doctrine of just desserts: the fire and its path were the fruits of its victims' own actions.

The previously articulated Karimpur consensus that the Brahmans were destroying the village laid the groundwork for the karmic explanation of the fire. In the villagers' views, these people had been sinning for years, and it was only reasonable that they now suffer. As Geertz (1973: 33–54) has reminded us, humans must retain a sense of meaning: the Karimpur community sought to put a tragic human experience into an orderly, meaningful framework. Building on their understanding of the local political economy, a meaningful rationale for the fire of 28 April developed. This rationale placed the blame, the evil, on the Brahman leaders of the village, and more diffusely on the bodies of which they were members—their houses and village. Rarely was there an attribution of cause to sin committed in a prior life.

One recurring imagery is critical to understanding why the villagers felt the fire occurred at all. Many saw the fire as the result of an overwhelming accumulation of sins. Sins, they say, are accumulated like water in a jar.

When the jar becomes too full, it breaks: some disaster occurs. Those who were unhurt by the fire had jars of sins that were not full, or had some merit which counteracted the sins. The fire was such a major disaster that it had to result from a large jar of sins. Perhaps, indeed, many jars of sins. One Brahman woman said,

> When there are lots of bad deeds done by someone, then it catches fire. When people do many sins then it catches fire. When all the sin comes together, then it catches fire.[12]

Only with the accumulation of sins of a large community does such a tragedy occur.

In this statement, as elsewhere in their comments about the fire, it is clear that Karimpur residents viewed the fire as a community punishment, not merely an individual one. One woman said, 'our village women don't give offerings to beggars. To feed the poor and guests is called *dharma*. If I advise them, they will beat me.' Likewise, this same woman much later said, 'Nobody [in village] knows Ram. See how many temples have been built in Aramgaon [a neighbouring village]. There are farmers with 100 acres in our village. None of them could build such a big temple. In this village, both temples were built by widows.'[13] The sin in this case is of the village: living in the village made people *adharmik*. Yet another man blamed the fire on the fate (*bhāgy*) of the village, saying 'it was written in our fate that the fire would occur.' E.V. Daniel (1984: 61–104) has shown that communities in south India have a nature and *karma* comparable to those of a human person, and that the community and persons living in it exchange and share substances. Though Karimpur is less clearly personified, here too we see sins attributed to a village unit. As we shall see below, the same transfer is also made between individuals and the house where they live.[14]

What were the sins of those destroyed by the fire? First, there was the curious fact of the fire's starting in House 7 and doing minimal damage there. However, there was the rocket-like ball of fire that then burned the stored grain of House 7 at a distance of one-quarter mile from the village. No one had any doubts: God had not succeeded in his punishment at their

[12] Possibly because the heat of digesting so many sins causes flames to erupt?

[13] In the 1970s, there were in fact three temples in the village, as careful readers of *Behind mud walls* (Wiser and Wiser 1971) will note. The third, too, was built by a widow, but has since been torn down by the residents of this *adharmik* community.

[14] Just as the consequences of sins and *adharmik* actions are shared by village, lineage, household and family, so are the consequences of ritual acts of merit. In fact, rituals in Karimpur are performed for the community (*khappar*, see Wadley 1975: 165), for the lineage (*siyāo mātā*, Wadley 1975: 171), for the household (women's Holi fire); for the family (*gobardhān*, Wadley 1975: 171) and finally for the individual (e.g., some women's *vrat*s such as Santoshi Mā are primarily for the worshipper).

house, so he tried a second tactic, burning the harvest. 'Think of this: the fire started from Mohan Lal's and everyone else's harvest was saved. If he was not a sinner, how did only his harvest burn?' This house too belonged to a recent headman. A sweeper claimed,

> I say this, he destroyed all the houses, he did. Otherwise how did the fire start there? I say—everyone kept their harvest near the village. His were kept [way out] there. And others were kept here. And all these were saved. Only his caught fire: what is the reason? Is there some defect? Or is there a lack of morality? Or sin? Or some other thing?

Some people believe this particular family actively worked to destroy the village. One person said, 'all along they have wanted to destroy this village. Now they just sat and watched it burn.'

The perceived sins of this family were enormous and thought to be directed against the whole community. Unlike the others, whose sins hurt only themselves or their family, this family took actions that, many believed, brought sorrow to a whole community. The resulting debate raised a contentious point regarding *karma*: to what extent is *karma* shared and to what extent do the misdeeds of one person affect the lives of others. Karimpur residents expressed the debate using the imagery of a boat containing one sinner and several innocent 'victims'. The issue here is different from the sharing of individual sin by house or village, as seen above: rather, because an individual death is involved, did that person sin or did he suffer from shared sin? One sweeper claimed,

> It's like this: when man's honesty becomes bad, he doesn't see anyone properly. When there is a sinner in the boat, then you sink. If there is only one sinner in the boat, all drown. One man causes all to drown because he is the sinner. Is dangerous because of this.

This latter point, about whether one person's sins resulted in a shared *karma* for all was disputed by others. A middle-aged farmer commented,

> Bhagvān might have thought this way—that his roof has only burned a little so he set fire in his harvest too. It is said that one sinner sinks a whole ship. But it is also said, 'Those who are not sinners do not drown, that they are able to get out.' Some devotees of Bhagvān are like this; they fall in the water and sink, but they reach the bank anyhow. I have heard that a boat sank in the Kali Nadi. Even though its boatman could not reach the bank, a woman took her boy in her lap and a man, they both went on a thatch roof which was also floating on the water and crossed that river. Some others were saved too . . . . But if they died, there must be a little bit of sin in the person . . . . It is not possible that there was no sin of the person who died with a big sinner.

By this logic, even if the major sin was attributed to the house where the fire started, the others who were hurt had to have sinned as well. This logic required villagers to define the sins of victims. Where whole houses were destroyed, the cause was the accumulated sin or lack of merit of the house: for this, the actions of all known former and current residents were mentally aggregated and tallied. The actions of public figures, usually male, were more critical in the village tally than were the actions of those hidden by *purdah*. As Figure 2 shows, the fire jumped one house (14) and stopped on the doorsteps of others (4, 8 and 25). Retribution for not giving alms to the sadhu (itself a sinful act) could have acted as an explanation for this seemingly erratic path. But the community sought a broader explanation.

Looking at these broader explanations is revealing, for we see how *karma* is shared among a kin group. House 8 is inhabited by a wealthy Brahman farmer, his wife, mother and sons. Although a money-lender, he is noted for decent interest rates and for even giving loans without interest on occasion. The owner and his family are respected for working hard and not indulging in liquor, sex, or gambling. One commentator said, 'He is not a sinner and that's why there was no fire there. Because this [fire] happens only at sinners' places', while another said, 'It was saved because he has done good deeds [*puṇya*]. You do good deeds and you will then find the fruits. And if we don't do good deeds, then we'll find that fruit too.' A third commented, 'The thing is, why was that house saved? Because they are devotees of god. They are god's servants.'

Opinions on House 25 varied. It is the house of a former headman who had been jailed in the late 1960s for embezzling government funds. One brother is a dacoit and another has deserted his wife for a mistress: all three currently support themselves by selling their land, their family inheritance, leading to the ultimate ruin of the whole family. The sons of the brothers, thus far all able and dutiful young men, are being disinherited by their fathers' profligary. A daughter of the same family returned home a few days after the fire in tears after someone had commented, 'All the other sinners' houses have burned, Now we'll have to burn yours.' Yet despite the blatant misdeeds of these brothers, their father was known to have been a good man: his *puṇya* saved the house.[15] One man said, 'Well, their jar of sins has not filled up as yet. You should understand that there is merit [*puṇya*] still.' Another said, 'His grandfather did *puṇya*. Now it's not like that. Om's grandfather did a lot of *puṇya*.' Someone else suggested that it was the *karma* of the lineage (*khāndān*) and that maybe there had been a *satī* at some early time, for 'then the whole family is saved. If there was one *satī*, then all your bad *karma* will be destroyed.' The house belonged to more than one person: the tally of sin and merit takes into account many current and past residents and only the total counts.

[15] Another factor was that this family lives in the house built by Charlotte and William Wiser. A few suggested that it was really *their* merit which saved the house.

The fire only slightly touched House 8, residence of a Brahman widow, who lives there with her youngest son and daughter. In this case, a woman's actions were tallied by the village 'accountants', for two reasons: first, she was acting household head, having a teenage son who only nominally owned the land. She was also a very public figure, known as the 'village Indira', a name given because of her recent political activities, often condemned in the community. Her older son's house (12) was completely destroyed. Once again the village found a karmic explanation. Here too there were visible sins, yet the fire left the house unscathed. The household head's widowhood had already marked her as sinful, and she had incurred additional evil in this life through a possible adulterous relationship, stinginess, etc. But, the house did not burn. The answer lay, so opinion decided, in her overt religiosity. One man commented,

> Ram's has burned a bit. Ram's wife [the widow] is very good at worshipping. She says, 'I always keep Bhagvān before me.' [She says], 'Look, he is standing there and telling me my work.' But you tell me what sorrow there is that she has not suffered [literally, 'had over her']. From her husband, from the children, from the land and now she is wandering about helplessly. She borrows money, does everything. Yet she says that Bhagvān knows me better than anyone else knows me. The main thing is this—who knows what is inside. Just like when a stove [*kuthilīyā*][16] has been whitewashed, who knows what is underneath? No one knows what is in the stomach. People have discovered the bottom of the ocean but nobody can see inside the stomach. So the meaning is this: who can say what is her condition?

Perhaps her known sins were cancelled out by her personal and unseen relationship with god. The evidence pointed that way.

The sins of yet others whose houses burned included gambling, lechery, drunkenness and usury. In only one instance were the sins not immediately obvious. The family in House 15 was hard-working and pious. The only possible act of wrongdoing was that a younger son's wife had run off with another man and that the family had finally brought her back without first obtaining the permission of the Brahman community. The adultery of the young wife was not held accountable for the family's suffering; rather, it was the father's decision to allow her return which was truly sinful. Another house was agreed to have burned because the owner had begun to plough the Brahman cremation ground, a horrifically sinful act. In only one case was there no obvious evil in this life and hence the explanation that the burning was 'due to something in his [the household head's] past life.'

Only those persons who died in the fire were considered to have fully

[16] A mobile clay stove kept in village houses.

eaten the fruits of their sins, and not to have shared their sins with others. Persons who suffered but survived were always seen as sharing sins, usually with a household of others. The washermen and their two dead wives illustrate this point. The older of the two brothers was said to have murdered his wife's first husband. He took too many loans. His sins were 'uncountable'. So he had to bear the sorrow of losing wife and children. At one level of explanation, the wives died because he sinned (the wife of his brother had previously been his wife, prior to his murdering the second wife's husband).[17] Yet that didn't seem to suffice, leading, we believe, to the common belief that the women died because they were greedy and they burned trying to salvage their pittance of money from their hidden stores. Somehow they too had to have sinned: one woman claimed, 'Bela's mother and those washerwomen died from greed.' Yet another said, 'If they [anyone] died, there must be a little bit of sin in the person.'

The Brahman widow (Bela's mother above) also died from greed. Although the man who dug her body out said she was nowhere near her precious box, everyone else believed otherwise. One woman remarked, 'Half the note had burned and half was in her fist. She went to take rupees from her trunk. People say [it was] to save her life but she gave her life. Those washerwomen also burnt the same way.'

We have seen that villagers find karmic concepts useful in developing plausible explanations for specific disasters. Sin and merit are flexible and especially useful concepts when they are conceived as capable of being shared among members of a family, among all the houses descended from a common ancestor, and potentially within a whole community—wherever there is a connected body of actions.[18]

To say that a consensus developed for karmic explanations in Karimpur is not to deny that other explanations were proffered. As noted earlier, the fire was initially attributed to the planetary God Sanīcar, who must have been offended by its victims. One man from the house where the fire started claimed that it was because the village Holi fire (a month earlier) had been lit a day late. Someone said that there had been a sadhu in the village the day of the fire, and that the fire hit those houses who had not fed him.

These other searches for understanding, all given in the first day or two after the fire, are what Hiebert (1983) has called 'middle-level' explanations: they attribute the fire to powerful gods, but specify no human moral

[17] No explanations were ever offered for the death of the children, suggesting that they were either counted with their mothers or that they themselves were too young to be capable of sin.

[18] S.B. Daniel (1983: 28–35) reports through many cases how Tamil villagers understand and calculate sharings of *karma* as well as the intrapersonal processes of its working. Our cases from Karimpur indicate a similar logic, although we cannot offer comparable evidence villagers' descriptions of their mental and moral physiology.

responsibility. We think it worth noting that in the Karimpur disaster there is no reference to yet lower-level agencies—ghosts and demons of sundry sorts. Clearly, the magnitude of the fire demanded an explanation at a higher level. As one man commented:

> The inevitable had happened before the machines [fire engines] reached. Later on, the machines extinguished the fire. However much trouble Bhagvān wanted to give, he had given before the machines reached. No one's power can help when Bhagvān wants to destroy something.

Yet the wrath of Sanicar, of a sadhu, or of a more impersonal Bhagvān was not the explanation that persisted. *Karma* was not the first explanation given in the village for this massive misfortune, but, as Sharma has noted, 'it is generally the last he [a villager] will abandon' (1973: 358).

More specific causal agencies of low or middle level are ruled out by the irreversibility and complexity of the Karimpur fire. Humans can take measures to reduce impending misfortune that may result from the ire of a god or the act of a demon or ghost: they can placate or exorcise the agencies and thus avoid or remove lesser misfortunes. But the Karimpur fire was over, the houses ruined and the dead gone. Human counteractions were no longer feasible or thinkable. Karmic interpretation at some higher, more comprehensive level could fit the helplessness and incomprehensibility of the disaster better than any collection of personal singularities. The strong village consensus that the fire had been brought on by the sins of village leaders—those higher-ups who guide the actions of all—is one step toward a more inclusive karmic interpretation. But so great was this disaster that reference became inevitable to the most comprehensive divine level.

At the highest level, the responsibility for dealing with moral complexity was ascribed to a remote god, usually designated as Bhagvān, the supreme object of devotion. It was Bhagvān who counted up sins and acts of merit by each one of this large population of sinners. It was Bhagvān who decided how to distribute the fruits of past action at this time, who determined who would eat and digest which sins. It was Bhagvān who started the fire after calculating village, lineage, household, family and individual *karmas*.

Given the overarching predominance of leaders and gods and Bhagvān, and given the accumulation of previous actions, can one still determine one's acts, or are all one's acts predetermined? Karimpur thought seems to confirm 'the conviction that human intentions really do matter' (Babb 1983: 180). The mystery of *karma* is 'Do your acts count, or are they all predetermined?' In discussing one known 'bad character', one of our friends summed up the argument thus:

A: . . . It's up to Bhagvān whether a man is good or bad.
Q: Yes, but shouldn't he [a man] be helpful [to others]?
A: If somebody doesn't have kindness in their heart what can you do?
Q: You mean to say he commits sins?
A: It is a sin when he's not devoted (religious). What can one do? One can only be devoted through acts of charity. Nowadays no one performs sacrifices, and no one is well-bred, and no one is religious. It's a question of your mind and heart. It's a matter of spirit [*bhāvnā*].
Q: Do you think that Kishenlal will come to a bad end?
A: That only Bhagvān knows. There's one thing to think about: if I do something bad I will obtain its fruits.

Our friend felt that the fire of 28 April proved his points: one does eat the fruits of one's actions, but the nature and scope of 'one' and the manner of one's eating may well transcend one's knowing.

REFERENCES

BABB, LAWRENCE A. 1983. Destiny and responsibility: karma in popular Hinduism. *In* Charles Keyes and E. Valentine Daniel, eds., *Karma: an anthropological inquiry*, pp. 163–84. Berkeley: University of California Press.

DANIEL, S.B. 1983. The toolbox approach. *In* Charles Keyes and E. Valentine Daniel, eds., *Karma: an anthropological inquiry*, pp. 27–62. Berkeley: University of California Press.

DANIEL, E. VALENTINE. 1984. *Fluid signs: being a person the Tamil way*. Berkeley: University of California Press.

GEERTZ, CLIFFORD. 1973. *The interpretation of cultures*. New York: Basic Books.

HIEBERT, PAUL G. 1983. Karma and other explanation traditions in a south Indian village. *In* Charles Keyes and E. Valentine Daniel, eds., *Karma: an anthropological inquiry*, pp. 119–30. Berkeley: University of California Press.

KEYES, CHARLES F. 1983. Introduction: the study of popular ideas of karma. *In* Charles Keyes and E. Valentine Daniel, eds., *Karma: an anthropological inquiry*, pp. 1–26. Berkeley: University of California Press.

LEWIS, OSCAR. 1965. *Village life in northern India*. Urbana: University of Illinois Press.

POTTER, KARL. n.d. Karma: the metaphor of making. Unpublished paper.

RAHEJA, GLORIA GOODWIN. 1988. *Poison in the gift*. Chicago: University of Chicago Press.

SHARMA, URSULA. 1973. Theodicy and the doctrine of karma. *Man* (n.s.) 8: 348–64.

WADLEY, SUSAN SNOW. 1967. 'Fate' and the gods in the Panjabi cult of Gugga: a structural semantic analysis. Unpublished master's paper, Department of Anthropology, University of Chicago.

———. 1975 (1985). *Shakti: power in the conceptual structure of Karimpur religion*. New Delhi: Munshiram Manoharlal.

WISER, WILLIAM H. 1958. *The Hindu jajmani system*. Lucknow: Lucknow Publishing House.

WISER, WILLIAM and CHARLOTTE V. WISER. 1971. *Behind mud walls 1930–1960 with a sequel: the village in 1970*. Berkeley: University of California Press.

7

Humoral transactions in two Tamil cults: Murukan and Mariyamman[1]

Manuel Moreno and McKim Marriott

Like the town's human residents, the two most popular deities in Palani[2] are understood to be humorally variable and humorally responsive to others. Murukan, most beloved god of the Tamil-speaking peoples and a son of the god Śiva, has his principal temple here; he draws thousands of pilgrims daily from all over southern India, and hundreds of thousands more during two of his six annual festivals. Mariyamman, a universally feared and loved goddess with hundreds of temples elsewhere, annually draws to her festival in Palani the greatest number of local residents and a total of worshippers second only to Murukan's. Both continue to draw such crowds to their festivals because their worshippers perceive and wish to remedy critical variations—"faults" (*doṣas*) in the deities' "humours" (another meaning of the word *doṣa*). The three festivals are interpreted here with the help of an ethnosocial psychology (Marriott 1989) that may claim special relevance because it builds upon an Indian humoral epistemology.

The humours and their metonyms

"Wind", "bile" and "phlegm", the three humours of Hindu biology (*āyurveda*), may seem from their names to have narrowly physiological

[1] The field research on which this study is based was conducted by Manuel Moreno from November 1979, to May 1981, with the support of a fellowship from the Social Science Research Council. Special thanks are due to Dr. P. Subramaniam of the Palani Andavar College of Indian Culture. The comments of Margaret Trawick are gratefully acknowledged.

[2] Palani town (population *ca*. 65,000) and *taluka* are in the northwestern corner of Madurai district within the region of western Tamil Nadu known as Konku.

referents. In fact, however, these three variable bodily substances are also metonyms of the physical "elements" (*bhūtas*) "air", "fire" and "water", respectively. They are further identifiable with the three "strands" (*guṇas*) of Indian natural philosophy and with three of the classical "principal aims" (*puruṣārthas*) of human life. Thus, three sorts of variations in personal biological functioning can be seen as homologous or metonymous with three similar sorts of variations in many other layers of an embracing classical cosmology.

Following Marriott's (1989) glosses and alignments of concepts, the three classical metonymic sets can be stated as:

> (1) "wind" (*vāta*), corresponding to "air", "darkness" (*tamas*), and "incoherence" (*adharma*)—Marriott's 'unmatching' variable;
>
> (2) "bile" (*pitta*), corresponding to "fire", "passion" (*rajas*), and "attachment" (*kāma*)—Marriott's 'mixing' variable;
>
> (3) "phlegm" (*kapha*), corresponding to "water", "goodness" (*sattva*), and "advantage" (*artha*)—Marriott's 'unmarking' variable.[3]

Classical thought postulates that each set varies independently of the others, and that all three sets of concepts are constitutive of all entities and actions, but in various and continually varying proportions. Marriott (1989) proposes adopting the common properties of these three sets as the fundamental 'variables' of an alternative social science for analysing Indian data, and we pursue his proposal here.

Tamil equivalents of these variables are known and currently used in Palani, especially in medical, dietetic and ritual discussions. In practise, attention may be directed to only one variable at a time or to one concept, leaving its metonymy with other concepts within that set implicit. Yet the classical triads and their equivalents remain universally available and are continually extended and applied to other areas of daily life.

(1) In colloquial Tamil the "wind" humour (termed 'unmatching' by Marriott) is commonly called "eruptive" (*kiranti*), referring typically to skin rashes and pustules (McGilvray 1982: 30). Much as classical Indian biology emphasises "wind" as the chief force and sees it in any movement—especially reversing movements, such as respiration or illness (Caraka *Sū*. 12; 20: 10–13)—so popular Tamil epistemology emphasises change and disorder as natural features of the social world with which humans have presently to cope (Pfaffenberger 1982: 95–146). Variations of heat may contribute to such movement and disorder. An excess of wind and its metonyms is suspected in any dysfunction—in any sudden change, or change for the worse that is felt to be "inauspicious", "unwholesome",

[3] Double quotation marks have been used to gloss Indian words, single quotation marks to indicate non-Indian words.

"diseased," "sinful", or "impure". Evil eye, spirits, ghosts, demons and certain goddesses are thought of as concentrated manifestations of wind. Psychic symptoms of wind include loss of control, drunkenness, sleepiness, trance, possession, madness and violence. Calmings of wind are effected by preliminary coolings and then by oppositions and separations—themselves unmatchings—and/or by careful timings and combinations—appropriate rematchings, such as are the preoccupations of astrology, medicine, dietetics, agriculture, ritual, and economic and political calculation.

(2) The "bile" or 'thermic' variable (Marriott's 'mixing') is omnipresent in Tamil popular perceptions that everything is more or less "hot" (*cūṭu*). Increases of heat are essential to life, love and the reproduction of life. Life thrives on an increased volume of blood, which generates strength, transactional activity, openness, expansion and mixture. The latter conditions in turn generate heat. An excess of heat may lead to hyperactivity—to profligate spending, greed, anger, lust, giantism and various diseases. Emphasising heat, popular humoral thinking sometimes treats wind as its consequence and water as its antidote, thus reducing the three distinct and intersecting classical humours to a simpler, single scale running from "hot" to "cold" (Mani 1981; McGilvray 1982).

(3) Equivalents of the "phlegm" or 'fluid' variable (Marriott's 'unmarking') are perceived by Tamils in all kinds of distinctions or directional movements between "high" and "low", "origin" and "end", "wet" and "dry" (Egnor 1978), "pure" and "impure", "subtle" and "gross", "essence" and "residue", etc. Such asymmetries, whether in head-to-foot bathing, food metabolism and peristalsis, preferences, ranked relations, or temporal sequences, are expected everywhere and are thought to give continuity to life. Classical Hindu biology lists "cold" as a secondary property of phlegm and water (and also of wind, contrasting both humours with the heat of bile) (Caraka *Sū*. 1: 59–61), but popular Tamil thought tends to treat "coolness" (*kuḷir*) as the primary property of this fluid constituent; hence wetness, coolness, highness and continuity are all sometimes treated loosely as metonyms.

Festivals as humoral crises

Crises of humoral excess ('mixing'), insufficiency ('unmixing'), and inappropriate combination ('unmatching') arise for both gods and humans in relations between their own humours and those of their environments. Such crises are brought on by the varied cyclings of astral time or earthly seasons in relation to personal constitution (Zimmermann 1979, 1980), or by interpersonal events. Management of the gods' humoral crises through compensatory transactions is a main concern of worshippers at the great festivals, since the god's crises both attract human sympathy and offer opportunities for human exploitation.[4]

One of Murukan's two greatest crises occurs when he experiences an insufficiency of heat at the intersection of the full moon of the "cold" month of Tai (January–February) with the Pucam constellation (*nakṣatram*).[5] His other great crisis occurs when he experiences an excess of heat at the intersection of the full moon of the "hot" month of Pankuni (March–April) with the Uttiram constellation. The pilgrimages of Tai Pucam and Pankuni Uttiram deal explicitly and massively with these two opposite thermic crises (Moreno 1984).

Mariyamman, too, exhibits thermic extremes during twenty-one days of the warming month of Maci (February–March), but her crises are not due only to the season. Her fluctuations between "hot" and "cold" moods show an excess in the wind variable, paralleling failures of matching in her previous interpersonal life (marriage to an ascetic, encounter with a demon, decapitation). Some of her worshippers attempt to compensate for her moods and thus to indulge her turbulence; others attempt to bring her fluctuations under control by rematching and remarking her through the rituals of marriage.

None of the festivals examined here is precipitated by a sudden lack of liquidity, but since all worship is asymmetric and all worship of embodied deities requires movements of substance between them and humans (as richly exemplified elsewhere by Babb 1970, 1981, 1983), most cults are continually concerned with this marking variable. Both icons are bathed regularly. Frequent fluidising pilgrimages are described below for Murukan, and episodic water rituals for Mariyamman. Too many worshippers can overheat a deity by an excess of love, too few by exciting the deity's lonely anger (e.g., Srinivas 1976: 327); either may result in drying up a deity's "unctuousness", a metonym for the superior's benign and flexible readiness to give. If endangered in any of these ways, deities may send personal messages via dreams and trances calling for help (Moreno 1985).

When attending the great festivals occasioned by the deities' major crises and also when making their routine daily obeisances, worshippers explicitly devote themselves to restoring or altering the deities' humors. Humoral differences among worshippers, gods, offerings, and the seasons make such restorations and alterations necessary and possible, and make the attendant transactions effective and often mutually rewarding.

Such transactions result in the gods' incorporation of properties conveyed by the worshippers and also create channels among the transacting parties. By those same channels worshippers incorporate substances from

[4] All festivals provide first honours to the temples' controlling authorities, for which offices there have been many struggles.

[5] Festival calendars are stated more fully for south India in general by Merrey (1982) and for Murukan by Clothey (1982).

the gods and thereby become more like them. Thus, a single, universal deity like Murukan can be said 'to ride at the crest of Tamil identity' (Clothey 1978: 2) because he interacts with and influences most Tamils, while a multiply localised deity like Mariyamman can be called more 'particular' because she is attached by name, residence and substance to a distinctive place and its people.

MURUKAN

At Palani's hill temple, Murukan's icon portrays him living as an "ascetic" (*āṇṭavar*) apart from his two spouses Teyvayanai and Valli, wearing only a loincloth and holding a spear in his right hand. According to the earliest sources, this icon was made from an alloy of nine poisonous metaloids tempered by various herbs and roots (Kavirayar 1903: 34). All these ingredients are said to have been taken from the Palani Hill itself, which is one of only six places in all the world where Murukan can exist in relative "compatibility" (*sātmya*) (Somacuntaranar Avarkal 1978).[6] The materials were collected and cast by a mathematical and alchemical "sage" (*siddhar*) named Pokar, who, some claim, was a pilgrim from China. These materials are said to have been combined in unique proportions by means of an ancient "catalytic agent" (*muppū*) peculiar to practitioners of the Tamil *siddha* medical system (Venugopal 1968).[7]

Murukan's legend declares that he was embodied in this image at Palani just at the beginning of the present Dark Age to serve people's special needs during this time of increasing disorder. His uniquely proportioned ingredients are said to give his Palani embodiment an extraordinary healing potency, much greater than that of the medicines which *siddha* doctors ordinarily prepare from similar poisons. The icon here is felt to be capable of healing any disease and of removing any misfortune (Somalay 1975; Somasundaram Pillai 1970). Thus, at Palani, Murukan is most commonly called "Doctor of the Dark Age" (*kaliyuga vaidyanātaṉ*). He is a master of matching.

Murukan's capacities for benefiting humanity are, however, contingent on appropriate (matching) circumstances. The wholesome proportions of his embodiment can be lost by excessive or insufficient thermic influences due to the changing of seasons, to the movements and realignments of astral bodies, and to depletions of his vital fluids as he attends to the continuous requests of his devotees. When such crises occur for Murukan, this otherwise incomparable source of life and well-being is in danger of becoming a source of death. His substance will then kill, just as *siddha*

[6] Immanence and territoriality as characteristics of some deities are examined by Shulman (1980: 40–55) and by Moreno (1985: 112).

[7] *Siddha* is a medical system claiming to be indigenous to south India. It is similar to *āyurveda*, but differs in emphasising the use of poisonous substances, especially minerals.

drugs are said to become poisonous if they are not handled properly (Shanmugavelu 1968).

Warming pilgrimage

At the extremely cold and moist juncture of Tai Pucam, pilgrims who are members of a "cold" caste bring a "hot" offering to the ascetic Murukan with a great display of their own austerity. Their hot offering is jaggery (unrefined sugar) which is mixed with other ingredients and poured over the god's body to warm him at the special festival "bath" (*abhiṣeka*). The god's excess of cold is absorbed by this hot mixture and the cold-bearing residue of the bath is returned to the pilgrims as a cool, edible "blessing" (*prasāda*) for their ingestion and enjoyment. By these thermic exchanges, a pair of complementary (unmatching) gestures, god and worshippers are also respectively unmarked and marked, relative to each other.

These cold-loving pilgrims are principally the Nāṭṭukkottais, a caste of Traders (Ceṭṭiyars) belonging to the historic "Left-hand" (*iṭaṅkai*) division of castes (Appadurai 1974; Beck 1972: 58; Rudner 1987: 365–69; Stein 1980: 196). Left-hand castes consider their natures to be affected only minimally by *rajas*, the "strand" or quality making for humoral heat, activity and bodily mixing with others (Daniel 1984: 186). They also claim a high proportion of *sattva*, the fluid constituent making for a discriminating mind and general excellence. They usually describe their own actual and preferred mode of behaviour as "cool" and "virtuous" (*sattvika*), and liken it to the behaviour of their revered ascetic teachers (Obeyesekere 1975: 466). For them, *sattva* implies not only goodness, but also the capacity to effect order and proportionality itself—to offset wind and darkness and to maintain the matching and "auspicious" (*nalla*) conditions. Nāṭṭukkottai Ceṭṭiyārs' achievements in their trading occupations, which require cool and careful calculation, prove that they are superior and disciplined as well as adept at expelling their own heat.

But they have not always been so cool or so successful. Indeed, during the recent past they had fallen in wealth and in others' esteem. As money-lenders, bankers and plantation contractors, Naṭṭukkottais had followed British imperial and commercial ventures all over Southeast Asia. When questioned about their way of life abroad they sadly say that many of them abandoned Hindu customs in order to mix with other, foreign peoples. But World War II and its aftermath brought ethnic antagonisms and expropriation in several countries, causing Traders great financial losses. With the exception of some who remain today in Malaysia and Singapore, most Naṭṭukkottais returned to India (Natarejan 1966).

Upon their return to India, Naṭṭukkottais made intense efforts to reconstruct themselves as a nonmixing, uncorrupted caste, and to regain their lost claim to the "quality of excellence" (*sattvaguṇa*). They call their strategy for doing the latter "greatness through goodness" (*sattvika perumai*) and define it as giving away a large part of their trading profits while refusing to accept gifts from others, except blessings from the gods. Naṭṭukkottais are now among the most prominent sponsors of temple reconstruction, patrons of vedic and shastric schools, founders of hospitals and modern colleges, and performers of the "gift of food" (*annatānam*), all of which are methods of unmarking themselves socially and of improving their karmic "merit" (*punya*) by transferring sin.

This renewed 'optimizing strategy' (Marriott 1976: 128–29) is concentrated in their great pilgrimage, which follows the annual closing of their financial books. At this time, most of the 60,000 Naṭṭukkottai Ceṭṭiyārs of Cettinatu (in Ramanathapuram district) come on foot to Palani, a distance of 160 miles. They refuse all food and drink offered by merit-seeking villagers along the way. By refusing to accept hospitality, the Traders also minimise opportunities for others to subordinate or bind them in continuing obligations (David 1974, 1977; Marriott 1976: 126–28). Instead, they apply their business earnings (which may have entailed sinning) to feasting as many thousands of local people as they can persuade to eat. The Traders' caste guru, an oracle-priest ("god dancer", *cāmiyāṭi*), also dispenses Murukan's trance-induced messages and blessings in the form of "pervasive" ashes (*vibhūti*) to villagers at worship each night.

Directed by the guru from his enclosed cart, a small corps of devoted Trader yoke-bearers marches swiftly each day at the head of the pilgrim column. Their shoulders are painfully loaded with collective offerings of jaggery. Members of this elite corps are cut off with great "strictness" (*kaṭṭāyam*) from contact with others while on the pilgrimage path. They consume none of the huge feasts that the Traders sponsor, but only food that has been previously offered to and transvalued by Murukan. The other Traders' dress, songs, dances, trance communications and general demeanour are similarly restrained, uniform and tightly centralised.

According to pervasive south Indian classifications of foodstuffs (Beck 1969: Ferro-Luzzi 1977, 1978), jaggery (crude sugar) is filled with heat—a quality that these pilgrims can happily alienate from themselves and that is urgently needed by the cold-shrunken Murukan at this time. The jaggery imparts heat to the whole mixture of ingredients that is used for the god's festival bath (Beck 1969: 570). But when Murukan's cold sweat is added, the chilled residue of the bath mixture becomes for the Traders truly an "[elixir of] immortality" (*amṛta*), recalling the product of the gods' primeval churning of the milky ocean (Mahabharata I, 15.5–13; 16.1–40; 17.1–30).

Cooling pilgrimage

At the contrasting time of Pankuni Uttiram, when Murukan is certain to become overheated by warming trends in both solar and astral cycles, large parties of "hot" pilgrims come in celebration of their spring harvest, bringing "cold" offerings of water from the river Kaveri for use in the god's festive bath. The bath water absorbs Murukan's excess heat, is drunk by the pilgrims as a return blessing, and thus helps to maintain and re-energise these worshippers' hot natures while also unmarking the god and marking them most enjoyably as his own people.

Hundreds of thousands of these pilgrims who come to Palani at Pankuni Uttiram are members of the "five [Right-hand] castes" (*añcujāti*) of Koṅku. They are led by the Koṅku Veḷḷāḷar Kavuṇṭars, who are Farmers by occupation. The caste name 'Kavuṇṭar' itself posts their claim to being the "lords of the land" in the Konku territory (Beck 1969: 50; Ganesh 1979: 49ff.; Manickam 1979: 36). But the Kavuṇṭars' territorial supremacy has recently come under bitter challenge: many labourers are working for daily wages or on non-agricultural jobs, rather than on long-term contracts with these landlords; more of the Untouchable castes are attracted by communist leaders than by the bosses of the Kavuṇṭar political parties; and other villagers can no longer be counted on to give wholehearted support to Kavuṇṭar-run village festivals. While the Kavuṇṭars seek other new measures to counter these threats (Manickam 1979: 39), they find their leadership of the summer pilgrimage to be one way in which their social mastery can still be substantially constituted and publicly demonstrated.

Kavuṇṭar Farmers come to Palani, all dancing and trancing, in rollicking, loosely organised, nocturnal stages that recreate the extravert social dominance which they formerly enjoyed in their respective villages. Members of other castes are included in the Kavuṇṭars' pilgrimage—allied Veḷḷāḷars to swell the size of the procession, Barbers, Washermen, Musicians, and other dependant castes to provide ceremonial services and entertainment. But only Kavuṇṭars and their allies are allowed the privilege of personally carrying water offerings for the god. Unlike the Traders, Farmers as 'maximal transactors' (Marriott 1976: 125–26) are happy to exchange meals with villagers along the pilgrimage path and thus to spread their networks of channels for mutual influence and obligation. For them their pilgrimage is thus socially, politically and personally recreative.

Farmers' natures are said to show a high proportion of *rajaguṇa*, the expansive, passionate quality which empowers external action and "hot-tempered" (*cūṭamai*) dealings in gross substance (Bech 1972: 11; Manickam 1979: 40). Heat is prominent in the stories that derive the origins of Kavuṇṭars and other Right-hand castes from a firepot that Śiva gave to Mariyamman as a weapon with which to kill a pernicious demon: 'From that fire (in Mariyamman's right hand) came some people to serve her and to cool her by caring for that fire' (Beck 1981: 93–94). Their inherent heat makes these castes the most suitable managers of the earth's fertility (Moreno 1987) and likewise of the gods' problems of thermic excess. Farmers thus have a natural symbiosis with Murukan each summer.

The Farmers' manipulative, demanding attitudes toward Murukan contrast almost as summer and winter with the sacerdotal attitudes of the Naṭṭukkottai Traders. Unlike the Traders, who salute the ascetic Murukan with formal respect and "devotion" (*bhakti*), Farmers address the god familiarly, either referring to him as "child" (*kuḻantai*) when attempting to soften him up for a later request, or calling him "father" (*appā, ayyā*) when actually requesting a boon. While Traders stress that they visit Murukan out of unconditional and undemanding "love", Farmers carry water only with explicit contracts in mind, wanting to get "what is needed" (*vēṇṭutal*) by them, such as relief from some present misfortune, or "to repay a debt" (*nērttikkaṭan*) that was pledged to the god for relief already received.[8]

Fluidising pilgrimages

Pilgrims of other contrasting humours—some high and wet (therefore unmarking), others low and dry (mark-receiving)—also seem needed if Murukan is to maintain his capacities for flexible response. Such pilgrims are respectively Brahmans and Cakkiliyans (*Mātāris*) and their transactions with Murukan especially concern not his thermic balance, but his fluid functioning. Brahmans function as a source of fluidity for Murukan while Cakkiliyans function as a container preventing its loss.

Devotees belonging to the Brahman and other high, demonstrably virtuous and phlegm-rich castes, commonly bring vessels of cow's milk to Murukan. They bring these milk offerings as contributions to the god's daily bath and also to his personal store of unctuous benevolence—his source of superior potency and virtue. They come at all seasons and without festival clamour, since milk is continually needed for bathings and since an excess of something so precious is inconceivable. The high quality of their offering helps to unmark the god. In return they receive and drink a portion of the "[water] mixture" (*tīrtam*) which is the residue of the god's daily bath. It marks them as lower than and appropriately blessed by him.

Cakkiliyan Leatherworkers, the largest Untouchable caste of the Left-hand in the region, make small, white, flowered shoes for Murukan's use and bring them to him similarly at intervals through the year. Footwear is recommended in Hindu medical books to maintain sexual potency and sharpen eyesight, evidently by helping to conserve the vital fluids that empower these functions. The books teach that semen and other vital bodily fluids are stored mainly in the head and chest, but may drain away by a sensory-motor channel that links the eyes directly to the feet (Caraka *Sū*. 5: 100; 20: 8); from the feet fluids may leak out unless restrained by shoes. As a cool, unmixing caste, Cakkiliyans should have an inherent

[8] These contractual aspects of Tamil worship are examined in more detail by Moreno (1985: 104–05).

talent for closing whatever is open; as low and dry, their natures should be ready to absorb marks; and as a somewhat peripheralised, unmatched caste they should be capable of stopping or reversing any directional movement. Thus, they are well suited to being Murukan's (and other persons') Cobblers.

With a purpose and by means apparently analogous to that of the shoes—conserving the god's vital fluids by constraining them—young girls of their caste are also brought to Murukan regularly by the Cakkiliyans of Palani town. Dedicated to the god as virgins, the girls are to remain as celibates in his service, a relationship which Cakkiliyans cite in substantiating their right to address Murukan as "sister's husband" (*maccaṉ*).

These fluid transactions move gravitationally—lighter, superior offerings rising from pilgrims to the god, and residues falling from the god to pilgrims—substantialising the fact that the transactors are higher and lower along a continuous stream of markings. Brahmans' 'optimal' strategy of nurturance and Cakkiliyans' 'pessimal' strategy (Marriott 1976) of podiatric or sexual service both construct channels through which help may be requested from the beloved god whenever needed.

MARIYAMMAN

Mariyamman is the goddess who in various circumstances has shown herself capable of erupting with smallpox, cholera and fevers (Elmore 1915: 20; Fawcett 1889; Francis 1906: 324; Whitehead 1921: 32), but also of bringing rain and prosperity (Arokiaswami 1953: 153). People in Palani say that she is both "too hot" and "too cold", as do other Tamils reported by Beck (1981) and Egnor (1984). Thus, they place Mariyamman unstably at three extremes of two variable constituents—heat (mixing) and wind (unmatching). Indeed, she arrives at a time of year when heat and epidemics are all expected to increase. Her name has been plausibly translated as "ambivalent lady" (Brubaker 1977: 60), "changed mother", and "mother of changes" (Egnor 1984).

Mariyamman's twenty-one day festival at Palani deals mainly with her volatility and flatulence, at first by opposing (unmatching) her thermic excesses externally (complementing her windy and overheated state with water and then her overcooled state with fire). Later it leads her through some matching rituals of a female life-course in which her turbulent, eruptive tendencies are to be more intimately united with, then divided from, the opposite, calming and ordering capacities of a husband. Tuesdays and Fridays—moments of her special accessibility—punctuate her passage from virgin to wife to widow with many reversals.

The complexity of the present festival results not only from the contrary nature of the goddess, but also from the diversity of her worshippers, who participate differently in most of the above actions and interpretations according to their natures. Some contradictory features may represent adjustments made over a long history of disputes. Multiple changes in ownership and a complex sharing in the management and ritual offices of her local temple now bring together persons of humorally diverse constitutions. The single festival of Mariyamman has thus become a composite like what might be imagined if all pilgrimages to Murukan were combined in one great festival.

Here as elsewhere, Mariyamman was probably once worshipped primarily by castes of the Right Hand (Beck 1972: 118); for them her slaying of a demonic buffalo was a critically important feature. But her clientele has recently expanded to include vegetarian Brahmans, castes of the Left Hand, and others who would not accept such a feature. Priestly liturgies from the Saiva canon now alternate with clamorous popular happenings, and the buffalo slaughter has been replaced by the goddess' wedding to a disappearing groom of disputed identity.

Preparations

Brahman priests (experts in matching) use canonical words to inaugurate the proceedings, which they and the Left-hand castes treat as a celebration of marriage between Mariyamman and the cool god Śiva. In deference to these participants' antipathy to violence and meat, the preparatory "pacification of the village site" (*grāma śānti*), which formerly included a scattering of blood to distract unwanted spirits, is done bloodlessly.

Gross physical preparations are conducted mainly by men of the Right-hand castes, who define the festival as a confrontation between the goddess and Karṭṭaviriya Arjuna, the handsome, lustful demon on whom she will ultimately take revenge for destroying her previous marriage. Under Right-hand direction the demon is embodied in a three-branched tree trunk (*kampam*), a form which some Left-hand observers prefer to see as Śiva embodied in his three-pronged spear. Men of the Right Hand bathe and worship the iconised demon, then accept as blessings some of his bodily adornments, his properties evidently being regarded as assets, at least for this occasion. Filled then with demonic energy, they rush the icon through the town and fix it upright in the temple hall so that it directly faces the goddess' chamber, a stance which only a very bold suitor might dare to take.

Cooling week

The danger of the impending confrontation between goddess and demon-groom—both of them superheated—is reduced by a week of coolings applied to both. The groom's heat is reduced largely by women of the cold-dispensing, Right-hand agricultural castes, who are almost the only worshippers in attendance during this week. They apply margosa leaves (considered especially cooling) to his "head" and pour water over it until they flood the temple. Some women roll on the ground around him in sexual obeisance, taking his heat and thus also cooling him. Most take back some of his heat-filled, vital drippings for use as medicinal blessings to benefit eyesight, promote reproductive health, and ward off skin diseases (for causing which the goddess is notorious). Evidently these women reckon themselves and the demon as mutually compatible in their opposition to the goddess' threats as well as in their sharing warm and somewhat windy humours.

The goddess separately receives cooling baths every day, administered privately inside the temple by her male professional attendants. Her critical state is indicated by her remaining thus in virtual seclusion. Some married women devotees emulate the goddess' sexual isolation by sleeping at the temple. During this still dangerous stage, those women worshippers who request the goddess' blessings are given only her ashes or her *kumkum*—not the usual residues from her Tuesday and Friday baths.

To please the goddess, crowds of women dancers circle and clap outside the temple on each night of this week. Some round the ambulatory of her shrine by successive prostrations. Many are possessed and speak with the goddess' small, breathy voice, usually expressing approval of the celebrations and answering other women's questions about future and far distant events.

Whenever they come to the goddess' temple during this dangerous week, those women who have newly harvested paddy at their homes throw handfuls of grain into the air at her gate. Throwing into the air directs offerings to disembodied, dissatisfied spirits and demons of which many are thought to fly or lurk about the goddess. The scattered grain is visibly collected by women of the town's Telugu-speaking Sweeper caste and by itinerant Beggars—beneficiaries whose heavily marked and unmatched natures resemble the dry, disarticulated offerings that they here receive. After such peripheral hungers are pacified, the remaining portion of the crop is expected to yield unimpaired prosperity to its owners, as in similar north Indian harvest rites reported by Raheja (1988: 162–69).

Ventilating drama

Pallans, who are Right-hand Untouchables and bound as a caste to the worship of her sister-goddess, offer themselves as channels by which Mariyamman's flatulence could be reduced[9] during the same cooling week. Enacting a myth of two drunken Pallan guards at Mariyamman's temple

[9] For the reduction of wind, enemas, cathartics and simple rectal ventilation are recommended in Hindu medicine (Caraka *Sū*. 7. 12–13; 20. 13).

who had once been accused of theft and sentenced to impalement, two Pallan men now sit atop "impalement posts" at her temple gates each night, awaiting terminal deflation. But in the myth the Pallans were exonerated after the goddess' intervention through a king's dream; here the votaries are released when, in the next week, their wives detect a blink and a smile from the cooled goddess' otherwise sleeping icon. The oneiric and ocular media used in these communications from Mariyamman are subtler than the impalement shaft, but show Pallans to be her very special servants, who are ready to receive even her grossest markings.

In these events Pallans' mark-receiving, 'pessimal' (Marriott 1976: 128) relation with Mariyamman approximates the form of Cakkiliyans' relation with Murukan. But as hot, perforable, disorderly, wind-disposing servants of the Right Hand and backside, Pallans contrast with Left-hand Cakkiliyans, who present themselves as cool, calm, continent and styptic.

From a point of view that emphasises matching, all rites to this point may be considered as preliminary calmings of disorderly forces. Thus, the Brahman priests of this festival (borrowed from the Murukan temple) do not raise the festival flag of Mariyamman's temple until the end of this week of cooling rituals. Only when her wind goes down does the flag go up, beginning the Brahmans' positive, orderly celebration.

Heating week

Providing the first fuel for this auspicious week of fire, Mariyamman's non-Brahman temple attendant places in the crotch of the tree trunk ("on the head of the groom") a huge earthen pot filled with firewood and clarified butter. When the attendant sets the pot afire with coals brought from the goddess' chamber, the music of pipes and drums soars to a peak of intensity. Worshippers call out praises to the goddess, raising their hands in high salutations as they would at the killing of an animal in sacrifice. Indeed, in the opinion of Right-hand worshippers, this event is a killing—the goddess' slaying of the demon groom by the burning of his head.

Repeatedly on each night of this week, male and female votaries of any caste carry pots of fire in their bare hands to the goddess' temple. Family members usually assist. The relative balance or at least the ambiguity of the goddess' humours at this stage permits many to approach her with less fear, trusting Mariyamman to allow them to do so with impunity. Although turbulent by nature, Mariyamman has been somewhat calmed for the time being by her previous week of bathing and ventilation, is now expelling much of her fire, and has become no hotter than a "pot of flowers" (*pūvōṭu*—a euphemistic word for the burning fire-pots now being given to her). Now she evidently craves more fire, either to reheat her overcooled self in preparation for marriage, or to continue her attacks on the demon-groom, which she does on succeeding nights. By either interpretation she adds to her network of devotees, blessing all with her now benign warmth, as well as with her warm *kumkum* or cooled ash, and again with her usual biweekly bath-washings.

In the middle of the week, Kavuṇṭar Farmers cook sweet rice—an auspicious, celebratory food—in the temple grounds for a ceremonial offering to the goddess; they themselves take back and eat the transvalued residue as her blessing, substantialising their intimate subordination to her. For this feast, they use auspicious grain from the same new crop whose negative components were thrown over the goddess' gate in the previous week.

De otion is confounded with revelry during the evenings of this complex but wholesome (for the goddess) week. It is a time of maximal interaction among people, and thus not surprisingly, some incoherence for them. Votaries carry their pots of fire; shops are crowded with women, especially those purchasing cosmetics while eruptive forces are quiet; intoxicated men dance wildly; and boys dressed as women enact farcical skits. In Mariyamman's temple it is now the turn of her male non-Brahman attendants to be possessed and to speak with the goddess' voice, and they do so repeatedly. In the midst of these contrasting events, the goddess in her moveable image is paraded around the town each night to be fed and entertained by competing host-groups of the Kavuṇṭar caste, and recently of other castes as well.

Wedding or funeral?

On the Tuesday of the third week of the festival, Mariyamman is deemed by some of her worshippers to be calm enough and warm enough (but not too warm) to be betrothed to whoever is embodied in the burnt tree trunk that stands before her. In contrast with the oppositional, unmatching responses applied in the cooling and heating rituals so far, a wedding is a matching, harmonious event: it attempts to bind separate entities and construct a new unity within which previous differences will be submerged. Members of the higher Left-hand castes prominently support this strategy by contributing to the wedding preparations: Florists bring garlands, Merchants bring an embroidered red silk saree for the bride, Traders bring *kumkum* for the couple's foreheads, and Artisans bring dolls to decorate the temple hall with representations of the goddess' divine family. These contributors receive in return various cool favours, such as the goddess' used garlands and sandalwood paste, that mark their castes as her principal marital well-wishers.

The wedding rites are performed by Brahman priests using an elaborate Śaiva agamic liturgy. Notably omitted from their performance are two rites that are present in the weddings of humans and of many other deities in south India—the "pounding of rice" and the "tying of the wedding badge".

Reasons given for these omissions are varied. According to the officiating priests and many worshippers of the Left-hand castes here, Mariyamman is in a state of "continual auspiciousness" (*nitya kalyāṇi*), an ambiguous term referring possibly to her perpetually married state, but here more plausibly to her perpetual virginity. This is a state that these castes think of as cool and peaceful, especially admirable for a woman. (Parvati, also a virgin goddess betrothed to the god Śiva, is often so described.) They hold therefore that Mariyamman may now be matched with her perfect groom, but need not be given in actual nuptial possession or consummation, for which the bodily-binding marriage necklace and the heat-producing rituals of pounding and grinding would be metonyms.

Farmers and others of the Right-hand castes offer a different interpretation of the missing rites, one especially sensitive to issues of dominance—heat, rank and conflict. They say that Mariyamman detests the pounding pestle and the grinding stone as signs of slavery. (In fact, they say that Mariyamman's temples should be built only away from human settlements, where such sounds of domestic drudgery will not reach her ears.) Their interpretation of the missing marriage badge, like that of the Left-hand castes, acknowledges the bride's reluctance, a mythic theme which is common in Tamil Nadu (Shulman 1980: 144–66) and elsewhere in India. But Farmers give this theme a special twist: they say that women who are long unmarried (as Mariyamman is) store up great amounts of heat, and that Mariyamman therefore remains too volatile to be successfully controlled (matched with and marked) by any male (cf. Shulman 1980: 166–92).

Whoever the groom may be—demon or Śiva—on the day following the defective wedding rites (always the lunar day of the full moon) Mariyamman is taken around the town, riding alone on a huge wooden chariot with the insignia of a queen. She is without a marriage badge but is otherwise dressed as an auspicious wife would be. Throngs of enthusiastic citizens rush to help drag the chariot by pulling the long ropes and chains attached to it. The glamour of the goddess' public appearance and the fervour of her devotees impresses many with Mariyamman's new coherence and accessibility, even as her moveable image is returned to its temple residence.

The festival does not quite end with Mariyamman's procession, for late in the night when nearly all worshippers are asleep, the tree trunk is inconspicuously uprooted and dragged by a non-Brahman temple attendant to a nearby pond, where it is immersed. This proceeding is witnessed only by the Paraiyan who beats the death drum. After the immersion, the festival flag comes down, and the goddess has her jewels removed and her red saree replaced by the simple, unbleached white saree of a widow. She remains so attired in her temple with the doors locked and with all worship suspended until the early hours of the next evening, when her donning of a yellow saree returns her to readiness for normal transactions with her worshippers.

Has there been a funeral? Most people of the Left-hand castes deny the death of Mariyamman's husband and interpret the immersion of the tree trunk as the routine, honorific cooling out of any temporary festival image. But people of the Right Hand, particularly Pallans, interpret Mariyamman as briefly polluted by the death of the suitor or mate whom she has murdered. They interpret the goddess' final condition as widowhood, which for her should be, and for them is, a humorally tolerable condition of moderate warmth and hope. According to Farmers of this area (who permit the remarriage of widows), the goddess becomes like those flourishing fields which lie fallow for some time after a harvest, waiting to be sown again.

The festival of Mariyamman at Palani is thus a composite of divergent actions and interpretations by castes of three-dimensionally contrasting natures. Thermic alternation and then an accelerated life-passage nevertheless enable the "mother of changes" to bestow her powerful blessings successively upon nearly all of Palani's residents. Neither her turbulence nor their diversity is compromised, for all are played out together, if ambiguously, through variable time.

Conclusions

A humoral Indian ethnosocial psychology has here been applied to the analysis of three great festivals which celebrate the cults of two very popular, but very different deities in one town. Palani's Mariyamman has an intense local following, while the Murukan at Palani draws adherents from a population of many millions. This Mariyamman deals mainly with issues of dominance and destruction, while Murukan here especially offers love, reciprocity and healing. Murukan changes gradually with the seasons and the stars, while Mariyamman fluctuates with the disjunctive and conjunctive interpersonal events of a female life. Celebrated by parts of one population in divergent ways, the cults of Murukan and Mariyamman each and together present examples of continuing Indian diversification that challenge conventional sociological explanation.

Different as they are, the cults of Murukan and Mariyamman can both be understood as working socially by variations in the same three elements or humours—fire, water and wind. Both Murukan and Mariyamman join by the corresponding transactional processes of mixing, marking and unmatching with their diverse worshippers, who are differentiated among themselves by the same three processes. Such cults would have few reasons for existence if gods or worshippers were simply ranked, or if either gods or worshippers were equivalent, invariant entities on which the other could rely without such continual and continually varied exchanges. A humoral ontology and epistemology provide many reasons for such variations and exchanges and for the cults' continued vigorous existence.

REFERENCES

Appadurai, Arjun. 1974. Right and left hand castes in south India. *Indian economic and social history review* 11: 216–60.

Arokiaswami, M. 1953. The cult of Mariyamman or the goddess of rain. *Tamil culture* 2: 153–67.

Babb, Lawrence A. 1970. The food of the gods in Chhattisgarh: some structural features of Hindu ritual. *Southwestern journal of anthropology* 26: 287–304.

———. 1981. Glancing: visual interaction in Hinduism. *Journal of anthropological research* 37: 387–401.

———. 1983. The physiology of redemption. *History of religions* 22: 298–312.

Beck, Brenda. E.F. 1969. Colour and heat in south Indian ritual. *Man* (n.s.) 4: 553–72.

———. 1972. *Peasant society in Konku: a study of right and left subcastes in south India*. Vancouver: University of British Columbia Press.

———. 1981. The goddess and the demon: a local south Indian festival and its wider context. *Puruṣārtha* 5: 83–136.

Brubaker, Richard L. 1977. Lustful woman, chaste wife, ambivalent goddess: a south Indian myth. *Anima* 3: 59–62.

Caraka. 1983. *Agnivesa's Caraka saṃhita* (trans. Ram Karan Sharma and *Vaidya* Bhagwan Dash). Vol. 1, *Sūtra sthāna*. Varanasi: Chowkhamba Sanskrit Series Office.

Clothey, Fred W. 1978. *The many faces of Murugan: the history and meaning of a south Indian god*. The Hague: Mouton.

———. 1982. Chronometry, cosmology and the festival calendar in the *Murukaṉ* cult. *In* G.R. Welbon and G.E. Yocum, eds., *Religious festivals in south India and Sri Lanka*, pp. 156–88. New Delhi: Manohar.

Daniel, E. Valentine. 1984. *Fluid signs: being a person the Tamil way*. Berkeley: University of California Press.

David, Kenneth A. 1974. And never the twain shall meet? Mediating the structural approaches to caste ranking. *In* Harry M. Buck and Glenn E. Yocum, eds., *Structural approaches to south Indian studies*, pp. 43–80. Chambersburg PA: Conocoheague Associates for Wilson Books.

———. 1977. Hierarchy and equivalence in Jaffna, north Sri Lanka: normative codes as mediator. *In* K.A. David, ed., *The new wind: changing identities in South Asia*, pp. 179–226. The Hague: Mouton.

Egnor, Margaret Trawick. 1978. The sacred spell and other conceptions of life in Tamil culture. Ph.D. dissertation, Anthropology. Chicago: University of Chicago Library.

———.1984. The changed mother or what the smallpox goddess did when there was no more smallpox. *Contributions to Asian studies* 18: 24–45.

Elmore, Wilbur T. 1915. Dravidian gods in modern Hinduism. *The university studies* 15: 1–149. Lincoln: University of Nebraska.

Fawcett, Fred. 1889. On some festivals of village goddesses. *Journal of the anthropological society of Bombay* 2: 261–82.

Ferro-Luzzi, Gabriella Eichinger. 1977. The logic of south Indian food offerings. *Anthropos* 72: 529–55.

———. 1978. Food for the gods in south India. *Zeitschrift für Ethnologie* 103: 86–108.

Francis, Winston. 1906. *Gazetteer of Madura*. Madras: Government Press.

Ganesh, Kamala. 1979. Vellalas: a socio-historical perspective. *In* R. Nagasamy, ed., *South Indian studies* 2: 47–58. Madras: Society for Archaeological, Historical and Epigraphical Research.

Kavirayar Balasubrahmaniya. 1903 (1628). *Paḻanittalappurāṇam* (ed., N. Kadiravar Pillai). Madras: n.p.

MAHABHARATA. 1973. *Vol. I. The book of beginnings* (trans. and ed., J.A.B, Van Buitenen). Chicago: University of Chicago Press.

MANI, SRINIVASA B. 1981. From marriage to child conception: an ethnomedical study in rural Tamil Nadu. *In* Giri Raj Gupta, ed., *The social and cultural context of medicine in India*, pp. 194–220. Main currents in Indian sociology, vol. 4. New Delhi: Vikas.

MANICKAM, SUNDARAJ. 1979. The Konku Vellalars of Coimbatore—a sketch of a dominant peasant community. *Journal of Tamil studies* 16: 34–47.

MARRIOTT, McKIM. 1976. Hindu transactions: diversity without dualism. *In* Bruce Kapferer, ed., *Transaction and meaning: directions in the anthropology of exchange and symbolic behavior*, pp. 109–42. Philadelphia: Institute for the Study of Human Issues.

———. 1989. Constructing an Indian ethnosociology. *In* this volume.

McGILVRAY, DENNIS B. 1982. Sexual power and fertility in Sri Lanka: Batticaloa Tamils and Moors. *In* Carol P. Macormack, ed., *Ethnography of fertility and birth*, pp. 25–73. London: Academic Press.

MERREY, KAREN L. 1982. The Hindu festival calendar. *In* Guy R. Welbon and Glenn E. Yocum, eds., *Religious festivals in south India and Sri Lanka*, pp. 1–25. New Delhi: Manohar.

MORENO, MANUEL. 1984. Murugan, a god of healing poisons: the physics of worship in a south Indian center for pilgrimage. Ph.D. dissertation, Anthropology. Chicago: University of Chicago Library.

———.1985. God's forceful call: possession as a divine strategy. *In* Joanne P. Waghorne and Norman Cutler, eds., *Gods of flesh, gods of stone*, pp. 103–20. Chambersburg, Pa.: Anima.

———. 1987. Agriculture as a sacrament: a new approach to the cycle of rice in south India. *Lambda alpha journal of man* 18: 53–62.

NATAREJAN, MANIKKAR. 1966. The Natukkottai Shettiyars of Chettinadu. *Proceedings of the First Tamil International Conference* 1: 251–60. Kuala Lumpur: International Association of Tamil Research.

OBEYESEKERE, GANANATH. 1975. The Left-Right subcastes in south India. *Man* (n.s.) 10: 462–68.

PFAFFENBERGER, BRYAN. 1982. *Caste in Tamil culture: the religious foundations of Sudra domination in Tamil Sri Lanka*. Foreign and Comparative Studies, South Asian series, no. 7. Syracuse: Maxwell School of Citizenship and Public Affairs, Syracuse University.

RAHEJA, GLORIA GOODWIN. 1988. *The poison in the gift: ritual, prestation, and the dominant caste in a north Indian village*. Chicago: University of Chicago Press.

RUDNER, DAVID WEST. 1987. Religious gifting and inland commerce in seventeenth century south India. *Journal of Asian studies* 46: 361–79.

SHANMUGAVELU, M. 1968. Mercury—the universal remedy for almost all diseases—according to Siddha's concept. *Proceedings of the second international conference—seminar of Tamil studies* 2: 531–34. Madras: International Association of Tamil Research.

SHULMAN, DAVID DEAN. 1980. *Tamil temple myths: sacrifice and divine marriage in the south Indian Saiva tradition*. Princeton: Princeton University Press.

SOMALAY. 1975. *Palani, the hill temple of Murugan*. Palani: Arulmigu Dandhayuthapani Swami Devasthanam.

SOMACUNTARANAR AVARKAL, P.V. 1978. *Tirumurukārruppaṭai*. Tamil annotated edition. Tirunelveli: Saiva Siddhanta Nurpatippu Karakana.

SOMASUNDARAM PILLAI, J.M. 1970. *Palani, the sacred hill of Murugan*. Palani: Sri Dandhayuthapani Swami Devasthanam.

SRINIVAS, M.N. 1976. *The remembered village*. Berkeley: University of California Press.

STEIN, BURTON. 1980. *Peasant state and society in medieval south India*. New Delhi: Oxford University Press.

VENUGOPAL, P.M. 1968. Muppu. *Proceedings of the second international conference—seminar of Tamil studies* 2: 541–44. Madras: International Association of Tamil Research.

WHITEHEAD, Rev. HENRY. 1921. *The village gods of south India*. Calcutta: Oxford University Press.

ZIMMERMANN, FRANCIS. 1979. Remarks on the body in ayurvedic medicine. *South Asian digest of regional writing* 18: 10–26.

———. 1980. *Ṛtu-sātmya*: the seasonal cycle and the principle of appropriateness. *Social science and medicine* 14B: 99–106.

8

The Kerala house as a Hindu cosmos[1]

Melinda A. Moore

In this paper I review my attempts to make sense of the complex structure of traditional high caste houses of Kerala, mostly Nayar houses in the Ernakulam and Palghat (formerly Valluvanad) districts, in which I lived for most of 1978–80 while studying family life.[2] I compare my observations of the houses and the highly patterned ways people live in them with some classic and regional prescriptions about buildings. As I assemble these observations and prescriptions, I find them approximating the multidimensional graphic metaphor for an Indian ethnosociology proposed by Marriott (1989). I go on to interpret the houses as models for dealing with the many-propertied, substantial Hindu universe that the modern West calls 'space'.

I became aware of some meanings of these older dwellings primarily by participating in everyday activities and in the annual round of life in three Nayar houses, and secondarily by noting or mapping similarities and differences in a total of about thirty other such houses that I visited. These were houses belonging to Nayar, Nambutiri Brahman, Ambalavasi, and kingly sub-castes.[3] Everywhere people's activities seemed to be patterned according to properties attributed to the houses themselves. I encountered many instructions from residents as to who and what should go where and

[1] The field research upon which this paper is based was supported by a grant from the American Institute of Indian Studies. Special gratitude for their assistance in India is due to Mr. C. Narayanan Nair of Adakkapputthur, Palghat district, and to his brother Mr. C.S.K. Nair. For criticism of earlier drafts of this paper, thanks are due to Michael Moffatt, Richard Kurin and Lee Schlesinger To McKim Marriott I am grateful for suggestions throughout, and for designing the drawings.

[2] My reports on Nayar family (*taṛavāḍ*) life (M.A. Moore 1983, 1985, 1988) argue that the house as a ritual entity plays a defining role in the Nayar and Nambutiri kinship systems.

[3] I did not gather detailed data on the houses of Tiyyas and lower castes but had the impression that these emulated the houses of Nayars and Nambutiris as far as was economically possible. Justification for my using the term 'Kerala Hindu house' for a generalised description of high caste houses lies in the economic and cultural dominance of these castes.

when, although I could elicit from them only fragmentary explanations of why matters should be so disposed. I was given many statements about the qualities of certain spaces (for example, 'the interior areas are safer'), but no comprehensive schemes. This lack of more general schemes may be due to the fact that houses of the older type ceased being built about fifty years ago.

Seeing my interest in the organisation of space in these houses and in the rules for building them, both residents and experts referred me to Malayalam-language building manuals. These manuals republish traditional prescriptions on house-building, apparently in order to preserve meanings that would otherwise be forgotten. My readings of such manuals led me from the observed architectural and behavioural evidence to several layers of ritual,[4] astral myth, and geometric formulation that in combination produce a structure much like the 'constituent cube' which Marriott (1989) constructs from the Hindu elements, humours, strands and aims.

The houses and their plans

The houses of which I write were constructed, usually for extended families, according to the Kerala science of house-building (*taccuśāstram*), which is digested in the Malayalam building manuals. 'Modern' houses are constructed differently—in the words of an expert informant, according to 'civil engineering principles'—and are usually smaller, being intended for a nuclear or only slightly extended family. The same informant told me that some of the old building customs—rituals, orientations, proportions—are still followed in rural areas, 'but not fully'.

A complete house in the manuals and in current Malayalam language consists of a "quadrilateral" or "four-sided" (*nālukeṭṭu*) structure centred on a "middle place" (*naḍumiṯṯam*),[5] or atrium (A in Figure 1). The Malayalam word for any building is *keṭṭiḍam*, literally a "tied" or "bound space". An atrium is itself open to the sky at the top and its stone-paved floor (with external drainage) is sunk into the earth below the level of the rest of the house. Writing about 1900, the observant Rev. Fawcett states that only in a four-sided house 'can all ceremonial be observed in orthodox fashion' (Padmanabha Menon 1937, IV: 162). The atrium was in his time used for making solemn contracts regarding membership in the house, land tenure and personal service; it continues to be preserved as a "sacred

[4] Daily rituals of the house will be mentioned in this paper, but the rituals of site selection, building and house entry are reserved for fuller discussion elsewhere (M.A. Moore n.d.).

[5] *Naḍumittam* in reference to the human body means the waist or the small of the back. Glosses of Malayalam and Sanskrit words are given in double quotation marks to distinguish them from quoted English words, which are given in single quotation marks throughout this paper.

place" (*tirumiṯṯam*) for festivals or other temporary worship, for growing jasmine flowers for the hair of Nambutiri and Ambalavasi married women, and in a few houses for the establishment of permanent specialised shrines.

Each of the four sides of the atrium or middle place is oriented squarely to one of the four directions. Any room or building standing beside the atrium or a courtyard is commonly given a directional name, being called "the northern", "the eastern", "the southern", or "the western" side (Malayalam *vaḍakkini, kizhakkini, tekkini* and *paḍiññaṯṯi*, respectively).[6] Added to the atrium's up-down orientation, this directional nomenclature completes a three-dimensional, cosmically oriented conception of the house.

A four-sided residence of medium size (one of the houses in which I stayed) is represented in Figure 1.[7] The structures forming the sides of the "middle place" may alternatively be unconnected buildings that do not touch each other at the corners as do the walls of this and most other houses which have enclosed atriums (Kanippayyur 1979: 79). In either case, the area between their wall lines is usually known as the "middle place".

Smaller houses which seem to lack an atrium or court are also very common. In the right half of Figure 1 is the plan of such a house, another one in which I have lived. Fawcett calls dwellings of this plan 'the ordinary Nayar's house that one sees all over Malabar'.[8] Residents of such a house generally consider their structure to be like the "west" side of a complete four-sided house; Raghavan (1932: 211) calls it a "west-side" house. They use a part of the ground at the eastern face of the house (here marked with a parenthetic A) for the special activities that take place in the atriums of four-sided houses.

Much larger dwellings used to be constructed by wealthy and noble families. These would often incorporate several atriums as well as have numerous separate buildings in their compounds, some of which would themselves have atriums. Two, four, or (very rarely) eight atriums may be found in one such large dwelling. (Odd numbers of such features are avoided.) Where there are many atriums, only one in the southern part of the house is considered to be the true "middle place" of the dwelling.

Houses of all sizes have rooms or areas that are dedicated to certain

[6] Additional buildings named for one of the four directions may even stand at some distance from each other, as do the "main house" (on the west) and the two "southern" side buildings of a Nayar dwelling mapped by Padmanabha Menon (1937: IV, 176A).

[7] The larger house at the left is the dwelling of a Nayar *taṛavāḍ* of medium rank—Asthikurissi (funeral priests)—in Valluvanad (now Palghat) district. The smaller house belongs to a branch of the same *taṛavāḍ*.

[8] Fawcett's drawing is reproduced by Thurston (1909: V, 361–64) and by Padmanabha Menon (1937: IV, 160–62).

FIG. 1 PLANS AND ORIENTATIONS OF KERALA HOUSES

A 'Four-Sided' House

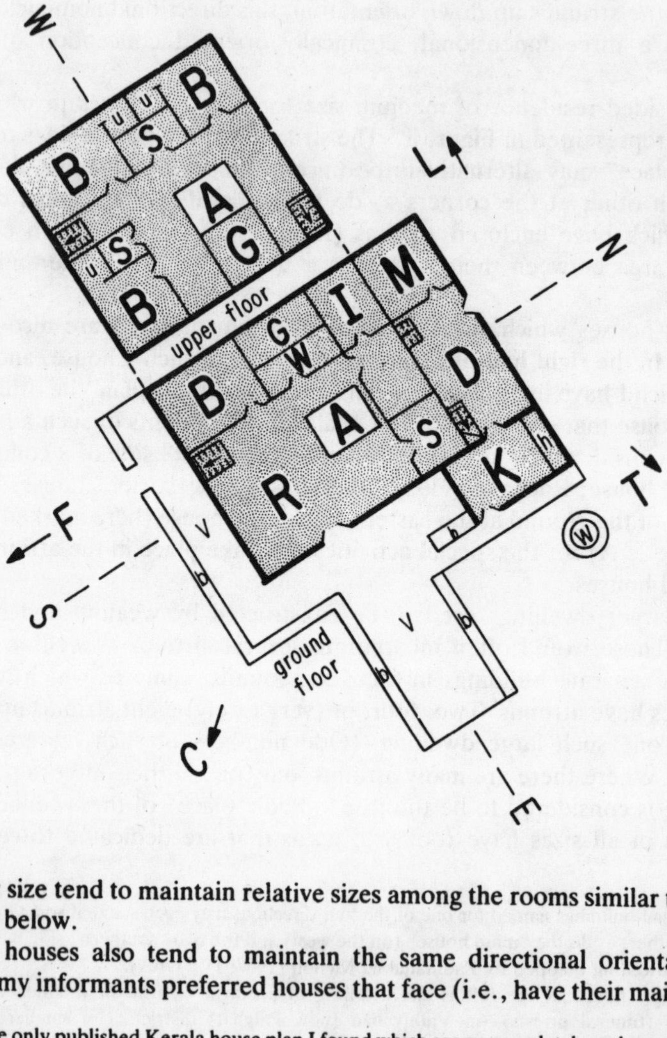

of any size tend to maintain relative sizes among the rooms similar to those noted below.

All houses also tend to maintain the same directional orientations.[10] Since my informants preferred houses that face (i.e., have their main doors

[10] The only published Kerala house plan I found which seems completely and systematically to violate the directional scheme of rooms presented here is a Nambutiri plan reproduced by Padmanabha Menon (1937: IV, 159). The residents' adaptations to its unusual orientations are unfortunately not known.

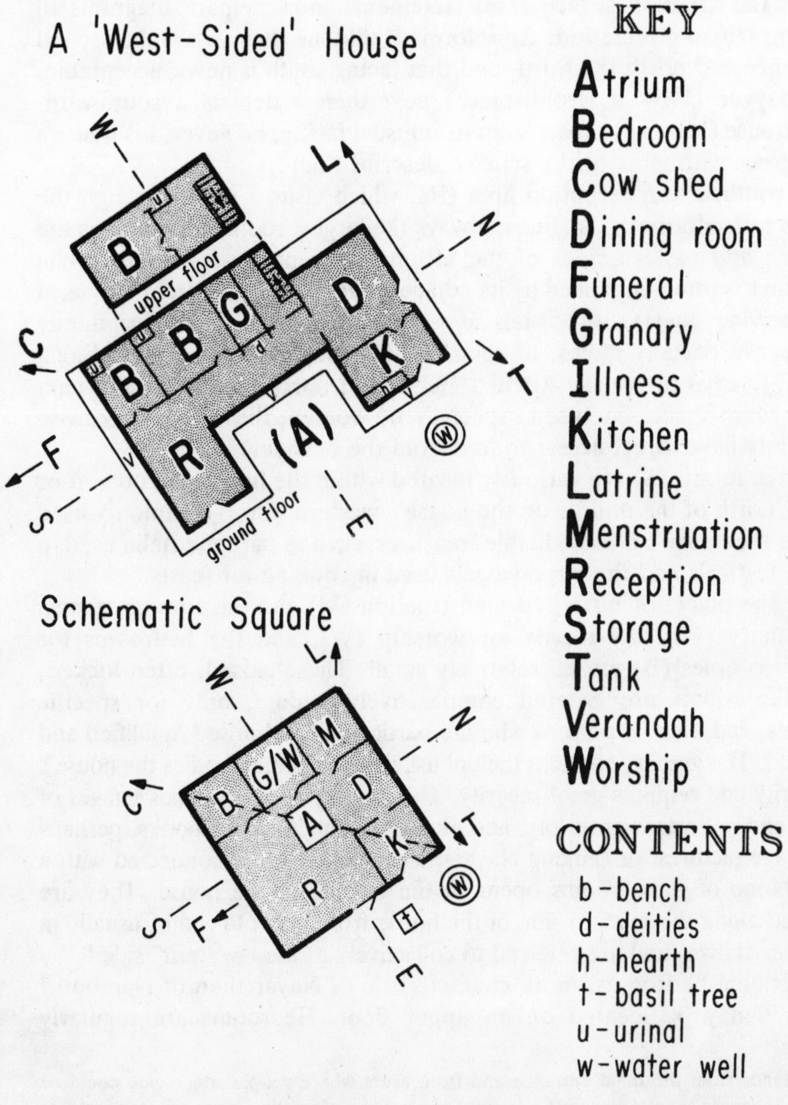

purposes. Larger houses provide separate rooms for purposes that smaller houses combine in a single area or room.[9] Thus, the larger house in Figure 1 provides a separate room for birthing and menstruating women (M) in its northwestern area, whereas the smaller house requires a menstruating woman to sit in the northwestern corner of the northwesternmost room (D)—a room used for family dining and for other purposes as well. Houses

[9] In general, Nambutiris have larger houses that are more differentiated in areas for rituals, dining and cooking.

opening toward) the east, and since my observations show that eastward is actually the commonest facing, my statements and schematic diagrams all refer to such an orientation. An informant told me that west is the second preference and north the third, and that facing south is never acceptable. Kanippayyur (1963: I, frontispiece) nevertheless depicts a southward-facing house (his own); apart from its unusual facing, however, his house's plan agrees with most of the scheme described here.

The southeastern reception area (R), which visitors enter through the house's main doorway, is almost always the largest room. It combines the southern and eastern sides of the atrium. Its capacity for larger social gatherings is often enhanced by its adjacency to a covered porch. It is used for receiving guests, for rituals and feasts, and as a place for family members, especially males, to socialise. On the north the family dining area (D), adjacent to the kitchen (K) at the northeast, offers the next largest room space, one used especially by women; these rooms likewise commonly have direct access to and from the outside.

Storage rooms (S) are variously located within the house. A room at or slightly north of the middle on the house's western side is commonly used to store the house's most valuable treasures, such as paraphernalia used in temple festivals and the large vessels used in cooking for feasts.

Like the place for birth and menstruation (M) and the storage rooms, the granary (G), any rooms for worship (W), and the bedrooms for married couples (B) are all relatively small. These closed, often locked, vault-like rooms are entered comparatively seldom, only for specific purposes, and then by persons who are particularly authorised, qualified and prepared. The granary contains the unhusked grain that embodies the house's prosperity and requires great security. The worship room contains images of deities and important ancestors, and may also contain sacred books, perhaps pilgrimage pictures, or (among Nayars) a protective sword connected with a deity. None of these rooms opens to the outside of the house. They are arranged along the western side of the house from north to south, usually in the order shown, and are referred to collectively as the "western" side.[11]

Additional bedrooms, more characteristic of Nayar than of Nambutiri houses,[12] may be located on an upper floor. Bedrooms are regularly

[11] Distance from the main entrance and from areas where people congregate could be stated as the more general principle governing the location of smaller, more private rooms, as in the urban, middle class Gujarati houses studied by Pramar (1987). In accord with this principle are the six Goan houses (presented by Ifeka 1987: 314–20) which face west and have their smallest rooms in the east. Kerala Hindus generally speak about rooms in directional terms, assuming that houses all face east; they do, however, also talk about the greater secludedness and protectedness of the interior spaces, regardless of direction.

[12] During the times when most of these older houses were being built, Nayar extended families retained their female, rather than their male members as residents, and also accommodated the husbands of those women; Nambutiri families, on the other hand, permitted only the eldest son to bring home a bride, and hence needed fewer private bedrooms.

equipped with private urinals, usually in closets. The menstruation room may be equipped with its own separate facilities for cooking, and in modernised houses with facilities for defecation and bathing as well.

Residents sometimes compared their houses with temples since houses always contain objects of worship which, like images in a temple, are usually placed on the western side and approached through an entrance-structure from the east. Temples need only have an east-west axis, but houses and compounds must be elaborated on a north-south dimension, too, in order to provide areas for human activities not essential to a temple, such as eating, sexual intercourse, birth, menstruation, defecation and cremation.

Along with their strong orientations to the four primary directions, houses and building manuals show concern with diagonals, and especially with the diagonal that runs from the southwest to the northeast corner of any house and compound. The southwest-northeast line (called simply *karṇasūtra*,[13] "the diagonal", literally "the ear" or "the corner line") is represented in some houses by a finger-sized hole through any wall that blocks its path. An informant told me that such strings of holes ("doors" in the manuals) are meant to facilitate flow (of wind, etc.) between the southwest and northeast corners.

Verandas (V) are most commonly attached to the eastern and northern faces of the house, but may be found also on the south and west. The southern and eastern verandas are used for sitting by day, and sometimes for sleeping by males at night. The northern veranda, especially its eastern end near the kitchen, is used by women for grinding and such activities related to food preparation. Persons who have eaten come there to spit and brush their teeth, leaning over its edge. Dishwashing may be done on the veranda outside the kitchen, where water from the well is handy and a drain carries the waste water off to the northeast. The compound area immediately northwest of the house is used for pounding and parboiling rice (thought to kill small creatures) and for killing and butchering meat animals.

Outside the house proper but within its compound (generally an unwalled, but clearly designated area), seven other features seem once to have been common: serpent grove, well for potable water (w), tank for bathing (T), tree of sacred basil (t), cremation ground (F), cowshed (C), and an area for defecation, or latrine (L). Larger dwellings may also incorporate whole temples in their compounds, if not inside the walls of the house. A compound's serpent grove has a variable location which is determined by local observation or divination.[14] Each of the other outlying features, like the

[13] For purposes of wider recognition, Malayalam words borrowed from Sanskrit are given in their standard Sanskrit spellings, rather than in their Malayalam forms.

[14] Innes (1951: 139) states that the serpent grove should be in the northeast; however, Thurston (1909: V, 364) cites a source saying that it is in the southwest, and Mencher's map (1966: 142) also positions it in this direction. I have seen such groves in practically every direction relative to houses.

rooms of the house, is said to require location in a certain direction which is appropriate to it. The appropriate direction for each of these is indicated around the 'schematic square'. Only two of these features—serpent groves and sacred basil trees—are missing from the actual compounds mapped in Figure 1.

Wells, tanks and any other out-buildings seem to be so located as to avoid the stresses that are thought to radiate out from the house along its centre lines and diagonals. Informants and Kanippayyur's manual (1979: 27–28) agree that nearby structures should not have their centre lines or diagonal lines coincide with those of the house lest they be "pierced" and damaged. The general tendency of a house to extend outward is also recognised as a problem in the building manuals, as detailed below and in Figure 5.

Where I found unusual directional orientations occurring in the compound, I also found residents aware of and apologetic regarding the violations. For example, a grossly inappropriate arrangement seemed to have been made at one house where the residents bathed in a tank and worshipped at a shrine in the northwest corner of their compound, the quarter generally reserved for defecation. When I queried a resident, he declared that the problem had been anticipated by ritually establishing a "namesake boundary" to the west of the house; that area having been redefined as part of another compound, the house's own tank and shrine could then appropriately be built there.

The 'schematic square' diagram (in the lower right-hand page of Figure 1) summarises the ways in which I found the plans of these older "four-sided" houses and compounds to be generally conceptualised and oriented.

Patterns of household activity[15]

The houses in which I lived had compelling routines of daily life as well as periodic ceremonies which all appeared to be somehow linked to particular properties of the houses themselves. Properties of the residents and their activities were felt to affect the house just as properties of the house manifestly affected the residents, much as reported by Daniel (1984:

[15] Some cultural analysts of domestic space (Bourdieu 1977; H. Moore 1986) emphasise contextuality, change, and the reflection of ongoing social relations. Similarly, Das (1977), Daniel (1984) and Khare (1976) emphasise process, flow, and interaction in the way South Asians give meaning to space. I find such emphases valuable, yet here rely more on conceptualisations that are relatively invariant across contexts. I must do so (*i*) because much of what is interesting about these houses can no longer be observed in ongoing social contexts, although it is remembered and located; and (*ii*) because I am relating memories and observations to formulas in certain texts which are relatively fixed and noncontextual. Other approaches that have been particularly valuable in South Asia include the search for spatial symbolism (e.g., Eck 1982, 1985; Kramrisch 1976; Meister 1986) and for ideological correlates of spatial arrangements (e.g., Ifeka 1987; Pramar 1987). I am unable to use either of these approaches fully here, but present data relevant to both.

105–62). I mention here only the most salient of the routine and life-cycle activities. Most of them involve movements of people and things from one area to another and thus indicate relationships in ways that static architecture may not.

Women generally precede men in rising, defecating and bathing. Defecation is done only in the northwestern latrine (L) area of the compound, which is usually approached by way of the house's northern exit.[16] Bathing is the immediately subsequent activity, and is accomplished at the compound's tank (T), near the northeastern corner; after bathing, the house is normally re-entered by the front (eastern) door. Exiting by the northern door when going on a journey is thought to have bad consequences.

Twice every day, at dusk and at dawn, the household's oil lamp (*viḷakku*ᵛ) is taken from the worship area or niche for deities (which is always near to the granary, G) by a woman who is in a pure state (bathed, fasting, not menstruating). It is filled and lighted by her in the kitchen, and is then carried through the rest of the house, moving toward the south; it is shown to the sun (at the eastern or western end of the southern veranda, if there is one) and finally returned to the worship area. Members of the house should view the lamp from the south, as it emerges from the kitchen; no person should look on this lamp from the north facing south, and to prevent this, the northern door of the house is closed when the lamp is brought out.

The kitchen is of course also the immediate source of the meals that sustain the family, meals that they ordinarily consume in the informal dining area (D) immediately adjacent to the kitchen. Formal meals and snacks are often presented to guests in the reception area (R), rather than in the family's dining area.

Married couples generally sleep in their respective private bedrooms (B). The southwesternmost bedroom (usually upstairs) is the one usually given to a newly married couple to promote conception on their wedding night.[17] The D and R areas are preferred for group sleeping by others who are unmarried or are without their spouses. Men sleep separately in one

[16] The latrines I observed were privies close to the house, where they were said to have been located for menstruating and parturient women to have easy, direct access. Their locations also shortened the distance to the tank for the bathing necessary immediately after latrine use. Mencher (1966: 142) and Padmanabha Menon (1937: IV, 179A) each present plans showing a latrine in the southwestern quadrant of the compound, far from their respective houses in the northeast quadrant. Latrines (called *kakkūs*, a word borrowed from Dutch) are undoubtedly an addition of the European period; their preferred locations are not mentioned in the building manuals.

[17] The Kerala preference for locating reproductive intercourse in the southwestern corner contrasts with Daniel's (1984: 119–20, 177) report from Tamil Nadu that the same location is prohibited because the house itself is always conceived by placing a stone or post there. In Kerala the place for "laying the first stone" (*śilāsthāpanam*) is not fixed, but is determined by drawing squares for the twelve Malayalam solar months around the outer edge of the house site, and counting from the current month to the tenth square (Kanippayyur 1968: 3).

group, women and young children in another, women taking the more interior (or upstairs), men the more exterior (or downstairs) places, such as a veranda, or the gatehouse of a larger dwelling.

Apart from family mealtimes, during both day and night, males tend to remain in the southern half of the house, females in the northern. A prohibition on the movement of women into the southern half (but no restriction on men's movement to the north) was observed in only one Nayar house of my experience—one that was said to have been imbued with this rule by its original residents, who were Nambutiri Brahmans. Separate northern and southern stairways are sometimes provided for males and females to reach the upper storey without leaving their respective halves of the house.

Menstruation presents conflicts between the need to seclude and protect the woman and the need to avoid spreading her pollutions around the house. Menstruating women were before the present generation required to keep apart from others in a special area or room. They could go out only to defecate and then only by the northern door until they had completed their days of pollution, when they could again bathe at the tank. Any woman entering the menstruation area or touching its occupants was required to bathe before returning to activities in other parts of the house.

When there is a death in the family, the deceased's body moves from north to south. Some householders customarily prepare the body in the northern (D) area, others in the southern (R), before carrying it to the cremation ground (F) in the south of the compound. The south of the compound is also used in death anniversary (*śrāddha*) observances, when *bali* offerings are thrown here to be taken by crows.

The atrium is kept clear of ordinary activities. In Nambutiri houses it usually contains worship facilities or even permanently installed deities. In Nayar houses it functions as a place for worshipping certain temporarily installed but important deities, such as Viṣṇu and Mahābali at the harvest festival of Onam, and the first sheaf of grain when it is brought in and worshipped at the ritual called "house-filling" (*illaṃniṟa*). The atrium has a generic quality. As a Nayar woman said to me, 'Any other offerings to gods may be placed here. For example, if the nearest temple is three miles away, one can avoid walking to it by placing offerings here.'

The atrium is also the place where rituals establish or reconfirm a relationship between the house and a person not born into it, such as a servant or (in a Nambutiri house) a bride. For example, the "ghee pitcher" (*naikkiṇḍi*) ritual, which was traditionally used to create a relationship of tenancy, took place there (Kanippayyur 1963: I, 28).

The walls, verandas and compound of the house distinguish three degrees of entry into the dwelling area that correspond with a triad of rules concerning acceptable distances between persons of different castes (Mencher 1966: 154). Persons who are merely "untouchable" to each other, like Nayars and Nambutiris, can enter each others' houses.

Members of a caste which is deemed "unapproachable" by a higher one, such as the Ceruman caste, who are agricultural serfs in relation to Nayars, can come onto the higher caste's verandas, but may not enter further. "Unseeables", such as Nayadi scavengers and beggars, cannot set foot in the compound of a Nayar house. The particular castes in these categories differ according to the caste of the house's residents.

In sum, these older Kerala Hindu houses impressed me with their microcosmic near-completeness. They contain areas not only for all daily activities, but for entire life passages from conception to cremation. They provide places for relating the residents to people of other social categories. They accommodate on their premises many or most of the beings that require worship or propitiation, and leave open spaces for the rest. Their comprehensive layouts led me to seek cosmic notions, such as those explored by Beck (1976), Das (1982, 1985), and Kramrisch (1976), to elucidate them. I began looking for such notions in the regional building manuals, where I found formulations that do not prescribe the locations of either rooms or activities, but speak of unseen divine presences, subtle slopes, and inherent proportions, as detailed below.[18]

Cosmic formulas in the building manuals

The "foundation man" (*vāstu puruṣa*)

The "Foundation Man" is a fallen antigod (*asura*) on whom a "Foundation Assembly" (*vāstu maṇḍala*) of controlling gods are seated. His myths, vedic and puranic, are known throughout South Asia (Beck 1976: 227; Kramrisch 1976: I, 7–97). His form is prominently displayed with a synopsis of his myth in most of the building manuals I examined. In the manuals that depict him (e.g., Kanippayyur 1979: 44, from which Figure 2 is derived) he lies supine with his head to the northeast,[19] pressed into a square whose sides are oriented to the cardinal directions. Over him in a standard pattern on the same square are inscribed the places and names of his controllers, usually forty-five gods, with eight more 'homeless' gods and demonesses at the outer corners and sides. Invoked and propitiated before any house or temple is constructed, the Foundation Man and Assembly together depict a world that is oriented to the directions horizontally and layered vertically, with gods triumphant over antigods, sky dominating earth, and aniconic presences controlling the visible body, but with possible trouble at the peripheries.

The position of the Foundation Man suggests the general character of

[18] The manuals deal with many other topics—with ritual, with types of soils that are suitable for the houses of various *varṇas*, with the measurements, etc. (M.A. Moore n.d.). Here I select only topics relevant to the form and uses of houses.

[19] Kramrisch (1976: I, 96) reports that a due east orientation of the head is found in some texts, but this does not appear in any of the manuals that I have examined.

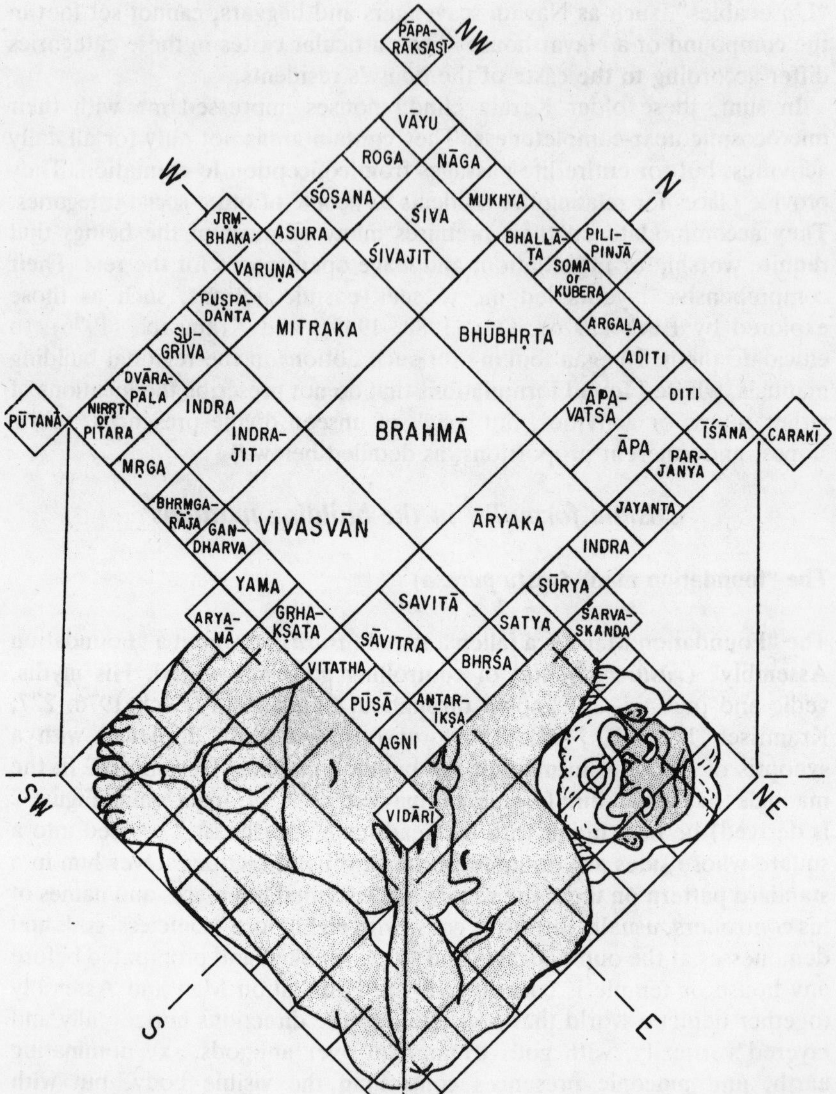

Fig. 2 THE GODS SEATED UPON THE FOUNDATION MAN

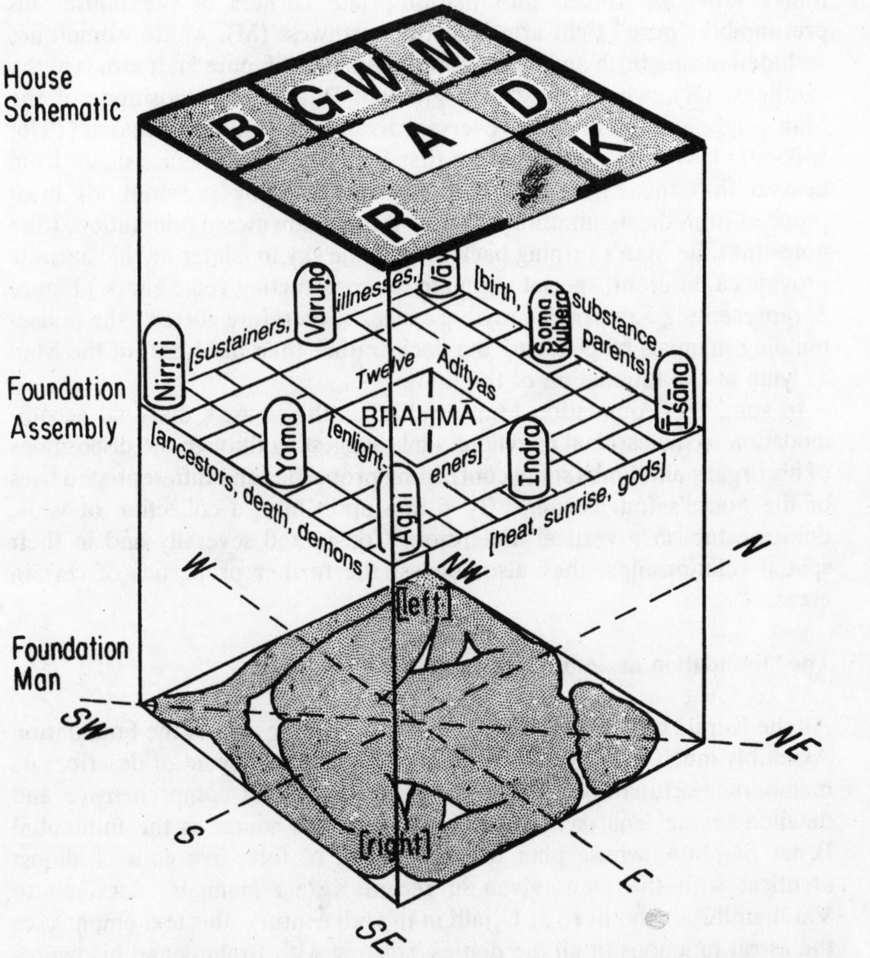

Fig. 3 HOUSE WITH GODS AND FOUNDATION MAN as interpreted by Kramrisch 1976:I:85–97

uses for the centre and four corners of the house. The Man's central organs—navel and waist—are depicted by the manuals at the middle of the square, where conceptually the architectural "middle place" arises. The Man's mouth in the northeastern corner could be said to demand food, and that is where the kitchen (K) is actually located. The Man's genitals are a prominent feature of the southwest corner where the most favoured bedroom (B) of the house also seems appropriately located.

If he faces upward, as shown in Figure 2 and in all the manuals, the

Man's arms are forced into inappropriate corners of the house: his presumably "pure" right arm is in the northwest (M), where women are secluded during birth and menstruation, and his "impure" left arm is in the southeast (R), where guests are greeted. But those dispositions of the Man's right and left must be reversed. Kramrisch's mythic research (1976: I, 85–97) leaves no doubt that he first fell head-first and face-down from heaven into the earth, and that ordinary building prescriptions must proceed from the assumption of his continued downward orientation. (She notes that the Man's turning back toward the sky in a later mythic episode provides a different, special template for constructing vedic altars.) Figure 3, representing Kramrisch's mythic exegesis, therefore corrects the house-building manuals by picturing the back, rather than the front, of the Man as lying at the foundation of the house.[20]

In sum, the Foundation Man establishes the house's diagonal accommodation to the cardinal directions while suggesting through the dispositions of his organs and limbs some contrasting properties and differentiated uses of the house's four corners. By sitting upon him, a collection of vedic deities establish a vertical dimension. Considered severally and in their spatial relationships, they also suggest the further properties of certain areas.

The "foundation assembly" (*vāstu maṇḍala*) of gods

All the Kerala building manuals present the seating plan of the Foundation Assembly much as in Figure 2, but none explains its layout or describes its members. Fortunately Kramrisch (1976: I) offers a comprehensive and detailed textual analysis of both. Her principal source is the influential Bṛhat Saṃhitā, whose plan for the seating of forty-five gods is almost identical with the plans given in recent Kerala manuals. Ascribed to Varāhamihira, who lived at Ujjain in the 6th century, this text emphasises the astral functions of all the deities, starting with Brahmā and his twelve attendants, seen as representatives of the sun. Kramrisch also searches through a wide array of largely earlier, vedic sources to elaborate on the attributes and mythic relations of these gods. My summary of what seems most relevant in her data and interpretations appears in Figure 3.

At the centre of the Assembly, sitting over what the Kerala manuals depict as the Man's navel, is Brahmā. Brahmā's location corresponds

[20] The corrected (downward) facing of the Foundation Man brings his limbs back into correlation with the apparently nearly universal association of right with male and left with female (Needham 1973). It also correlates with the Tamil and Telugu distinction between the Right-hand groupings of castes, who maximise inter-caste mutuality (which would be appropriately realised in the open and spacious southeast of the house), and the Left-hand grouping of castes, who minimise it (as would be favoured by the house's closed and secluded northwest) (Marriott 1976).

closely to the conceptual "middle place" of the house (A). That the first of the gods and the original power of the universe sits in this location seems to encourage treatment of the atrium as a nodal "sacred place" that is filled with undifferentiated power.

Kramrisch observes that the sun is seen as carrying light 'from the centre to the corners' (1976: 90), evidently with the help of the subordinate deities and along the square's diagonal lines. Correspondingly, the light coming from its "middle place" is also often remarked on by residents of a Kerala atrium house.

The gods' heliocentric seating plan suggests a ranked ordering among them starting from the largest seat offered to Brahmā, and stepping down through two grades of large but lesser seats given to his twelve lieutenants, the Āditya enlighteners and their spouses. Thirty-two small spaces are allowed for all other gods on the perimeter, plus eight more for demons on the square's projections. The rules of approach for various persons and castes treat the Kerala house as if it had three or four such ranked layers—atrium, rooms, verandas, compound, and beyond.

Among Brahmā's four attendant deities with the largest squares, two—Āryaka (due east) and Mitraka (due west)—are arcs of the sun's apparent path. They sit symmetrically opposite each other in the directions where the sun rises and sets, respectively. The solar path between them is depicted in the Kerala building manuals as the "Brahmā line" (Figure 4) and is celebrated in the ritual of showing the household lamp to the sun at both dawn and dusk. But only if the seating plan of these deities is interpreted as asymmetrical can it be said to suggest the large differences evident in both architecture and activities between the east and west sides of the house.

The seat for Mahīdhara (= Bhūbhṛta) to the north of Brahmā, according to Kramrisch, is the place where the *vāstu puruṣa* is 'most firmly fixed in his nature' (1976: 90). Kramrisch equates Mahīdhara with Ananta, the serpent on whose head the world rests, a deity who is invoked in the ritual of "laying the foundation stone" (Kanippayyur 1968: 5). I could find no special associations of greater fixity or firmness with this area of Kerala houses, nor did informants refer to an underlying serpent. Many houses do, however, partition the northern side of the atrium and some use it as an area for worship.

Vivasvān, who is seated due south of Brahmā, 'is Mārtāṇḍa, the mortal form of Brahman, whom "Aditi bore hitherward into repeated birth and death" (RV. X. 72.9)' (Kramrisch 1976: 90). His location and this quotation suggest a north-south cycling of human lives and indicate connections of the south with death that are confirmed by many other textual and actual usages.

The thirty-two deities around the Assembly's perimeter are divided by Kramrisch into sub-groupings whose attributes suggest other properties of the house. Thus, the group of deities on the eastern side are generally linked with fire (and hence with *kāma* or desire), with the sun, and with light (and hence also with *dharma*). Such properties are consistent with uses of this side of the Kerala house for daytime activities, for cooking, and for external relations, such as receiving guests.

In the south, next to Vivasvān and flanking Yama, god of death, are other 'divinities associated with the Ancestors (*pitṛ*) and . . . divinities of evil portent' (Kramrisch 1976: 92). But locally the Ancestors (alternative or joint occupants of the southwestern corner seat with Nirṛti in Figure 2) are not regarded as implacably 'evil'; they are demanding, but will not cause harm if their demands are satisfied.

Along the west side of the Assembly, the deities to the south of Varuṇa differ greatly from those to his north. The southwestern group includes Sugrīva, or Manu, 'the primordial and universal law-giver'; it also includes the vehicles of the gods Śiva and Viṣṇu (Dauvārika [Nandi] and Puṣpadanta [Garuḍa], respectively) (Kramrisch 1976: 93–94). Although law-giving and vehicles suggest little about the specific purposes to which this area is put (bedrooms, granaries, rooms and niches where deities are installed), their formative, facilitating, life-sustaining natures are at least not incompatible with the constructive character of these parts of the house. In noting some positive attributes of these west-by-southwestern deities, I am interpreting Kramrisch's data, rather than reporting her own characterisation; I am specifically setting aside her further exegesis of the goddess Nirṛti as 'destruction, decomposition, the exit from life'—associations which I did not hear from people in Kerala, whose manuals describe the area of Nirṛti as the "quadrant of the gods" (as in Kanippayyur 1979: 26).

In sharp contrast to my positive reading of these deities' traits are the clearly menacing natures of deities to the north of Varuṇa—Śoṣa ("drying up"), Asura or "antigod" (Kramrisch has Pāpayakṣman, "consumption"), and Roga ("disease"). These deities are directly suggestive of uses of the northwestern area by persons who suffer from such depleting and disorganising processes as birth and menstruation.

The deities seated on the northern perimeter are, according to Kramrisch, those who provide the materials of human life. These include serpents (Nāga, Argaḷa) in their generative aspects, the gods of human fluidity (Soma) and wealth (Kubera), the god of making (Mukhya, equivalent to Viśvakarman), and the goddesses Aditi and Ditta or Diti (mothers of the Ādityas and Daityas, respectively). In the Kerala house, the west end of this side (M) is indeed the corner of birth, while the east end is the kitchen corner (K) from which nourishment is made to emerge. From the kitchen corner the household lamp is also made to emerge when a woman carries it through the house at dawn and dusk. Although female functions and some female presences are thus indicated by the Assembly for the K area, the actual preponderance of women all along the north side is not specifically presaged in the divine seating plan.

Summary. Following Kramrisch as in Figure 3, I could thus interpret some attributes of the vedic deities in the Assembly as suggesting the present uses and purposes of sides and corners of the Kerala Hindu house. These attributes confirm some (eastern openness, southwestern generativity, northwestern impurity) and add other (central light, concentric rank, solar ritual, southern death, etc.) suggestions to those that could be provided by the Foundation Man alone. Yet because different readings of the deities' attributes are also possible, and because few deities of the Assembly or their loci on the plan are known to residents, it seemed to me that their possibly causal and meaningful connections with perceptions of the house remained remote. To supplement the historical scholarship of Kramrisch and the largely unexplicated seating plans in the building manuals, I looked for formulations that are more consciously and demonstrably present and meaningful to the residents. One such formulation is that of the well-known deities called "guardians".

The guardians of the eight directions (*aṣṭadikpāla*)

The eight deities in the Assembly called "guardians of the eight directions", can by themselves suggest most of the lateral, if not the central properties of the house that the larger Assembly suggests. As shown in Figures 3 through 5, these guardians are Indra, the sun god (east); Agni or "Fire" (southeast); Yama, god of death (south); Nirṛti, a goddess (southwest); Varuṇa, god of waters (west); Vāyu or "Wind" (northwest); Kubera, god of wealth, or Soma, a lunar and ritual "elixir" (north); and Īśāna, the upward-looking face of the god Śiva (northeast). In a village temple a few miles from the houses in Figure 1, these deities were represented as icons on a temple ceiling; their locations and their names, unlike the names of many other gods of the larger Assembly, were known to many of my informants.

Brenda Beck (1976: 232–35), following her informants in Konku, Tamil Nadu, and referring also to Kramrisch and other textual sources, proposes a naturalistic rationale for the guardians' placement based on movements of the winds as well as of the sun. The rising sun, which Beck notes is on most days a bit south of due east, is the most prominent natural phenomenon of both the southeast (Agni) corner and the due east (Indra) direction. The due west (Varuṇa) direction, to which Beck gives the specific interpretation of 'rain' (rather than the more general meaning of "water"), she says, is associated with darkness not only through the sunset but through the black clouds that come with the monsoon rains.

Beck makes little reference to Tamil domestic architecture, but her interpretation of the meanings of the directional guardians reiterates what the larger Assembly shows and fits with some uses of the southeastern corner of a Kerala Hindu house: the room for greeting guests is appropriately located at the southeastern corner from which the sun rises and is greeted. In Kerala the room for birth and menstruation, which makes the person undergoing them unfit for contact with most other persons and places, seems well-placed in the area that is most remote from these guests. Yet, this scheme says little about important areas like the atrium or kitchen and seems to be contradicted in Kerala by the location of deities and other worshipped entities in rooms of 'dusk and darkness' along the west side.

Beck also argues for more dynamic diagonal interpretations:

> wind is diagonally paired with fire, and water is paired with the earth. This fits with the popular idea that the chariot of Agni (fire) is drawn (upward) by Vayu (wind) (Gopinatha Rao 1916: 524) and that the earth 'draws' water downward from the sky. Furthermore, these ideas link the southeast to upward movement and the southwest to the opposite (Beck 1976: 234).

Kerala house-building manuals do give attention to diagonals, as shown in the ground-plan of Figure 4. Houses and compounds are both discussed as comprising four "corners" or "quadrants", each belonging to its guardian, either "Īśāna", "Fire", "Nirṛti", or "Wind". Some houses facilitate communication along the southwest-northeast diagonal between the Nirṛti and Īśāna corners by holes through their walls. But contrary to Beck's interpretation of close relations between "fire" and "wind", the slopes that tilt the house in either southeast or northwest directions are both listed in the Kerala manuals as highly destructive (Figure 4), and no attempt is made in houses to open a physical passage between these corners.

As for the southwest-northeast diagonal, no manual and none of my informants support Beck's tentative identification of the southwest corner's deity Nirṛti with "earth", or of the northeast corner's deity Īśāna with "water" (Beck 1976: 233), although wells are preferably located to the northeast of houses in Kerala as they are in Konku (ibid.: 221). The manuals' discussions of "slopes" assume that Nirṛti in the southwest corner is higher (for which see below), contrary to Beck's implication; moreover, a lower position for Īśāna is more consistent with the 'upward-looking' iconography that Beck finds for him (ibid.: 221 fn. 16). In other words, a reversal of Beck's hypothesised movement is indicated: in Kerala, if not also in Konku, Īśāna appears to draw water downward from the direction of Nirṛti (and Varuṇa).

Summary. The loci and attributes of the divine presences—the guardians of the eight directions, the Foundation Man, and the gods of the Foundation Assembly—establish the general orientation of the house and suggest some appropriate uses of its areas. The diametric and diagonal relationships of these further suggest some sorts of internal processes. But the gods' many attributes and narratives leave ambiguities that themselves seem to need further clarification by data from an ethnographic context, and their placements alone are unable to provide much information on relationships and processes.

Slopes

I was surprised at first to find so little in the Kerala manuals regarding the up-down dimension of building. From E.V. Daniel (1984: 138) I had learned that in the denser, clustered villages of Tamil Nadu the relative heights of houses and temples are carefully calculated, since the higher structure is assumed to influence the lower structure, and not vice versa. If one wishes to gain the blessings of a deity, one should build one's house on lower ground or build it to a height less than that of the deity's temple. But if one wishes to avoid being dominated by an enemy domiciled nearby, one is advised to build a taller house, or one on higher ground.

The Kerala manuals that I surveyed have nothing to say about the relative height or gross height of buildings, but they do presuppose inequality and asymmetrical influence. Their views on these relations are contained, I found, in formulations that ostensibly concern not altitude, but the house's lateral and frontal placement vis-a-vis temples, the slope of the plot of land on which the house is to be built, and the quadrant within the compound on which the house is best built.

One Kerala manual (Kanippayyur 1979: 16–17) considers quite subtle lines of dominance when it urges builders to place their structures in front and to the right of the temple of a deity with a beneficient aspect, but to the rear and left of one having a "malign icon" (*ugramūrtti*). Evidently a diagonal cline of subtle influence is presumed to exist on what may otherwise appear to be level ground. Assuming that the deity or house in question faces east, as is usual, the presumed universal and underlying cline may be restated directionally as running from southwest to northeast. This cline coincides with three other diagonals which I had previously taken to be horizontal—the foot-to-head axis of the Foundation Man, the main "corner line" of the manuals, and the string of holes through the walls that some old houses have. If one follows the manuals, all these southwest–northeast diagonals must be taken as naturally sloping toward the northeast.

In effect, no land is expected to be level and level plots are not advised by the manuals. Instead, the manuals treat sloping land systematically and provide rationales for preferring one slope to another. Figure 4, which was developed from one manual's table (Kanippayyur 1979: 11), predicts that five of eight possible directions of slopes will yield decidedly negative consequences. A slope from south to north and one from west to east will both yield positive consequences, and a slope from southwest to northeast will yield the best consequences of all.

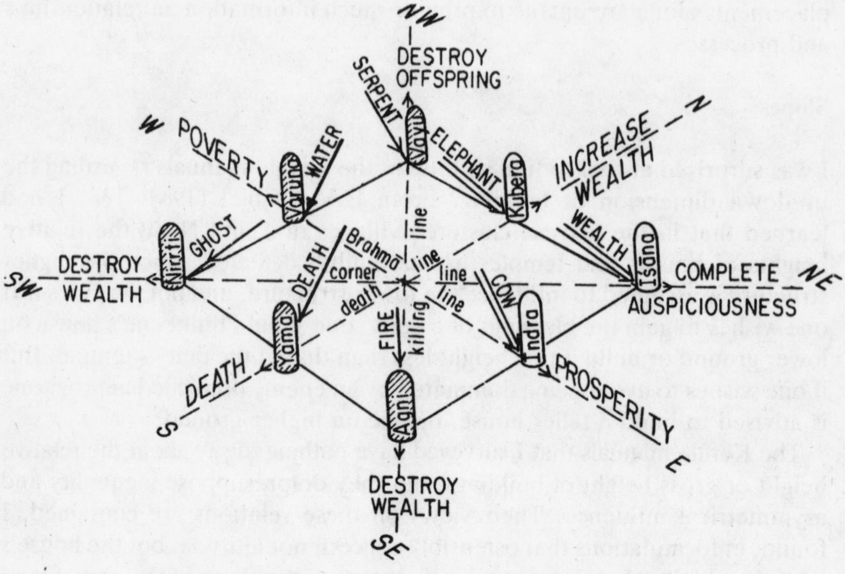

Fig. 4 Slopes and their Consequences

Accompanying this advice on slopes, Kanippayyur offers two analogies: (1) consider the direction(s) in which it is best for oneself to face and see that the house plot does likewise; and (2) consider the direction(s) in which it is best for water to flow and see that this is the slope of the ground on which you build. Kerala Hindus prefer to face eastward, toward the rising sun; they also favour facing northward in contexts like the daily crepuscular viewings of the household lamp.[21] Facing northeast gains the visual advantages of both north and east. Water is presumed to move most easily in the same southwest-to-northeast direction, given the universal subtle cline presupposed by the manuals.

Kanippayyur's comparison between vision and the flow of water struck me as odd until I applied a *saṁkhya* and *advaita vedanta* theory of perception, by which 'the mind (*antaḥkaraṇa*) goes out to the object and assumes its form' (Sinha 1986: I, 136). Seeing is thus understood to involve a substantial emanation of light from the mind through the eyes (Babb 1981), an emanation that seems to move like the flow of water, gravitationally.

Assuming the underlying universal cline, if a house's ground slopes to

21 The eastward facing of a sacrificer is an ancient rule, and so is the northward facing of his priest. Das (1977: 106–07) provides examples from Gṛhya Sutra texts of the auspiciousness of looking and moving eastward and northward. Manu (6: 31) advises forest-dwelling Brahman ascetics to end their lives by moving northeastward, presumably upward into the Himalayas.

the west, then flood and waste waters might not drain away from the house. Similarly, the residents of a westward-sloping house site may have their view obstructed on the east, and thus be deprived of witnessing auspicious events such as the sunrise. The gods of a household shrine or temple are particularly insistent on having such a view (Logan 1951: I, 83); thus, they are kept in the western side of any structure, facing eastward, and their worshippers must take the less desirable westward view in order to face them. A southern slope would have the same hydraulic disadvantages as a western slope and would further cause the house undesirably to face always toward the god of death and place of cremation, to trend always in their direction.

At the northeastern pole of the preferred slope—in the earthen depths of the well and the tank—a recycling of impure into pure water seems to take place. Waste water bearing bodily effluents should not flow back to the house, but assisted by rain water should flow toward these reservoirs in the north and east, where it will merge with the universal waters, which are by definition pure.

Discussions in the manuals of where to build one's house on a plot of land similarly assume an underlying flow of good influence from the southwest toward the northeast (e.g., Krishnavariyar 1975: 17). Choices are made in terms of "quadrants" (*khaṇḍam*). Innes (1951: 139), writing in 1908, describes such discussions as follows:

> The compound being divided into four by imaginary lines running due north and south and east and west, the house should occupy the southwest angle of the northeast quarter. Thus it is practically in the centre of the garden.[22]

Kanippayyur (1979: 26) agrees that the northeast and southwest quadrants (those which are along this main diagonal) are the best for houses. but seems to approve both quadrants equally:

> The northeast (Īśāna) section of a plot of land which has been divided into four sections is called 'the section of human beings.' One who builds a house in it will obtain offspring, wealth, and prosperity in every respect. The southwest Nirṛti section is called the 'section of gods.' If one builds a house here, he will obtain all of his desires. These two sections are auspicious for the building of houses. The section in the southeast Agni corner is called the 'section of Yama.' Because of this, it is productive of death. It should be avoided in all circumstances by all *jātis*. The northwest Vāyu section is called the 'Asura section.' As this name suggests, it too is not good.

[22] Such a placement is nicely illustrated in the house and compound drawn by Mencher (1966: 142).

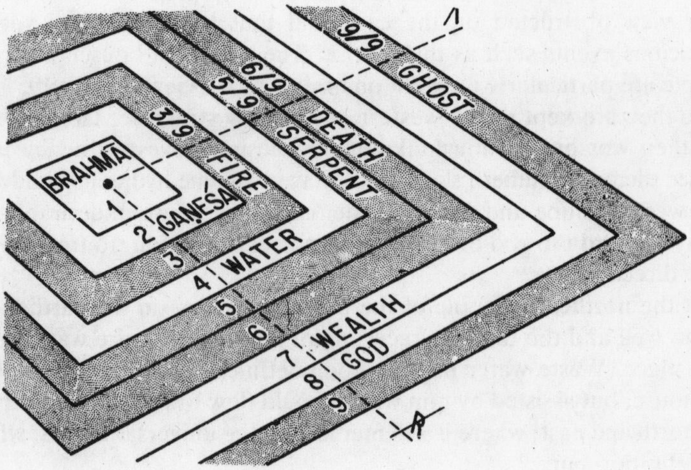

FIG. 5 HOUSE/LAND RATIOS
(after Krsnavariyar 975:23 and Kanippayyur 1979:31)

Proportions: external relations

In keeping with the Nayar tendency to seek "good fruits" like prosperity and increase, houses are assumed naturally to expand. But extension in space is fraught with subtle dangers. The manuals offer no formulas by which external dangers increase in regular correlation with increased distance, contrary to the expectations one might have from the caste rules of approachability sketched above. However, several manuals do offer a formula by which the extent of a house over its compound may be evaluated for possible losses and gains.

The formula for relating extension to loss or gain is expressed in ratios of house to land, as shown in Figure 5. To calculate these proportions, one must first measure the compound and divide both its width and its length into eighteenths. The resulting series of eight rectangular zones, all nested around the centre (the 9th zone), are labelled with auspicious (Brahmā, water, god, Kubera, Gaṇeśa) or inauspicious (snake, fire, ghost, death) names according to whether the zone is "blameworthy" (*nindyam*) or not.

One blameworthy ratio of house to land (in the 5/9ths zone of the figure) recalls the forces (noted above) radiating from a house's midlines and diagonals which can split any nearby structure in two. The other blameworthy ratios occur at weak points where the ratio of the expansion is divisible by its inherent prime number (here 3)—in the 3/9ths, 6/9ths and

9/9ths zones. Ratios that are not blameworthy, but strong and positive in their consequences, are those which are not so easily divisible.

Estimating the vulnerability of an expansion ratio by the ease of its denominator's divisibility, as is done here, is similar to a technique used extensively elsewhere in the manuals for determining the points at which walls and pillars should not be located when building a house. Weaknesses occur at points of denser intersection among diagonals drawn over the house site on a 9 × 9 or other grid. Called *marmams*, these points are analogous to the weak points of the human body against which surgeons are warned in the books of Hindu medicine and which combatants seek to strike in the Kerala martial arts. Such formulations illustrate general tendencies to calculate proportionally, to make graduated evaluations, and to anticipate negative transformations.

Summary. The building manuals present spaces imbued with divine attributes to which human purposes may be variously adapted. They give formulas for cosmic orientations, both horizontal and vertical, viewed from a household centre with lines and layers extending indefinitely outward. Through their formulas for evaluating diagonal slopes and proportions they suggest other subtle external influences and connections. But they do not deal with patterns of human aetivity such as I had observed within Kerala houses, nor do they provide a comprehensive scheme.

Cubing the house

The three-dimensional cube of Hindu constituents (Marriott 1989) offers a larger conceptual framework in which I found that I could assemble most of the manuals' spatial formulations and relate them both to the patterns of household activity that I had observed and to some larger patterns of Hindu cosmology.

Marriott's cube is a graph of five postulates, intended as the core metaphor for possible Indian social sciences. It is constructed from cultural variables (such as "high" and "low", "hot" and "cold", "auspicious" and "inauspicious", and the varied concerns with "purity" and "impurity") that are prominent in many rural ethnographies. It is also constructed from classical Hindu categories (such as the five elements [*bhūtas*], three humours [*doṣas*], three strands [*guṇas*], and four aims [*puruṣārthas*]), which are seen as implying similar underlying variables. Its postulates are thus both physical and social and are widely shared among Hindus. The cube was constructed about 1978 without reference to Hindu architecture. Yet its attention to physical elements and its three-dimensional form invite comparison with the forms of Kerala houses, while its postulated social-relational features invite comparison with patterns of household activity.

My uses of the cube may be divided into (1) correspondences, in which the house's plan and its activity patterns are seen as congruent harmonious with the cube's constituents, and (2) dialectics, in which activity patterns are seen as opposing the constituents.

1. Correspondences

Figure 6 depicts the Kerala house as it might be mapped into the theoretical Hindu constituent cube. The mapping is achieved by identifying formal and conceptual features of the house with Marriott's formal definitions of the cube's dimensions (mixing, unmarking, unmatching) and with the Hindu variables that the cube summarises.

Two sorts of cubic mappings of any entity are possible, one more concrete, the other more abstract. The more concrete sort here identifies the house's walls with the cube's sides, the house's geophysical orientations with the cube's dimensions, the house's atrium with the cube's centre, etc., as in Figure 6. It identifies humans as bodies and their activities as physical movements. A second, more abstract sort of mapping identifies general properties of the house and its activity patterns with general properties and processes of the cube. Both sorts of mappings are considered below, primarily the more concrete.

Mixing. The lateral dimension of the cube called 'mixing and unmixing' by Marriott is defined by nonreflexive relations. 'Mixing' refers to more or less intersecting, opening, and expanding (irreflexive) physical and social processes. This dimension is modelled on that metonymic set of Hindu variables which consists of the element "fire" (*agni*), the humour "bile" (*pitta*), the strand "passion" (*rajas*), and the aim "attachment" (*kāma*), and their greater or lesser incidence in any entity or situation.

Clearly this 'mixing and unmixing' dimension corresponds physically to the east-west dimension of the Kerala Hindu house. The house opens its doors and expands largely toward the east, has its largest and (horizontally) most open interior areas on this side, and promotes mingling with visitors here. The house's room spaces close and shrink in size as one moves toward the guarded areas for privacy, security and seclusion on the west.

The house's and residents' external attachments are cultivated on the east, where fire is the cube's dominant element. Fire is eponymously present there in the guardians Agni and Indra. Heat is physically increased on the east by the doors opening toward the rising sun and decreased on the west by thicker walls and an absence of doors. Fire and heat are physically present in the cooking fires of the kitchen. Within the kitchen, the hearth is almost always against the east or north wall (cf. Ifeka 1987: 321), replicating the kitchen's northeastern place in the plan of the house; storage is on the west or south of that room, as it is generally in the house.

Considered as an abstract variable property, mixing also predicts the actual concern with houses' greater or lesser external vulnerability and influence, regardless of direction. Mixing in general, like heat, is controlled

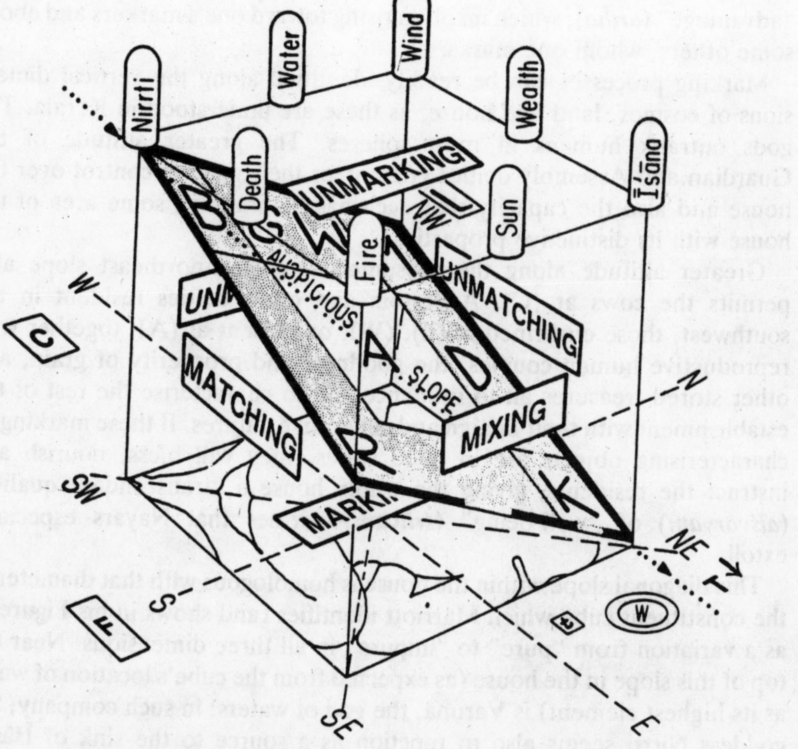

Fig. 6 House Schematic in Hindu Constituent Cube

by walls, doors, verandas and compound. The potential force or fragility of any structure's central lines and the anticipation of consequences from incursions or extensions (Figure 5) can all be understood as examples of the universally present mixing variable.

***Marking*. A second dimension of the cube—the vertical dimension called 'unmarking and marking' by Marriott—is defined by nonsymmetrical relations. It refers to asymmetrical social processes of outranking others by pervading them with markings while reducing or neutralising the marker's**

own relative markings. This dimension is modelled on the metonymic set of Hindu variables consisting of the element "water" (*apaḥ*) and the humour "phlegm" (*kapha*), which both tend to descend from high to low and to penetrate what they fall upon; it is also modelled on the strand "goodness" (*sattva*), which is an evaluative or 'up' idea, and on the aim of seeking "advantage" (*artha*), which involves rising toward one's markers and above some others, whom one marks.

Marking processes can be readily identified along the vertical dimensions of cosmos, land and house, as these are understood in Kerala. The gods outrank humans in most spheres. The greater altitude of the Guardian and Assembly deities guarantees their general control over the house and also the capacity that each has for imbuing some area of the house with its distinctive properties.

Greater altitude along the presumed southwest-northeast slope also permits the cows at (C), Ancestors and other deities resident in the southwest, those enshrined at (d), (W), or present at (A), together with reproductive human couples, the goodness and prosperity of grain, and other stored treasures all to influence and to characterise the rest of the establishment with their benign and generative natures. If these marking or characterising objects are in good states, they will bless, nourish and instruct the residents, giving the whole house a "transcendant quality" (*aiśvāryam*) of "well-being" (*śrītvam*)—virtues that Nayars especially extoll.

This diagonal slope within the house is homologous with that diameter of the constituent cube which Marriott identifies (and shows in his Figure 2) as a variation from "pure" to "impure" in all three dimensions. Near the top of this slope in the house (as expected from the cube's location of water as its highest element) is Varuṇa, the god of waters; in such company, the goddess Nirṛti seems also to function as a source to the sink of Īśāna, beside the well; and in such company, Death, a god of each life's final reckonings, seems to function more especially (like the Ancestors and Sugrīva, the universal law-giver, nearby in the Assembly)[23] as a source of household morality. Reversing this slope would produce a general state of physical and moral pollution along with the dessication and destruction of wealth anticipated by the "ghost" cline of the building manuals (Figure 4).

'Unmarking' as a neutralising of specificities in the upper region is physically best realised in the structures of Nambutiri houses, which often have large, general-purpose halls, rather than bedrooms, on their upper floors. The higher location and character of these less differentiated rooms is analogous to the conceptually elevated, although not top location of the southeastern areas (R) of Nayar houses.

[23] Marriott's model thus helps to select relevant meanings from among the many divine attributes collected by Kramrisch.

Unmatching. A third, back-to-front dimension of the cube, called 'unmatching (sometimes also "messing") and matching' by Marriott, is defined by nontransitive relations. It refers to the likelihood of social and physical processes of negative transformation, such as separations, reversals and destructions. This dimension is modelled on a metonymic set of Hindu variables consisting of the element "air" (*vāyu*), the humour "wind" (*vāta*), the strand "darkness" (*tamas*), and the aim "incoherence" (*adharma*)—the last variable being more usually stated from its positive (front) end as "coherence" (*dharma*).

The unmatching, wind-dominated region of the metaphoric cube includes what householders of Kerala actually consider to be the domain of the guardian deity Wind, who is known for moving about and thereby possibly disordering any situation. If any side of the Kerala house and compound may be called especially 'messy', it is this windy north. Still, Kramrisch's (1976: 94) description of the north as the region where life emerges fits the guardian deities Wealth (and Soma) and the north side's uses for activities that are necessary to give life its substance. Women, whose bodies are most productive, but whose substances are also frequently somewhat disarticulated are appropriately concentrated here.

Within the house, the menstrual, dining and kitchen areas are all specialised for such vital, if messy operations. Here are concentrated human birthing and dying, as well as the most frequent activities of grinding, cutting, cooking, feeding and eating. They occur near an exit door and a veranda specialised for acts (spitting, washing) that separate bodily substances already loosened from the person. Beyond in the compound there occur separations of feces from people and of life from living animals. The whole north side can also be called an area of "darkness", being conceptually most distant from the atrium, from the southward-tending sun, and from the divine light of the household shrine.

At the opposite, south side of the house are found the forces of unity. Here are the objects that encode and give order and coherent form to the substances provided at the north. South is the side for matchmaking and marriages, for controlled couplings of spouses, performances of worship and other ceremonies, and for the conduct of other formal meetings, feasts and bondings. It is the place of greatest light. The Ancestors (Nirṛti's double), Death as a personification of moral reckoning, and Fire as a witness of these proceedings are all present in the coherent south.

Without reference to geographic directions and taken by itself (apart from combination with the mixing variable [R], such as occurs in Figure 5), the unmatching variable (T) of the theoretical Hindu property space is to be understood as increasing with distance from any central point (abstractly represented by the cube's front). Distance is the natural abode of less matched others—diners, cleaners, ghosts, demons and castes whose unmatching properties (as killers or removers of loose substance, or as perverse and corrupted people) make them unsuitable for union with the well-matched people at the cube's front.

Three-dimensionality and "purity." The three variables listed above separately define the main dimensions and sides of the house in ways that recognise what the Hindu residents and building manuals regard as real distinctions. Intersecting as they do in the cube, the mixing, unmarking and unmatching variables form a group whose permutations accurately differentiate many other household areas and processes. They work particularly well in defining issues of "purity".

The greater precision of such triadic analyses was exemplified for me by comparing them with the uncertain distinctions afforded by a previous, one-dimensional 'organic' identification of pollution or impurity with the products of human biology (Dumont 1980: 46–61; Stevenson 1954). Observing bloody 'irruptions' such as birth and menstruation there, I could readily identify one corner—the northwest—as a place of such impurity. But many other north-side activities regarded by residents as "impure"—eating, grinding, pounding, cooking and dishwashing, for example—could escape the 'organic obtrusion' definition. What makes north-side activities alike and "impure" is not their specific production of human effluvia, but more generally their splittings of entities, their reversals of properties, their transformations of substances—all unmatching processes.

The imprecision of an organic definition of impurity would raise further difficulties for distinguishing the north from the south of the house. Cooking and dishwashing at the north side look less 'organic' than certain human bodily processes located on the south—sexual intercourse and cremation—although the latter are regarded by Hindus as conducive to "purity" in so far as they promote *dharma* (matching).

If I abandoned the organic definition and redefined "impurity" as simple unmatching, I could correctly distinguish the impurity of the north from the purity of the south. But if I did so, I would then miss the contrast in another kind of impurity—mixing—that distinguishes the eastern and western corner areas on both the northern and southern sides of the house. These corner areas are better defined by combining two or three Hindu variables.

Thus, the northwest simultaneously provides closure—seclusion and protection—(unmixing) and separation (unmatching) for women when their bodies are in unmatched or unmatching states of menstruation or parturition. It is not located directly on the subtle cline, and is thus less likely to be heavily marked from above. Being at an intermediate altitude equal with that of the southeast corner (R), this M area also avoids the movement of markings either way between the secluded women and guests. These undesirable movements are not labelled by the manuals as "serpent"-like (toward the vulnerable women) and "fire"-like (carrying the women's heat toward the men) (Figure 4).

Contrasting with the northwest corner, the kitchen (K) and the northern informal dining area (D) are relatively open places for mixings of both substances and people (fire, foods, cooks, eaters, kitchen visitors). At the lowest point on the subtle cline, the kitchen is also in the corner most influenced by the house's markings. On all three dimensions the kitchen, with its notoriously unmatching operations, is thus logically the most impure corner of the house—more impure than the northwest corner.

In the southeast corner, mixing with outside guests threatens the hosts with a kind of impurity, but guests are pre-selected to be of matching castes and to be in nonmixing, well-matched (bathed, appropriately dressed) bodily conditions, so that mixing with them will not alter the hosts' purity. Not being at the lowest point, the southeast is not so heavily marked with the house's characterising features as is the kitchen, although accepting the host's food may mark the guests with the hosts' markings. The southeast corner is thus to be rated less impure than the northeast, and about equal in impurity to the northwest.

The southwest corner must be reckoned to be the purest area by three-dimensional analysis. The bedroom, granary, worship and storage areas—all characterising loci—are in the upper region and thus less marked. By their walls and doors, all these areas and their contents are well protected from external mixing, as the open southeast area is not. Sexual intercourse there is an act of unity calculated to occur only between well-matched partners. Anything whose exact markings are wanted on everything else in the house must be kept pure here in the southwest—unmixed, unmarked and matched—as in fact it is.

With its three graduated dimensions of contrast, the cube thus permits many more distinctions than does a unidimensional contrast of 'pure and impure'. Three kinds of purity-impurity are evidently present in the Kerala house, four combinations of them occur in the house's corners, and many further permutations are conceivable between and among the cube's eight corners. The cube further permits a rational analysis of the house's internal slopes and inherent movements.

2. Dialectics

All of the above correspondences place certain objects, activities, people, or states at domestic loci which resemble them in their respective properties. But the same objects, activities and people have some properties that are felt to need moderation, and these are deliberately disposed in domestic loci that have properties different from their own.

Thus, outdoor bathing, which can be a chilling activity in the early morning, is located at a tank on the sunny east side of the house, where at least a little warmth may be available. Guests, who may not initially be amenable to exchanges, are entertained in the household area of greatest warmth, which has the property of mixing—the capacity to open them.

On the other hand, sexual intercourse, a heating, intensely mixing activity, along with childbirth and menstruation (which are understood to entail great releases of bodily heat), are all relegated to rooms on the conceptually cooler, closed, mixture-retarding western side. Such heat-releasing activities also put women into highly markable and mixable (because open) states from or to which alien substance should not be allowed to spread, with possibly marking effects.

Bodily death, a state of drastic incoherence initially dealt with on the unmatching north side at (D), is transformed into carefully rematched coherence by rites conducted at the south side of the house (R), followed by cremation further south in the compound at (F). The gross body's constituents are remanded to the elements, the spirit to unity with the ancestors.

The most massive dialectic movement in the house is the infusion of the most impure corner of the house with goodness from above. This triumph of purity occurs along the subtle cline from southwest to northeast. The contents of the southwestern corner unmark themselves and mark (or characterise) everything else by directing their influences downward to the two sides and the one corner opposite to their own location—to the east, to the north, and to the northeast. The process of unmarking and marking must correlate with either the mixing (west-to-east) or the unmatching (south-to-north) slopes, never with their opposites. The southwest-to-northeast slope which meets both these conditions simultaneously yields what the manuals and Figure 4 call "complete auspiciousness"

Any of the five other possible cardinal and diagonal slopes would prevent some or all of the desired unmarking and marking from occurring. They would make more difficult the residents' daily efforts to supply the kitchen with the auspicious subtle influences of grain and the gods' grace. They would prevent that underlying movement and recycling of waters that is necessary for the house to retain the purity and auspiciousness of its overall orientation.

Being directly on the main incline, the kitchen and its food products are readily marked by the house's most desirable, characterising features; and through the food these markings may be conveyed to all who consume it, relatively unmarking the cooks. Thus this hot, low and messy (mixed, marked, unmatched) area, initially defined as the corner of greatest impurity, is converted through the householders' counteraction (planning, ritual, material success and hospitality) into a main channel for purification and self-elevation.

The daily rites of illumination celebrate this continual achievement. At dawn and dusk the shrine's lamp floods the otherwise conceptually dark north side of the house with light from the shrine lamp and from the eyes of the lamp's viewers, who are careful to look northward at these times. That the lamp is repeatedly refuelled from the kitchen and reignited from the kitchen fire asserts the complementarities of north and south, east and west, high and low, and the variable properties of the cosmos that these parts of the house contain and sustain.

Conclusion: the empty centre and the Hindu cosmos

Apparently unaffected by these movements is the atrium, an orientation to which provides a definition of the "four-sided" Kerala house. It is in some ways treated as the most essential and "sacred" place. Like the western rooms, the atrium is set apart. Like the southwestern rooms, its contents may at times be said to mark or characterise the house and its members. Unlike the western and southern sides, however, the middle place is not high—its floor uniquely extends somewhat into the earth; and unlike the western side, it is not closed but open—on four sides to other rooms and on the fifth to the sky.

Interpreted concretely as the geometric centre of the Hindu constituent cube, the "middle place" is a point of reference for all the directions. It is also a point of balance among the cube's three variables, each of them being at half strength here. Such a perfect, three-way equilibrium would resemble the condition of the mind of God before the world's emergence—before its expansion as differentiated and variable substance—as understood by E.V. Daniel's Tamil village informants (1984: 3–5). The centre so understood is inactive and constant, like some notions of the universal soul (*brahman, ātman*). Thus interpreted abstractly, the centre corresponds to the zero element in Marriott's table of five Hindu postulates. Its non-differentiation and indifference to the world's variations suggest rather the 'empty set' of pure consciousness—an interpretation consistent with the atrium's use as an area for personal meditation.

But the atrium is not only an empty place symbolising for some the aim of release from the variations of the phenomenal world. It is also a physical structure—an axis between earth and ether (sky)—and its physicality continues to link it with the repertoire of substantial Hindu elements. As the element which provides gross bodies to all entities, earth is the specific locus and the material synthesis that is the house itself. As the element which provides the space in which all specific entities must exist, ether directs attention more subtly to the house's abstract structure, to its analytic homologies with the general processes of the universe.

Marriott's diagram (in his Figure 1) depicts earth and ether as a pair of terms beside the cube, "earth" summarising the whole cube as a triad of gross elements in contrast with the subtler, unpicturable but omnipresent spatial element of "ether". I argue that this pair of terms belongs in the centre of the cube that represents the Kerala house. Earth and ether are the "middle place", the axis of this microcosm. The notion of microcosmicity—of homologies between the concrete house and subtle, implicit universal structures—in this axial symbol is what holds together the diverse dimensions and variable elements of the Kerala Hindu house.[24]

Here my search for models to elucidate the house is reversed: the house itself becomes a model of the Hindu macrocosm, presenting its residents with understandings about the possibilities of action in that universe which may not be available to them in other ways.

[24] Readers of Paul Wheatley's (1969) analysis of medieval Asian urban geography will recognise in the Kerala house a largely similar set of principles—axiality, cardinality and micro/macrocosmic orientation.

REFERENCES

BABB, LAWRENCE A. 1981. Glancing: visual interaction in Hinduism. *Journal of anthropological research* 37: 387–401.

BECK, BRENDA E.F. 1976. The symbolic merger of body, space, and cosmos in Hindu Tamil Nadu. *Contributions to Indian sociology* (n.s.) 10: 213–43.

BOURDIEU, PIERRE. 1977. *Outline of a theory of practice*. Cambridge: Cambridge University Press.

DANIEL, E. VALENTINE. 1984. *Fluid signs: being a person the Tamil way*. Berkeley: University of California Press.

DAS, VEENA. 1977. *Structure and cognition: aspects of Hindu caste and ritual*. Second edition. Delhi: Oxford University Press.

———. 1985. Paradigms of body symbolism: an analysis of selected themes in Hindu culture. *In* Richard Burghart and Audrey Cantlie, eds., *Indian religion*, pp. 180–207. London: Curzon Press.

DUMONT, LOUIS. 1980. *Homo hierarchicus: the caste system and its implications*. Chicago: University of Chicago Press.

———. 1982. *Banaras: city of light*. New York: A.A. Knopf.

ECK, DIANA L. 1985. Banaras: cosmos and paradise in the Hindu imagination. *Contributions to Indian sociology* (n.s.) 19: 41–55.

IFEKA, CAROLINE. 1987. Domestic space as ideology in Goa, India. *Contributions to Indian sociology* (n.s.) 21: 307–29.

INNES, C.A. 1951. *Madras district gazetteers: Malabar*. Madras: Government Press.

KANIPPAYYUR SANKARAN NAMBUTIRIPPAD. 1963. *Ente smaraṇakaḷ*. Kunnamkulam, Kerala: Pancangam Press.

———. 1968. *Gṛhārambhavum gṛhapravēśavum*. Kunnamkulam, Kerala: Pancangam Press.

———. 1979. *Manuṣyālaya candrika*. Kunnamkulam, Kerala: Pancangam Press.

KHARE, R.S. 1976. *The Hindu hearth and home.*. Durham, NC: Carolina Academic Press.

KRAMRISCH, STELLA. 1976. *The Hindu temple*. 2 vols. Delhi: Motilal Banarsidass.

KRISHNAVARIYAR, JYOTSYAN PARAYKKAL. 1975. *Gṛhanirmmānapaddhati*. Kunnamkulam, Kerala: Pancangam Press.

LOGAN, WILLIAM. 1951. *Malabar*. 2 vols. Madras: Government Press.

MANU. 1969. *The laws of Manu* (trans. Georg Bühler). New York: Dover Publications.

MARRIOTT, MCKIM. 1976. Hindu transactions; diversity without dualism. *In* Bruce Kapferer, ed., *Transaction and meaning: directions in the anthropology of exchange and symbolic behavior*, pp. 109–42. Philadelphia: Institute for the Study of Human Issues.

———. 1989. Constructing an Indian ethnosociology. *In* this volume.

MEISTER, MICHAEL. 1986. On the development of a morphology for symbolic architecture. *Res* 12: 33–50.

MENCHER, JOAN P. 1966. Kerala and Madras: a comparative study of ecology and social structure. *Ethnology* 5: 135–71.

MOORE, HENRIETTA L. 1986. *Space, text, and gender*. London: Cambridge University Press.

MOORE, MELINDA A. 1983. Taravad: house, land, and relationship in a matrilineal Hindu society. Ph.D. dissertation in Anthropology. Chicago: University of Chicago Library.

———. 1985. A new look at the Nayar taravad. *Man* 20: 523–41.

———. 1988. Symbol and meaning in Nayar marriage ritual. *American ethnologist* 15: 254–73.

———. n.d. Rituals of house and land. Unpublished manuscript.

PADMANABHA MENON, K.P. 1937. *History of Kerala*, 4 vols. Ernakulam: Cochin Government Press.

Pramar, V.S. 1987. Sociology of the north Gujarat urban house. *Contributions to Indian sociology* (n.s.) 21: 331–45.

Raghavan, M.D. 1932. A ballad of Kerala. *Indian antiquary* 61: 9–12, 72–76, 112–26, 150–54, 205–10.

Sinha, Jadunath. 1986. *Indian psychology*. 3 vols. Delhi: Motilal Banarsidass.

Stevenson, H.N.C. 1954. Status evaluation in the Hindu caste system. *Journal of the royal anthropological institute* 84: 45–65.

Thurston, Edgar. 1909. *Castes and tribes of southern India*. 7 vols. Madras: Government Press.

Wheatley, Paul. 1969. *The city as symbol*. London: University College.

About the contributors

Bruce Woods Derr has written on the economic and social history of Karimpur village for the Ph.D. in Anthropology (Syracuse 1979). He is on the staff of the Academic Computation Centre of Syracuse University, Syracuse NY 13210.

Nicholas B. Dirks (Ph.D. History, Chicago 1981), is Associate Professor of both Anthropology and History at the University of Michigan, Ann Arbor MI 48109–1382. Experienced field researcher in Tamil Nadu, he is currently conducting archival studies on the ethnographic and historical materials collected by Colin MacKenzie, an early 19th century British soldier and official in peninsular India.

McKim Marriott, Ph.D. in Anthropology (Chicago 1955), is Professor in the Department of Anthropology and in the Social Sciences Collegiate Division of the University of Chicago, 1126 E. 59th Street, Chicago IL 60637. He has done fieldwork in Uttar Pradesh and Maharashtra, edited *Village India*, and authored varied studies of rural social organisation and change. He is concerned with formulating and simulating indigenous sociologies and psychologies in India, Japan, and other cultures.

Diane Paull Mines (M.A. Chicago 1985) has undertaken fieldwork on prestations and the networks they form in rural Tamil Nadu. She is a candidate for the doctorate in the Department of Anthropology, University of Chicago, 1126 E. 59th Street, Chicago IL 60637.

Melinda A. Moore, Ph.D. in Anthropology (Chicago 1984), is a Lecturer in The College, University of Chicago, 5845 S. Ellis Ave., Chicago IL 60637 and an Associate of that University's Committee on Southern Asian Studies. From her field studies in Kerala she is preparing one monograph on Nayar social organisation and another on Kerala Hindu households and their rituals.

Manuel Moreno, Ph.D. in Anthropology (Chicago 1984), is Associate Professor of Anthropology at Northeastern Illinois University, St. Louis at Bryn Mawr Avenue, Chicago IL 60625. He specialises in the anthropology of religion and has written elsewhere on agriculture, astrology, and other aspects of the culture of Tamil Nadu.

Gloria Goodwin Raheja, Ph.D. in Anthropology (Chicago 1985), authored her contribution as an Associate of the Committee on Southern Asian Studies of the University of Chicago. She is now Assistant Professor of Anthropology at the University of Minnesota, 224

Church Street S.E., Minneapolis MN 55455. Her current researches are on women in north Indian kinship systems and on language use.

A. K. Ramanujan, Ph.D. in Linguistics (Indiana 1963), folklorist, poet, and translator, is William A. Colvin Professor in the Department of Linguistics and in the Committee on Social Thought as well as in the Department of South Asian Languages and Civilisations at the University of Chicago, 1130 East 59th Street, Chicago IL 60637. The latest of his many books are *Poems of love and war* and (as editor, with Stuart Blackburn) *Another harmony: new essays on the folklore of India*. He is currently writing on Kannada folklore.

Susan Snow Wadley is Professor in the Department of Anthropology at Syracuse University, 308 Browne Hall, Syracuse NY 13244. Her doctoral dissertation (at Chicago in 1973) is the book *Shakti: power in the conceptual structure of Karimpur religion*. Author of many researches in north Indian folklore and demography, she is now preparing a social and cultural history of Karimpur village which will include personal narratives gathered from a variety of its residents.

Index*

adharma, 16, 20, 150, 195
Alexander Wilder, 46
Allen, N.J., 20n, 34
Amarasingham, Lorna Rhodes, 7, 34 (also see Rhodes)
anachronism, 33
Anantha Murthy, U.R., 117, 127
Appadurai, Arjun, 60, 76, 80, 99, 154, 165
Apthorpe, Raymond, 30, 34
Arokiaswami, M., 158, 165
artha, 9, 13, 13n, 20, 28, 51, 54, 113, 125, 150, 194
āśrama, 4, 6, 23, 23n, 114–16, dharma, 48
āyurveda, 12, 29

Babb, Lawrence A., 8, 34, 141, 147, 148, 152, 165, 188, 201
Bakhtin, 75
Barnes, R.H., 41
Basso, Keith H., 101
Baudhāyana, 47
Bayly, C.A., 63, 76
Beals, Alan R., 7, 34
Beck, Brenda E.F., 31, 34, 154–56, 158, 159, 165, 179, 185, 186, 201
Benjamin, Walter, 41
Berger, Peter L., 112, 128
Berreman, Gerald D., 60, 76
Bhagavad Gītā, 9n, 11, 13, 34, 113, 128
Bhattacharya, Ram Shankar, 36
birth, 22, 26, 85, 103n, 105, 110, 114, 140; rebirth, 22; rites, 103n, 105
Bloch, Maurice, 112, 128, 129
Blunt, E.A.H., 92, 99
Borgatta, Edward F., 17, 36
Bourdieu, Pierre, 75, 81, 99, 176n, 201
brahmacārya, 54
Brahman/Brahmin, 11, 26n, 30, 31, 44, 46, 47, 50, 51, 59–62, 64–66, 72, 80, 82–99, 104, 106, 106n, 115, 118, 120, 125, 136, 137, 139–41, 144, 145, 157–59, 161, 162, 188n; ascetics, 188n; priest, 64, 162
Breckenridge, Carol, 60, 76, 80, 99
Bṛhadāraṇyaka, 50, 53
Bṛht Saṃhitā, 182
Brubaker, Richard L., 158, 165
Buck, Harry M., 35, 165
Buckley, Walter, 33, 34
Buddhism, 42
Buddhists, 44, 53, 140
Buhler, George, 37, 129, 201
Burghart, Richard, 80, 99, 128, 201
Burke, Kenneth, 50, 57

Cannadine, D., 99
Cantlie, Audrey, 201
Capra, Fritjof, 33, 34
Caraka, 11–13, 16, 21–23, 27, 29, 34, 150, 157, 160n, 165
Carman, John B., 30, 34
Cartwright, Dorwin, 36
caste, 8n, 23, 26, 26n, 28, 32, 59, 61, 62, 64–66, 68–74, 79–83, 80n, 85, 87–89, 93, 95–98, 106, 106n, 108, 133, 137, 156, 159, 160, 162, 164, 179, 182n, 183; authority, 73; dominant, 65, 71, 77, 80, 82, 87, 93, 95, 96, 98; hierarchy, 71; ideology of, 72; interaction of, 72; nature of, 79; network, 26, occupational, 28; organisation of, 59, 72; the politics of, 59; royal, 62; sub-caste, 66, 68–70; system, 80n, 108; village system of, 81
centrality, 26, 79–101
Chakravarti, Anand, 3, 13, 34
Channabasavanna, S.M., 39
Chase, Ivan D., 21, 34
Chaudhuri, Nirad, 42

Damle, Y.B., 5, 34
dān, 83–88, 92, 95, 97–99
Daniel, de-Coppet, 34
Daniel, E. Valentine, 8, 29, 32, 35, 38, 51, 57, 103n, 113, 117, 128, 142, 148, 154, 165, 176, 176n, 177n, 187, 199, 201
Daniel, Sheryl B., 7, 9n, 19, 35, 44, 47, 57, 146n, 148
Das, Veena, 16, 18n, 20, 35, 103n, 112, 113n, 120n, 121–23, 128, 176n, 179, 188n, 201
David, Kenneth A., 19, 35, 37, 77, 129, 155, 165

* The Preface and the Introduction are not covered in this.

Davis, Marvin Gene, 8, 9n, 23, 28, 35, 113–16, 115n, 118, 128
death, 22, 23, 26, 85; impurity, 103–29
Denning, G., 75, 76
Derr, Bruce W., 19n, 23, 26, 28, 39, 131–48
dharma, 3, 11, 13, 13n, 48, 51, 54, 96, 97, 99, 105, 107, 113, 117, 126, 139, 142, 184, 195, 196
dharmaśāstra, 5, 11, 13, 13n, 103, 104, 106, 109, 111, 114, 126
Dirks, Nicholas B., 8n, 23, 27, 30, 32, 35, 59–77, 79, 80, 100
division of labour, 29
Doreian, Patrick, 17, 35
Douglas, Mary, 108, 128
Dravid, Raja Ram, 53, 57
Dumont, Louis, 4, 6, 20n, 30, 31, 35, 51, 58–62, 68, 72–74, 76, 77, 79–81, 83, 87, 88, 92, 93, 96, 100, 104, 105, 108, 112, 120n, 128, 196, 201
Durkheim, Emile, 2, 29, 35

Eck, Diana L., 176n, 201
Egnor, Margaret Trawick, 7, 32, 35, 51, 58, 119, 120, 120n, 128, 151, 158, 165 (*see also* Trawick)
Eliot, T.S., 56, 58
Elmore, Wilbur T., 158, 165
Emerson, 55
Evans-Pritchard, E.E., 47
evolution, cultural, 44; social, 42

family, 16, 16n, 52, 53, 64, 82, 85, 86, 95, 142n, 143, 162, 170; divine, 162; extended, 170, resemblances, 16n, royal, 64
Fawcett, Fred, 158, 165, 170, 171, 171n
Fernandez, James W., 5, 35
Ferro-Luzzi, Gabriella Eichinger, 7, 35, 155, 165
Foster, Edward Morgan, 45, 58
Focault, Michel, 59, 75, 77
foundation assembly *(vāstu maṇḍala)*, 179–86
foundation man (*vāstu puruṣa*), 179–83, 182n, 185–87
Francis, Winston, 158, 165
Freed, Stanely A., 20, 35
Frits Staal, 53
Fuller, C.J., 93, 100
functionalism, 111, 112

Gandhi, 55
Ganesh, Kamala, 156, 165
Garbett, G.K., 20, 35
Gautama, 46
Geertz, Clifford, 4, 5, 36, 47, 58, 67, 74, 77, 141, 148
Gītā, 43
Gold, Ann Grodzins, 16, 22n, 36, 114n, 122n, 123, 128
Gonda, J., 80, 86n, 100
Good, Anthony, 93, 95, 100
Gramsci, 75
Gṛhya Sutra, 188n
Guha, R., 100
guṇas, 6, 7, 21, 53, 113, 115–17, 150, 166, 191

Hage, Per, 17, 19, 27, 36
Harary, Frank, 17, 19, 27, 36
Harper, Edward B., 44, 58, 108, 128
Heesterman, J.C., 60, 77, 83, 86–88, 87n, 93, 96, 100
Hegel, G.W.F., 46, 47, 58
Heginbotham, Stanley J., 3, 36
Herbert, Risley, 80n
Hertz, Robert, 105, 111, 112, 128
Hiebert, Paul G., 9, 20, 29, 36, 146, 148
hierarchy, 11, 13, 20, 20n, 26, 29–31, 61, 62, 67–69, 71–74, 76, 79–101; of caste 62, 72; of deities, 20; nature of, 76; political, 67, 68, 72–74; revolving, 11; of status, 73; value, 11, 13
Hindu, 3, 5, 6, 8n, 9, 11—13, 16–22, 26–33, 44, 48, 53, 54, 59, 64, 103–29, 140, 141, 169–203; biological thought of, 27; concepts, 29; cosmic myths, 122; cosmos, 169–203; death, 103–29; ethnography, 13; iconography, 12; postulation, 17; property space, 26, 27; spatio-temporal terms, 27; tradition, 33; variables, 17; *varṇa*, 29
Hobsbawm, E., 100
Hocart, A.M., 66, 77, 80, 81, 88, 100
Hubert, Henri, 86, 100

Ifeka, Caroline, 174n, 176n, 192, 201
impurity, 26, 59, 83, 103–29
Inden, Ronald B., 8, 16, 36, 37, 50, 58, 60, 71, 77, 111, 116–20, 128, 129
Innes, C.A., 175n, 189, 201
inter-caste relations, 11, 19, 23, 30, 79–99
Islam, 42

Jadhav, Sushrut S., 39
Jain, R.K., 128

Jaini, Padmanabh S., 32, 36
jajmān, 27, 31, 83–90, 97–99, 116, 137, 137n
jajmāni system, 65, 79, 81–83; relationship, 93, 95, 96, 99
Jameson, Fredric, 75, 77
Jean-Claude, Galey, 34
Kakar, Sudhir, 45
kaliyuga, 51
Kallars, 27, 62, 64, 65, 68–73, 76; royal sub-caste of, 64, 72, 73
kāma, 11–13, 13n, 19, 51, 54, 113, 150, 184, 192
Kāmasūtra, 53
kamīn (service caste), 80, 82, 84–87, 90, 91, 95
Kane, P.V., 103n, 104, 106, 117, 118, 120n, 121, 122, 128
Kanippayyur, S.N., 171, 174, 176, 177n, 178, 179, 183, 184, 187–89
Kant, 46, 47
kanyādān, 95
Kapferer, Bruce, 37, 129
Kapp, K. William, 5, 36
Karimpur, 19n
karma, 3, 8, 44, 116, 138–44, 140n, 146n, 147
Kaushik, Meena, 112, 120n, 121, 122, 128
Kavirayar, Balasubrahmaniya, 153, 165
Kemeny, John G., 17, 36
Kemper, Stephen E.G., 11, 27, 36
Keyes, C.F., 35, 38, 57, 139, 140
Khare, R.S., 7, 32, 36–38, 121, 128, 176n, 201
kinship system, 5, 23, 62, 67, 68, 72, 73, 95, 107, 111, 112, 117; American, 5; central organisation of, 72; domain of, 72; Dravidian isolation of, 62; south Indian, 72; as spiritual impurity, 108, 109
Kissinger, 44, 45, 52
Knipe, David M., 123, 128
Kolenda, Pauline, 105, 129
Kramrisch, Stella, 176n, 179, 194n, 195, 201
Krishnavariyar, Jyotsyan Paraykkal, 189, 201
Kurin, Richard, 32, 36

Langer, Susanne K., 17, 36
Larson, Gerald James, 8, 11, 21, 28, 36
Leaf, Murray John, 5, 36
Lebra, Takie Sugiyama, 5, 36
Leslie, Charles M., 34
Lévi-Strauss, Claude, 2, 17, 36, 47, 58, 108
Levinson, Stephen C., 19, 27, 36
Lewis, Oscar, 141, 148
Lindzey, Gardner, 17, 36
lineage, 26, 62, 66, 69, 71, 73, 82, 95, 142n, 147
Linget, Robert, 48, 58
local political economy, 141
local social organisation, 26
Logan, William, 189, 201
Ludden, David E., 62, 77
Lyons, John, 58

Mackie, John Leslie, 46, 58
Macormack, Carol P., 37
Madan, T.N., 13, 21, 37, 115, 116, 118–21, 120n, 129
Mahābhārata, 48, 49, 51, 60, 117, 155, 166
Mahar, Pauline M., 20, 37
Malamoud Charles, 11, 37
Mānavadharmaśāstra, 60
Mani, Srinivas B., 151, 166
Manickam, Sundaraj, 156, 166
Manu, 9n, 13n, 16, 21, 37, 45–47, 54, 55, 58, 96, 97, 104, 106, 129, 184
Marglin, Frédérique Apffel, 34, 104, 105, 128, 129
Mariyamman, 149–67
Mark Sainsbury, 35, 128
Mark Twain, 42
marriage, 72, 73, 80, 85, 95, 119, 161–63, 195; polygynous, 72; rites, 105, 118; rituals, 152
Marriott, McKim, 1–38, 52, 58, 60, 129, 149–66, 169, 170, 182n, 191–95, 199, 201
Marx, Karl, 2
Mauss, Marcel, 86, 96, 100
Max Muller, 44, 53
McClelland, David C., 5, 37
McGilvray, Dennis B., 8n, 32, 37, 60, 77, 150, 151, 166
Meggitt, Mervyn J., 5, 37
Meister, Michael, 176n, 201
Mencher, Joan P., 175n, 177n, 178, 189n, 201
Merrey, Karen L., 152n, 166
metonymy, 16, 149, 150
Mines, Diane Paull, 3, 22, 23, 26, 27, 30,37, 103–30
Mitchell, J.C., 9, 27, 35, 37
Moffatt, Michael, 32, 37, 120n, 121, 122, 128, 129
mokṣa, 13, 51, 54, 108, 114
Moore, Henrietta L., 176n, 201

Moore, Melinda A., 23, 27–31, 37, 169–202
Moreno, Manuel, 9n, 23, 26, 27, 29, 32, 37, 115n, 149–66
Morton, A., 128
Motwani, Kewal, 5, 13n, 37
Mukerji, Dhurjati Prasad, 4, 37
Mukherji, Partha N., 37
Muller, Max, 46, 58
Murukan, 149–67
mutuality of inter-caste relationship, 88–91, 182n

Nagasamy, R., 165
Naipaul, V.S., 45, 58
Narayana, Vasudha, 39
Natarejan, Manikkar, 154, 166
Needham, Claudia, 128, 182n
Needham, Rodney, 128
Nehru, J.L., 42
Newtonian revolution, 52
Nicholas, Ralph W., 16, 36, 103n, 111, 117–20, 128, 129
Nichter, Mark, 7, 37
Norman, Robert Z., 36

Obeyesekere, Gananath, 154, 166
O'Flaherty, Wendy D., 38, 96, 100, 108, 129
Oommen, T.K., 37
Orenstein, Henry, 104, 105, 107–12, 114, 114n, 117, 123, 126, 129

Padmanabha, Menon K.P., 170, 171n, 173n, 177n, 201
Pandy, Raj Bali, 120n, 129
Parkin, R.J., 34
parochialism, 33
Parry, Jonathan P., 32, 37, 82, 83, 100, 105, 112, 120n, 122, 123, 128, 129
Parsons, T., 3–5, 37
Pederson, Poul, 80n, 100
Peirce, C.S.S., 50, 58
Pfaffenberger, Bryan, 29, 38, 111, 116, 123, 129, 150, 166
Piatigorsky, Alexel, 6, 38
Pillai, N. Kadiravar, 165
piṇḍa, 105, 123
pitṛ, 184
Plato, 48, 55
Pocock, David, 81, 93, 100, 105, 108, 128
Pollock, Susan, 128
Potter, Karl H., 3, 8, 19, 38, 128, 148
power, 59, 60, 61, 63, 65, 67, 80, 96; of the dominant caste, 92; political, 23; royal, 87, 93; secular, 93; structure of 72; temporal, 83, 88; web of, 76
Pramar, V.S., 174n, 176n, 202
prestation, 82, 84–86, 86n, 89, 91–93, 95–97; inter-caste, 95, 96; *muṭṭhī*, 84; pattern, 79; *sāvṛī*, 83, 84, 89
Price, P., 80, 100
Price, S., 99
Prigogine, Ilya, 33, 38
Pugh, Judy F., 6, 7, 26–28, 38
purity, 29–32, 59, 61, 72, 79–81, 104, 105, 114
puruṣārthas, 6, 7, 11, 12, 113, 191

Radhakrishnan, S., 56
Raghavan, M.D., 171, 202
Raheja, Gloria Goodwin, 6, 8n, 11, 23, 26–32, 38, 79–100, 116, 120n, 121, 129, 139n, 148, 160, 166
Ramanujan, A.K., 2, 6, 7, 18, 26n, 33, 38, 41–58, 127, 130
Ranger, T., 100
Rao, Gopinatha, 186
Rao, M.S.A., 37, 38
reincarnation, 44
Reining, Priscilla, 37
Renou, Louis, 52, 58
renunciation, 108, 110
Reynolds, Frank E., 129
Ṛg Veda, 106n
Rhodes, Lorna Amarasingham 28, 38 (*see also* Amarasingham)
Richards, J.F., 77
ritual, 21, 29, 32, 50, 52, 64, 66, 80, 82, 85, 97, 98, 103n, 111, 142n; centrality, 85, 97, 98; incapacity, 103n, 111; function, 82; occasion, 64
Rizvi, Najma, 7, 38
Roland, Alan, 52, 53, 58
Rosaldo, Michelle Zimbalist, 5, 38
Roth, Gunther, 39
Rudner, David West, 154, 166
Rudolph, L.I., 118, 130
Rudolph, S.H., 118, 130
Russell, Bertrand, 43

sacrifice, vedic, 50, 52
Said, Edward, 44, 45, 58
Saksena, R.N., 5, 38
saṃsāra, 3, 18, 52
saṃskāra, 19, 117, 118, 122
sanīcar, 132, 132n, 133, 146, 147
sannyāsa, 54

Sanskritisation, 69
sapiṇḍa, 105, 107, 109–11, 114, 123, 125
Saussure, 81
Schneider, David M., 5, 38
Schutz, Alfred, 57
Schweder, Richard, 58
Selby, H.A., 101
Selwyn, Tom, 16, 38
Shanmugavelu, M., 154, 166
Sharma, Ram Karan, 34, 165
Sharma, Ursula, 141, 147, 148
Shils, Edward A., 3–5, 37, 38
Shulman, David Dean, 27, 29, 38, 80, 83, 101, 122, 130, 153n, 163, 166
Shweder, Richard, 52, 58
siddha, 153, 153n
Silverstein, Michael, 81, 101
Simpson, George, 35
sin, 26, 145, 146, 146n, 147
Singer, Milton 37, 57, 58, 99, 100, 129
Sinha, Jadunath, 188, 202
Śiva, 149, 156, 159, 163, 184
smṛti, 48
Snell, J. Laurie, 36
social stratification, 5
Somacuntaranar, Avarkal P.V., 153, 166
Somalay, 153, 166
Somasundaram Pillai, J.M., 153, 166
śrāddha, 122, 123, 178
Srinivas, M.N., 81, 101, 106, 108, 130, 152, 166
śruti, 48
Stanislavsky, 41
static reflectionism, 111, 112
Stein, Burton, 80, 92, 101, 154, 166
Stengers, Isabelle, 33, 38
Stevenson, H.N.C., 108, 130, 196, 202
Stevenson, S., 120n, 130
svadharma, 48, 116
Swain, Joseph Ward, 35
Szanton, David L., 4, 39

talaividi, 44
Tambiah, Stanley J., 104, 105, 130
Thompson, Gerald, 2, 36
Thorp, John Putnam, 39
Thurston, Edgar, 171n, 175n, 202
Thurston, William P., 12, 39
Trautmann, Thomas R., 11, 39, 60, 77, 83, 101
Trawick, Margaret, 6, 7, 12n, 32, 39, (*see also* Egnor)

Uberoi, J.P.S., 2n, 29, 39
Uttar Pradesh Zamindari Abolition and Land Reform Act, 98

Vaidya Bhagwan Das, 34, 165
van Buitenen, J.A.B., 166
varṇa, 4, 6, 23, 23n, 28, 31, 79, 96, 97, 99, 103, 104, 106–11, 106n, 114–16, 125, 126, 179n
Vatuk, Sylvia, 121, 130
vedas, 41
Venugopal, P.M., 153, 166
Viṣṇu, 178, 184
Viṣṇu Purāṇa, 113, 115n, 130
Viśvāmitra, 48

Wadley, S.S., 13, 19n, 20, 23, 26, 28, 39, 44, 98, 101, 131–48
Waghorne, Joanne P., 3, 39
Waugh, E.H., 129
Weber, Max, 3, 39, 47
Weeks, Jeffrey R., 12, 39
Weiss, Mitchell G., 7, 39
Welbon, G.R., 165, 166
Western dualistic structuralism, 8n
Wheatley, Paul, 202
White, Merry I., 120
Whitehead, Rev. Henry, 158, 167
Williams, 75
Wilson, H.H., 130
Wiser, Charlotte V., 144n, 148
Wiser, William, 81, 98, 101, 131n, 137n, 144n, 148
Wittgenstein, Ludwig, 16n, 39
Wittich, Claus, 39

Yama, 121, 184, 185, 189
Yocum, Glenn E., 35, 165, 166

Zaehner, R.C., 34, 128
Zimmer, Heinrich Robert, 45, 58
Zimmermann, Francis, B., 11, 18, 23n, 27, 39, 52, 58, 151, 167